BRING BACK THE REAL REPUBLICAN PARTY

A CASE AGAINST DONALD J. TRUMP

AND HIS TRUMPUBLICAN PARTY

OF

IGNORANCE, HATRED, RACISM, TREASON

WARNING: HONEST AND DESERVING BIASED VIEWS OF THOSE WHO WANT TRUMP GONE.

Compiled

by

ROBERT A. NOWLAN PH.D.

A SCRAPBOOK OF EVIDENCE PROVIDED BY ARTCLES, MEMES, AND POLITICAL CARTOONS

ISBN:9798683049904

PREFACE

This work began as a chapter in my not yet completed book, In My Opinion, Vol. III, N-R, part of a planned five-volume memoir. However, with so many sources available, it became clear there was enough material for a standalone book. I am both author and compiler of the material found in this work. As author my opinions direct material due to others to be included in the story I am telling. My bias is meant to be seen. I am not so much trying to convert readers to share my opinions and positions, as it is to compile some, hopefully informative information on the numerous subjects covered. It will be noted that I share many quotations of other Republican Presidents to remind readers as to what kind of people once led a proud GOP.

"The two major U.S. parties (now called Democrats and Republicans) went through many changes in American history as support from geographic locations, party leaders, political factions, stances on key voter issues, and platform planks switched between the two major parties and third parties throughout the different 'party systems.' Democrats and Republicans, switched platform planks, ideologies, and members many times in American history. These switches were typically spurred on by major legislative changes and events, such as the Civil War in the 1860's, and Civil Rights in the 1960's." (https://thecompletepilgrim.com/how-the-democrats)

Over a long life of voting in election at every level, who I voted for depended on which party embraced nearly the same principles and objectives for the country I love and respect. I haven't changed much in my beliefs, but the parties have. I admired the founding fathers of this nation in setting it along a righteous path, even though the admirable sentiments laid out in the Declaration of Independence have still not been shared by all Americans. Progress has been made at various times, but there has also been reversals, which can only be attributed to that which seems obvious – the United States people are filled with hatred. Will the country come to the promise land where all men and women, no matter their race, ethnicity, religion, gender, sexual orientation, and any other thing that has often separated the people because some just don't want everyone to share the inalienable rights of life, liberty, and the pursuit of happiness.

How to choose your candidate for President of the United States (October 10, 2020)

I have never missed an election, national, state, and local in which I was eligible. Now, as I prepare to vote in the Presidential in the eighth decade of my life, I recall my first opportunity to exercise this great privilege and duty. I trusted my Dad's judgment, so I asked him what criteria he used to choose who to give his vote? He responded that always vote for the individual, not the party – you want to know who to hold responsible if you are later disappointed in your candidate. You might find one honest, intelligent, and trustworthy politician, but a group of them, no way. Dad also advised: "Make a list of positive traits you would like to see in the candidate of your choice, and another list of the negative traits you don't wish to see." I asked to know his lists, but he said, "No, you must make your list, try not to be swayed by others, judge the candidates for yourself, and adjust the lists as more information about the candidates becomes available."

I followed Dad's advice ever since. My candidate didn't always win, but at least I knew why I voted the way I did. My first presidential election was in 1956, a rematch between Republican Dwight David Eisenhower and Democrat Adlai Stevenson. (I was ineligible to vote in 1952, not being twenty-one.) I made four lists, one of the positive traits and one of each man's negative qualities. It became a tough choice. I found both candidates to have almost all the positive characteristics I sought and nearly none of the negative. Finally, I went with the incumbent, war hero, Ike. I decided I would not be disappointed no matter which one won. I've never had that luxury ever again at a presidential election. Sometimes I voted Republican, sometimes Democrat, and sometimes for a third-party candidate, which meant making an additional two lists.

My list of traits changed over the years, but a few kept popping up, election after election: Honesty for one positive, lying, or cheating for a negative. I want a president who takes the people into his confidence and tells them the truth about matters that do and should concern them. I don't want a cheerleader who tells the people what he wants them to believe, not what they need to know. My candidates have to understand the Constitution and protect it at all costs. I don't want one who will wish to ignore the ideals found in that precious living document to his or her benefit. My President's choice realizes that he or she represents all the people and is answerable to them. George Washington warned of the danger of political parties in his Farewell Address. Parties in power often seek advantage, not progress. We need a government that produces results, not gridlock, and compromise rather than ideology. The President has the responsibility to lead the way in making this happen.

Presidents need to admit that the U.S. has long been a racist nation, with bigotry and hatred rampant. A President must work to change this cancer on our national character and honor. There is much to do, and not nearly enough has been accomplished. Presidents should proudly enforce the separation of church and state. To do so is to protect the religious rights and beliefs of all, even those who don't believe. Over the centuries, religions have proven to be most sinful when they are intolerant of individuals or groups that don't think as they do. Just remember, the Christian Right is neither Christian nor right.

Presidents must honor the balance of powers of the three branches of the federal government; the executive, the legislative, and judicial branches. These are co-equal, and the nation must not tolerate attempts to subjugate one to another. It would be unconstitutional.

In choosing a presidential Cabinet and members of the President's administration, the number one qualification is that they have the experience, training, and skills to qualify for the job they are to fill. Patronage is not now and never should be a qualification. Consider Abraham Lincoln's Cabinet, given the title, Team of Rivals: The Political Genius of Abraham Lincoln (2005), written by historian Doris Kearns Goodwin. Lincoln first stunned the nation when he won the Republican nomination for President by prevailing over three prominent rivals— William H. Seward, Salmon P. Chase, and Edward Bates. Perhaps equally surprising was that

Lincoln appointed all three rivals to his Cabinet, where they served brilliantly as Secretary of State Seward, Secretary of the Treasury Chase, and attorney general Bates. Admittedly, Lincoln wasn't as fortunate in his choice of Vice President, Andrew Johnson.

I rather admired both John F. Kennedy and Ronald Reagan, for choosing their major competitor for their party's presidential candidate, Lyndon B. Johnson and George H.W. Bush, respectively. I'm afraid that some presidents have chosen their running mates carelessly, with no clear evidence, that they were qualified to take over the reins of Chief Executive if that becomes necessary. (Don't just choose a couple of midwest boys to capture votes to balance the ticket).

I consider myself a feminist, and so my choice for President will be one who champions the very just causes of women, who they hold in great respect. For far too long, half of the world's population, females, have been denied their full rights as citizens. The intolerant belief, championing over the centuries by religions, that women are naturally inferior to men and should subjugate themselves to the males pure bullshit. This belief is reason enough to disqualify some politicians from holding public offices.

Robert A. Nowlan, SR.

In preparing this material, my purpose is to be informative about my belief and fear that Trump has destroyed the Republican Party that I once knew and respected, and if re-elected he will work diligently to destroy the United States of America and the ideals it represents, even though its citizens have fallen very short of entitling all Americans, with no exceptions to have the rights Thomas Jefferson described in the Declaration of Independence. The U.S. has not obtained these rights for all its people, but progress has been made, until Trump put on the brakes. Trump and his enablers in the new Republican Party are behaving unconstitutional, and their virus must be eliminated.

I have tried to include alternative opinions if they are made with some degree of logic, respect for facts, and not resort to the famous cop-out, "well, so-and-so was worse." Give reasons not emotions. I'm not even trying to bring converts to my o pinions. I'm just trying to be informative. The upcoming presidential election November 3, 2020, is not between the Democrats and

Republicans. It is an important race between Americans, who love this nation, be they Democrats, Republicans or Independents, who understand, and honor the Constitution and the TRUMPUBLICAN Party of Donald Trump, who are determined to reelect an unfit, ignorant, insulting, womanizer, friends of dictators, failure to take the lead in the fight against the Coronavirus, and a man with no honor, no integrity, and no one other than me, Donald Trump.

True patriots must join together to expel this dangerous and unhinged man, to the island of forgotten people. Won't you be pleased to turn on the news and not see the smirking face of a man, who has no redeeming virtues and a very long list of vices. Members of the old GOP must join with Democrats and Independents to cut out the caner in our government, Trump and Pence. Getting rid of these two has the bonus of also ridding the United States, of Trump's enablers, who will even commit treasonable acts, in support of Trump's intention of destroying what makes America great.

In the articles and images that are throughout this book, Republicans often are taken to the woodshed for some needed spanking. However, these refer to the TRUMPUBLICANs, not the old GOP. The appeal to members of the party for whom I have frequently voted to help rid the nation of Trump and his Enablers, by voting Blue.

Trump's lack of empathy is worsened by his preference for style over substance. His daily press briefings promise miracle cures that don't work, sweeping action that falls far short, and imminent relief that never appears. When news organizations catch on to the snake-oil salesmanship, he attacks. "I watch and listen to the Fake News, CNN, MSDNC, ABC, NBC, CBS, some of FOX (desperately & foolishly pleading to be politically correct), the @nytimes, & the @washingtonpost, and all I see is hatred of me at any cost," he wrote on Twitter on Sunday evening. "Don't they understand that they are destroying themselves?" *(https://newrepublic.com/article/157022/trump-coronavirus-response-doesnt-care)*

R.A.N.

MEMORIAM

In Memory Of Those Who Lost Their Lives To Covid 19.

Because the President first considered the pandemic a hoax created by the Democratic Party to make him look bad. And then he refused to take any responsibility for combatting the pandemic by having a nation-wide plan, To do so is a chore that is indeed part of the job description of the president of the United States. Trump was too busy playing golf at a tremendous cost to taxpayers, and lying about the severity of the virus. He refused to adopt the views and recommendations of noted scientists because he thought he knew more than they did.

DEDICATION

To The Medical Practioners, Who Constantly Risk Their Lives To Care For Those Who Contracted The Virus. They Are Heroes.

Also, To Those Low Wages Americans Who Continue To Serve The Nation And Its Citizens By Risking Their Own Lives As Essential Workers

To The Scientists That Try To Inform The Public Of The Serious Results Of The Virus If Safeguards Are Not Followed, Despite Trump Undercutting Their Findings And Recommendations, Because He Is Ignorant, Jealous, And 'It's All About Me.'

To The Media For Reporting Trump's Stupid Missteps In The Time Perhaps The Greatest Crisis In USA History, Rivalling Its Wars.

ACKNOWLEGMENTS

To my wife and best friend, Wendy, our aging Black Lab, Jezebel (Jessie), and my family and friends. May they all remain safe during this pandemnic.

CONTENTS

INTRODUCTION

I was born during the Great Depression, but didn't take much interest in political parties until the 1940s, when Franklin D. Roosevelt was president. My parents at the time favored the Democrats, so I did too. I felt a patriotic obligation during the war, although I was aware that not everyone shared this view, as my playmates mouthed the anti-Roosevelt statements they heard from their parents. When Harry S. Truman became President on FDR's death, I had no idea who the man was and how he could replace the only president I ever had known. However, I was delighted when Truman upset Thomas Dewey in 1952. I stayed up all night listening to the radio as election figures for each state were updated each hour. I have never made up the lost sleep. I think I associated Dewey and his mustache with Hitler. Political philosophies didn't mean much to me and my playmates at that time. We still were following the family ticket.

Over a long life of voting in election at every level, who I cast my ballot for depended on which party embraced nearly the same principles and objectives for the country I love and respect. I haven't change much in my beliefs, but the parties have. I admired the founding fathers of this nation in setting it along a righteous path, even though the admirable sentiments laid out in the Declaration of Independence have still not been shared by all Americans.

Progress has been made at various times, but there has also been reversals, which can only be attributed to that which seems obvious – the United States people are filled with hatred. Will the country come to the promise land where all men and women, no matter their race, ethnicity, religion, gender, sexual orientation, and any other thing that has often separated the people because some just don't want everyone to share the inalienable rights of life, liberty, and the pursuit of happiness.

The two major political parties of the present Republican and Democrat have overgone changes in their political principles, in many ways moving from liberal to conservative and visa-versa. The reasons for these switches is complicated, yet interesting.

"The years leading up to the American Civil War were some of the most divisive in American history. Many northerners favored the abolition of slavery. Others supported accommodating the southern states. Most southerners favored maintaining the institution of slavery and favored the power of state governments over that of the federal government. These disagreements split existing political parties and led to the formation of new parties that vied for control of the U.S. and Confederate governments during the Civil War." (https://classroom.synonym.com/civil-warera-political-parties-north-vs-south-8901.html)

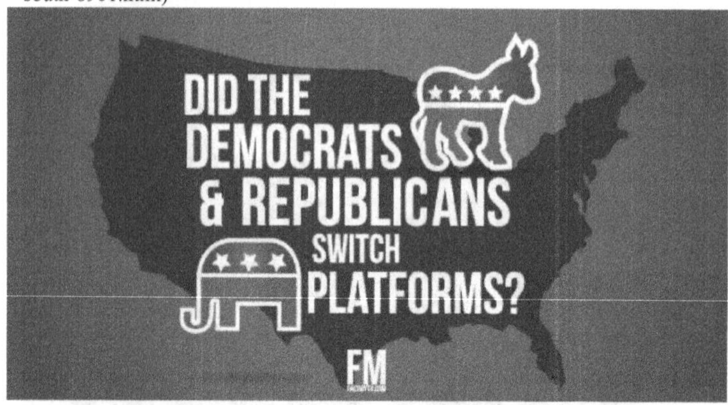

At its founding in 1856, the Republican Party opposed the expansion of slavery, supported more money for public education, and advocated a more liberal immigration policy. The Democrats started out as the conservative party but are now the liberal party. "The Democratic and Republican Parties have made a long transition from their founding ideological principles. The Democratic stronghold was the conservative South, while the Republican stronghold was the liberal North. The Republicans, once the liberal party, are now the conservative party.

Part of the reason for the two parties switching polarity was due to the tremendous wave of immigrants that arrived in the late 19th and early 20th centuries.

"Many immigrants came to America from all over the world. Irish, Chinese, Italians, Russians, Scandinavians, Germans, Japanese and Jews made up the majority. Most of the immigrants came from Northern and Western Europe. Almost 4.5 million Irish immigrants came to the United States, accounting for 1/3 of the total European immigrant population. 5 million Germans settled mostly in the Midwest. The California Gold Rush also attracted over 25,000 Asian immigrants."
(https://www.sutori.com/story/immigration-in-the-19th-century--y2rd9xbiKHP5DWcN7BP12zMw)

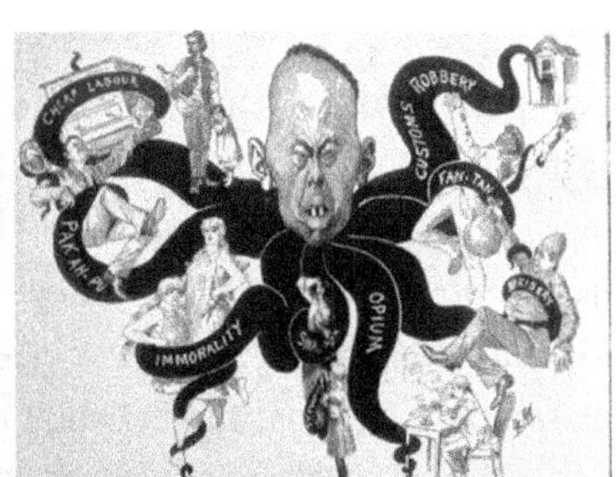

"Political parties perform various tasks within their nation states, their roles and existence have been subject to heated debates for many generations. Notable figures in U.S history such as the first president of the United States George Washington viewed them in a rather pessimistic fashion as he once famously warned against the "continual mischiefs of the spirit of party". In hindsight we can see how his warning was not heeded by the political class of America. Nevertheless, a study of the United States is almost impossible without looking at the history of the political parties that functions within them. These parties are not constants, they form, change over time and ultimately break away. Not a single party in the entirety of U.S history has maintained the exact same stance on specific policy issues throughout its lifespan. Parties are ever changing political organisms that are subject to various factors that lead to them adjusting from time to time. The ideology of the members that combine to form these parties is what ultimately leads to parties not only forming, but also changing.

Political parties do indeed carry with them certain benefits to the governmental systems that adopt them. Some of their most notable contributions involve serving as intermediaries as they create a communication channel between like-minded people within society to the government. They transmit the policies and ideology of the specific groups that they represent. In addition, they nominate candidates for various positions within government, this is vital as political parties help decrease the choice range for the various positions that exist and compete for a specific position, hence providing the voters with the best choices available from the various political parties available. They provide public accountability and manage conflict within the government as well.

Political parties form as a result of a shared group of peoples unified set of ideas regarding how a government should function. However, the changes that occur over time are due to the same reason that lead to the formation of political parties, the distinct groups that form them. These groups are made up of members of similar ideological classes, however these people change their ideological leanings based on a wide range of external factors such as social class, income levels, geographical location, ethnicity, religious affiliation, etc. As and when these factors change the political parties core values adjust as well.

Basically, parties form and change due to ideology. They form when their core group of founding members agree on a set of issues, consequentially they change or divide when those unifying ideologies begin to diverge from each other. Another common reason why political parties change over time occurs when their supporter base changes. Basically, this is due to the party changing their policies which attracts voters that normally would not have voted for that specific party and alienating their previous voters who do not agree with the policy shifts. The New Deal is a very common occurrence whereby African American voters who were very known to have been loyal Republicans switched to Democrats as the Democrats were willing to implement policies that were more aligned with what they wanted. This is the most influential aspect that leads to changing political parties.

A common mistake most people make is claim that the Republican Party freed the slaves and use that fact to claim that the Republicans are more in line with African American rights. False, this misconception occurs when one does not take into account the fact that the ideological leanings of the members of the Republican party back then would now be classified as democratic, over the years many members of the democratic party joined the Republican party due to internal policy and ideology changes, same goes for Republicans.

Sometimes immense external pressure leads to parties having to change over time. Regardless of whether one was a democrat or a republican, segregation and racism was a bipartisan issue. Both parties were guilty of allowing it to spread and prosper throughout the country as both had their fair share of the blame. These policies led to some of the most shameful chapters in U.S History, and within that dark time rose the civil rights movement. The situation was so heinous during that time due to "Jim Crow laws at the local and state levels" which "barred them from classrooms and bathrooms, from theaters and train cars, from juries and legislatures".

The civil rights movement which lasted for more than a decade brought about such an immense shift in public opinion regarding racial segregation and equal rights that it led to the government in its entirety to shift its policies regardless of party lines. To this day both Democrats and the Republicans advocate equal rights with regards to their policies and seek to portray themselves as being unbiased towards the race of their constituents.

 Another way could be the advent of certain minority groups gaining immense power over a specific party as was seen with FDR when he became president and completely rebranded the Democratic party in the 1930s with his New Deal policies. In modern times this is shown with the advent of Donald Trump and the Republican party whereby although he is advocating ultra-conservative policies as reflected by his cabinet choices up until the date of this essay. Regardless, of how he shifts over time, Trump on his own has led to immense shifts in the political landscape in the United States such that we should definitely expect to see major changes over the coming years. (How U.S political parties formed and changed over time, The Cerebrum; Oct 1, 2017; Nasser Ali, https://medium.com/@thecerebrumschool/how-u-s-political-parties-formed-and-changed-over-time-17ff2a1fcfd1)

BIRTH OF THE REPUBLICAN PARTY

The Republican Party was born on March 20, 1854, in a little schoolhouse in Ripon, Wisconsin by a small group of dedicated abolitionists, ex-Whigs, ex-Free Soilers and former Democrats gathered to fight the expansion of slavery. The Republican Party name was christened in a June 1854 editorial written by New York newspaper magnate Horace Greeley.

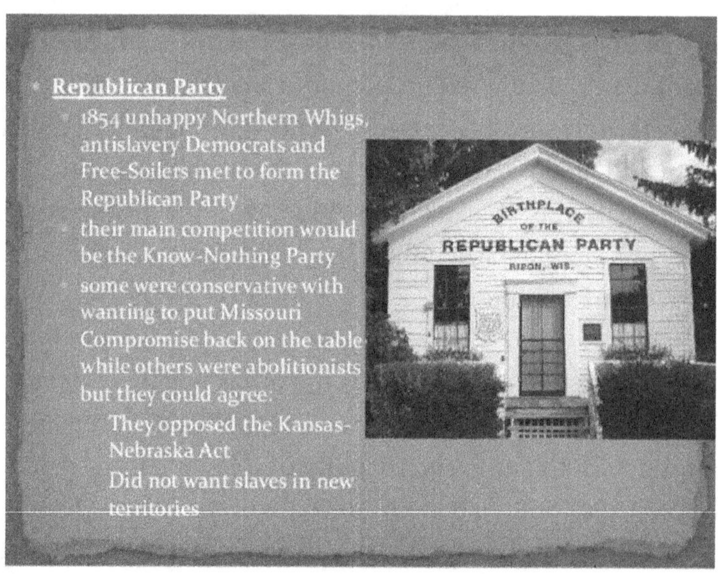

"We should not care much whether those thus united (against slavery) were designated 'Whig,' 'Free Democrat' or something else; though we think some simple name like 'Republican' would more fitly designate those who had united to restore the Union to its true mission of champion and promulgator of Liberty rather than propagandist of slavery." (Horace Greeley quote: We should not care much whether ...https://www.azquotes.com/quote/792173)

The name "Republican" originated with Thomas Jefferson's Democratic-Republican Party, which was commitment to the inalienable rights of life, liberty, and the pursuit of happiness.

FEDERALISTS VS. DEMOCRATIC REPUBLICANS	
Federalists	**Democratic Republicans**
Led by Alexander Hamilton	Led by Thomas Jefferson
Thought rich, educated people should lead nation	Thought more people should have political power
Wanted strong federal government	Wanted strong state governments
Wanted to encourage manufacturing and trade	Wanted to encourage farming
Supported loose interpretation of the Constitution	Supported strict interpretation of the Constitution

The Party was formally organized on July 6, 1854, when a state convention of anti-slavery men was held in the outskirts of Jackson, Michigan, to found a new political party. Upwards of 10,000 people turned out for a mass meeting. Since the convention day was hot and the huge crowd could not be accommodated in the hall, the meeting adjourned to an oak grove on "Morgan's Forty" on the outskirts of the town known today as "Under the Oaks," (www.dublingop.org/about.html)

This led to the first organizing convention in Pittsburgh on February 22, 1856. And two years later, the first Republican National Convention took place in the Philadelphia Musical Fund Hall from June 17 to June 19, 1856, where the Republicans nominated their first presidential candidate John C. Fremont, an American military officer and an early explorer and mapmaker of the American West.

"Fremont was one of the principal figures in opening up that region to settlement and was instrumental in the U.S. conquest and development of California. The Know-Nothing Party nominated former President Millard Fillmore, of New York. In the election, Fremont and his running mate William Dayton of New Jersey were defeated by Democrats James Buchanan and John C. Breckinridge but came closer to uniting the electorate of the North and West against the South than had any previous candidate." (https://www.britannica.com/biography/John-C-Fremont)

Born: January 21, 1813, Died: July 13, 1890, at the age of 77

The Compromise of 1850 was clearly beginning to fall apart by the campaign of 1856. The popularity of Taylor (1848) and the unpopularity of Scott (1852) had disguised the increasingly sectional divide in American politics. The escalating violence in Kansas underscored the danger to the nation inherent in the slavery issue.

The two established parties were proving incapable of addressing the issue. The Whigs had unraveled leading to the formation of a new party completely opposed to the expansion of slavery. The Democrats remained together only by pandering to Southern slave interests. President Pierce failed to garner enthusiasm for his renomination. James Buchanan had been a leading contender for the nomination in 1852 and emerged as the front runner at the Cincinnati Democratic convention (June 1856). Like Pierce, his lack of involvement in the heated issues, especially slavery, was a major asset. It took 17 ballots, but Buchanan was nominated unanimously.

The Democratic platform supported the Compromise of 1850, opposed any Federal limitations interference in slavery, and came out for the transcontinental railroad. The new Republican Party emerged as a union of anti-slavery Whigs and Free-Soil Democrats. It was a sectional party with no support in the South and very little in the Border States. The Republicans nominated John Fremont who made a name for himself in California during the Mexican War.

The Republicans were initially a single-issue party. They were opposed to the expansion of slavery. They sharply criticized President Pierce for not acting forcefully to stop the violence in Kansas. The Know-Nothing Party emerged as another single-issue party. They were opposed to immigration and Catholicism. (Irish immigrants in the 1840s had substantially expanded the Catholic population in America.) The Republicans campaigned on the slogan party in the candidate was "Free Speech, Free Press, Free soil, Free Men, Fremont and Victory!"

The Democrats warned that the South would not accept a Republican victory and would secede. They also incorrectly charged that Fremont was Catholic. The South voted in a bloc for Buchanan who also carried most of the border states as well as northern states like Illinois, Indiana, Pennsylvania, and New Jersey. It is unclear to what extent the vote was a referendum on slavery in the north or northern concern over Southern secession. Buchanan won with 174 electoral votes. Fremont amassed 174 votes, a respectable showing for a new party. Former President Filmore only carried Maryland with 8 electoral votes, but over 20 percent of the popular vote."
(https://www.histclo.com/country/us/hist/elect/19/e1856p.html)

In the following political cartoon, Candidate Fremont is shown taking calls from advocates of "popery", free love Fourierism, Racial Equality and Women's Rights. *

This Louis Maurer political cartoon was published by Currier & Ives during the 1856. The man at the right is Republican nominee John C. Freemont. Maurer was lampooning the various elements Freemont was supposedly collecting under the Republican banner, including anti-tobacco and liquor preachers, suffragettes, immigrants, free lovers, Catholics, and blacks. Interestingly there was no abolitionists pictured. Perhaps picturing a black man covered the slavery issue. Note the suffragette and how she is dressed. The outfit looks rather like something a young boy would wear. I am not sure if this is what Maurer was trying to depict. This was not, however, how women dressed in the 1850s.

(https://www.histclo.com/country/us/hist/elect/19/e1856p.html)

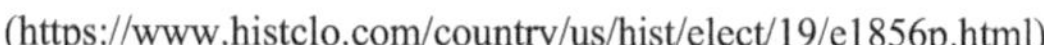

THE RIGHT MAN FOR THE RIGHT PLACE.

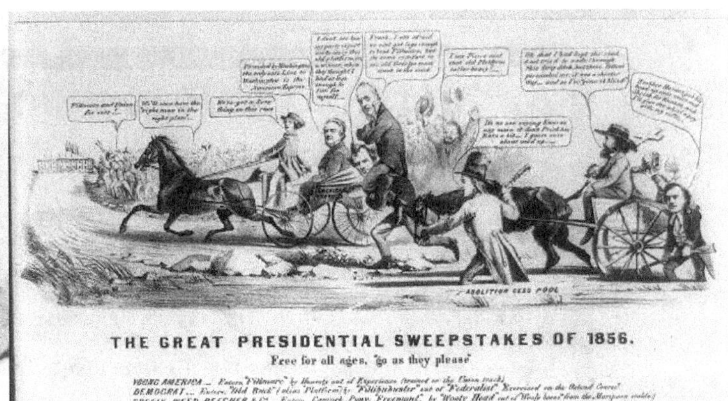

Nominee	James Buchanan	John C. Frémont	Millard Fillmore
Party	Democratic	Republican	Know-Nothing
Home state	Pennsylvania	California	New York
Running mate	John C. Breckinridge	William L. Dayton	Andrew J. Donelson
Electoral vote	174	114	8
States carried	19	11	1
Popular vote	1,836,072	1,342,345	873,053
Percentage	45.3%	33.1%	21.6%

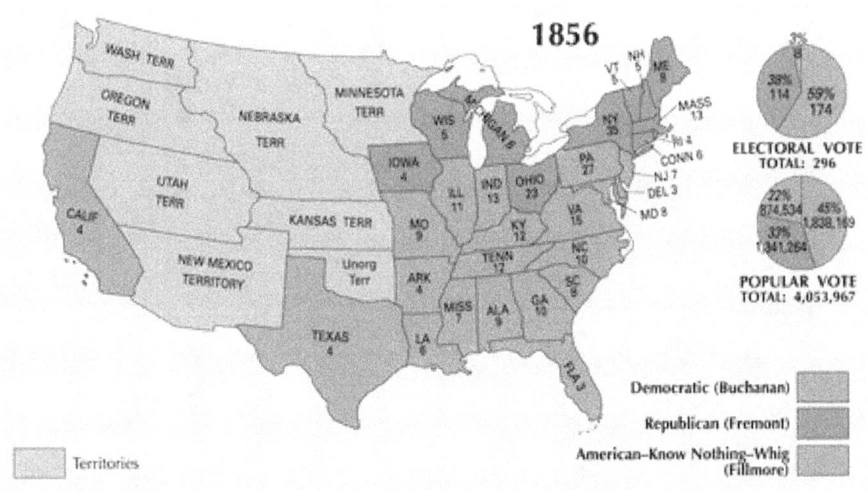

Are These Pillars Still Standing in the TRUMPUBLICAN Party?

QUOTATIONS ABOUT THE REPUBLICAN PARTY

(Source of the following ten quotations: https://www.goodreads.com/quotes/tag/republicans?)

"I recognize the Republican party as the sheet anchor of the colored man's political hopes and the ark of his safety" — Frederick Douglass

"Have you ever wondered why Republicans are so interested in encouraging people to volunteer in their communities? It's because volunteers work for no pay. Republicans have been trying to get people to work for no pay for a long time. " — George Carlin

"The Republicans believe in the minimum wage -- the more the minimum, the better." — Harry Truman

"We had a choice between Democrats who couldn't learn from the past and Republicans who couldn't stop living in it..." — P.J. O'Rourke

"How did sex come to be thought of as dirty in the first place? God must have been a Republican. " — Will Durst

"Think about it...The Republicans have gone from Abraham Lincoln to Sarah Palin to Donald Trump. No wonder they don't believe in evolution." — Andy Borowitz

"Younger white Southerners are more republican not because they are more conservative but because their attachments formed during a period when Republicans were more likely to be regarded as an attractive social group." — Donald P. Green

"The Republican Party today has a catechism. If you want to be a candidate, with very rare exceptions, you have to repeat the catechism in lockstep uniformity: global warming isn't happening, no taxes on the rich. There are about ten things that you have to repeat, whether you believe them or not. Anybody who departs from them is in trouble." — Noam Chomsky

"Anarchists have taken over (the GOP)." — Harry Reid

"For an entire wing of the G.O.P., a dysfunctional government, whose only visible activity is mismanaging crises, is not an embarrassment but the vindication of a worldview." — Amy Davidson

The nickname of the Republican Party "Grand Old Party" (GOP) wasn't introduced until 1888. After the Republicans won back the Presidency and Congress for the first time since the Grant administration, the Chicago Tribune proclaimed: "Let us be thankful that under the rule of the Grand Old Party ... these United States will resume the onward and upward march which the election of Grover Cleveland in 1884 partially arrested."
(https://www.history.com/topics/us-politics/republican-party)

REPUBLICAN ECONOMIST
BRUCE BARTLETT:
"I love Donald Trump because he exposes everything about the Republican Party that I have frankly come to hate. It's just filled with people who are crazy, stupid, and have absolutely no idea what they're talking about."

Occupy Democrats

We Are REPUBLICAN Because...

We believe the strength of the nation lies with the individual and that each person's dignity, freedom, ability and responsibility must be honored

We Believe in equal rights, equal justice and equal opportunity for all, regardless of race, creed, sex, age or disability.

We believe free enterprise and encouraging individual initiative have brought this nation opportunity, economic growth, and prosperity.

We believe government must practice fiscal responsibility and allow individuals to keep more of the money they earn.

We believe the proper role of government is to provide for the people only those critical functions that cannot be performed by individuals or private organizations and that the best government is that which governs least.

We believe the most effective, responsible and responsive government is the government closest to the people.

We believe Americans must retain the principles that made us strong while developing new and innovative ideas to meet the challenges of changing times.

We believe Americans value and preserve our national strength and pride while working to extend peace, freedom and human rights throughout the world.

Finally, we believe the Republican Party is the best vehicle for translating these ideas into positive and successful principles of government.

ANYTIME SIGN 1-800-582-1554

Does Trump and his loyalists hold these beliefs?

(http://www.cnn.com/2010/POLITICS/08/30/obama.economy/index.html?npt=NP1)

Personal Political Positions

In 1952, I was 18, but not eligible to vote. However, I following the election campaign with great interest. To my mind, both parties had chosen admirable candidates, Dwight D. Eisenhower for the Republicans and Adlai Stevenson for the Democrats. I attempted to learn what principles they stood for, and in which way they differed. I listen to their words and was impressed. Both addressed the issues and did not just mouth some rhetoric they and their managers believed would appeal to voters. I heard what the two thought was important, discussed the problems in the country as they saw them and offered some solutions. I believe that was the next to last presidential election in which I admired both the candidates. (Eisenhower was elected and so I would have four years before I could finally vote to judge his performance). The only other time was in 1956, when the Eisenhower and Stevenson matched up again. Eisenhower was a hero, and I liked Ike, especially when I read some of his beliefs, which I share here: (Sources: https://www.brainyquote.com/authors/dwight-d-eisenhower-quotes; https://www.quotationfun.com/author/dwight-eisenhower-quotes-753; www.eisenhowerlibrary.gov/eisenhowers/quotes)*

DWIGHT D. EISENHOWER'S QUOTES

"Every gun that is made, every warship launched, every rocket fired signifies in the final sense, a theft from those who hunger and are not fed, those who are cold and are not clothed. This world in arms is not spending money alone. It is spending the sweat of its laborers, the genius of its scientists, the hopes of its children. This is not a way of life at all in any true sense. Under the clouds of war, it is humanity hanging on a cross of iron.”

“Don't join the book burners. Don't think you're going to conceal faults by concealing evidence that they ever existed. Don't be afraid to go in your library and read every book...”

“Never waste a minute thinking about people you don't like.”

“In preparing for battle I have always found that plans are useless, but planning is indispensable.”

“Leadership is the art of getting someone else to do something you want done because he wants to do it.”

“A people that values its privileges above its principles soon loses both.”

“Extremes to the right and to the left of any political dispute are always wrong.”

“If you want total security, go to prison. There you're fed, clothed, given medical care and so on. The only thing lacking... is freedom. ”

“The search for a scapegoat is the easiest of all hunting expeditions.”

“You do not lead by hitting people over the head -- that's assault, not leadership.”

“Get it all on record now - get the films - get the witnesses -because somewhere down the road of history some bastard will get up and say that this never happened.”

“Should any political party attempt to abolish social security unemployment insurance and eliminate labor laws and farm programs you would not hear of that party again in our political history. There is a tiny splinter group of course that believes you can do these things. Among them are a few other Texas oil millionaires and an occasional politician or business man from other areas. Their number is negligible and they are stupid.”

“In the councils of government, we must guard against the acquisition of unwarranted influence, whether sought or unsought, by the military industrial complex. The potential for the disastrous rise of misplaced power exists and will persist. We must never let the weight of this combination endanger our liberties or democratic processes. We should take nothing for granted. Only an alert and knowledgeable citizenry can compel the proper meshing of the huge industrial and military machinery of defense with our peaceful methods and goals, so that security and liberty may prosper together.”

“What counts is not necessarily the size of the dog in the fight- it's the size of the fight in the dog.”

“Never question another man's motive. His wisdom, yes, but not his motives.”

“The supreme quality for leadership is unquestionably integrity. Without it, no real success is possible, no matter whether it is on a section gang, a football field, in an army, or in an office.”

“Never let yourself be persuaded that any one Great Man, any one leader, is necessary to the salvation of America. When America consists of one leader and 158 million followers, it will no longer be America.”

“A sense of humor is part of the art of leadership, of getting along with people, of getting things done.”

“No man is worth your tears, but once you find one that is, he won't make you cry.”

“May we never confuse honest dissent with disloyal subversion. ”

“Never send a battalion to take a hill if a regiment is available.”

“Pessimism never won any battle.”

“You are about to embark upon the Great Crusade, toward which we have striven these many months. The eyes of the world are upon you. The hopes and prayers of liberty-loving people everywhere march with you. In company with our brave Allies and brothers-in-arms on other Fronts, you will bring about the destruction of the German war machine, the elimination of Nazi tyranny over the oppressed peoples of Europe, and security for ourselves in a free world. Your task will not be an easy one. Your enemy is well trained, well equipped and battle hardened. He will fight savagely. But this is the year 1944! Much has happened since the Nazi triumphs of 1940-41. The United Nations have inflicted upon the Germans great defeats, in open battle, man-to-man. Our air offensive has seriously reduced their strength in the air and their capacity to wage war on the ground. Our Home Fronts have given us an overwhelming superiority in weapons and munitions of war, and placed at our disposal great reserves of trained fighting men. The tide has turned! The freemen of the world are marching together to Victory! I have full confidence in your courage and devotion to duty and skill in battle. We will accept nothing less than full Victory! Good luck! And let us beseech the blessing of Almighty God upon this great and noble undertaking." (D-Day)

"The problem in defense is how far you can go without destroying from within what you are trying to defend from without."

"As we peer into society's future, we -- you and I, and our government -- must avoid the impulse to live only for today, plundering for our own ease and convenience the precious resources of tomorrow. We cannot mortgage the material assets of our grandchildren without risking the loss also of their political and spiritual heritage. We want democracy to survive for all generations to come, not to become the insolvent phantom of tomorrow."

"We are going to have peace even if we have to fight for it."

"The history of free men is never written by chance but by choice - their choice."

"I like to believe that people in the long run are going to do more to promote peace than our governments. Indeed, I think that people want peace so much that one of these days governments had better get out of the way and let them have it."

"I hate war as only a soldier who has lived it can, only as one who has seen its brutality, its futility, its stupidity."

"Pull the string and it will follow wherever you wish. Push it, and it will go nowhere at all."

"Leadership consists of nothing but taking responsibility for everything that goes wrong and giving your subordinates credit for everything that goes well."

"An intellectual is a man who takes more words than necessary to tell more than he knows."

"Always try to associate yourself with and learn as much as you can from those who know more than you do, who do better than you, who see more clearly than you."

"Only Americans can hurt America."

"Every gun that is made, every warship launched, every rocket fired signifies, in the final sense, a theft from those who hunger and are not fed, those who are cold and are not clothed. This world in arms is not spending money alone. It is spending the sweat of its laborers, the genius of its scientists, the hopes of its children. The cost of one modern heavy bomber is this: a modern brick school in more than 30 cities. It is two electric power plants, each serving a town of 60,000 population. It is two fine, fully equipped hospitals. It is some fifty miles of concrete pavement. We pay for a single fighter plane with a half million bushels of wheat. We pay for a single destroyer with new homes that could have housed more than 8,000 people. This is, I repeat, the best way of life to be found on the road the world has been taking. This is not a way of life at all, in any true sense. Under the cloud of threatening war, it is humanity hanging from a cross of iron.... Is there no other way the world may live?"

"The world could be fixed of its problems if every child understood the necessity of their existence."

"When I was a small boy in Kansas, a friend of mine and I went fishing. I told him I wanted to be a real Major League baseball player, a genuine professional like Honus Wagner. My friend said that he'd like to be President of the United States. Neither of us got our wish."

"All generalizations are inaccurate, including this one."

"I despise people who go to the gutter on either the right or the left and hurl rocks at those in the center."

"Freedom has its life in the hearts, the actions, the spirit of men and so it must be daily earned and refreshed - else like a flower cut from its life-giving roots, it will wither and die."

"Neither a wise nor a brave man lies down on the tracks of history to wait for the train of the future to run over him."

"What is important is seldom urgent and what is urgent is seldom important."

"An atheist is a man who watches a Notre Dame - Southern Methodist University game and doesn't care who wins."

"In most communities it is illegal to cry "fire" in a crowded assembly. Should it not be considered serious international misconduct to manufacture a general war scare in an effort to achieve local political aims? "

"Peace and justice are two sides of the same coin."

"Humility must always be the portion of any man who receives acclaim earned in blood of his followers and sacrifices of his friends."

"We seek peace, knowing that peace is the climate of freedom."

"Preventive war was an invention of Hitler. I would not even listen to anyone seriously that came and talked about such a thing."

"Don't join the book burners. Do not think you are going to conceal thoughts by concealing evidence that they ever existed."

"This conjunction of an immense military establishment and a large arms industry is new in the American experience. The total influence -- economic, political, even spiritual -- is felt in every city, every State house, every office of the Federal government. We recognize the imperative need for this development. Yet we must not fail to comprehend its grave implications. Our toil, resources and livelihood are all involved; so is the very structure of our society.

In the councils of government, we must guard against the acquisition of unwarranted influence, whether sought or unsought, by the military industrial complex. The potential for the disastrous rise of misplaced power exists and will persist.

We must never let the weight of this combination endanger our liberties or democratic processes. We should take nothing for granted. Only an alert and knowledgeable citizenry can compel the proper meshing of the huge industrial and military machinery of defense with our peaceful methods and goals, so that security and liberty may prosper together."

"The world is more like it is now then it ever has before."

"How far have we come in man's long pilgrimage from darkness toward light? Are we nearing the light—a day of freedom and of peace for all mankind? Or are the shadows of another night closing in upon us?"

"Worry is a word that I don't allow myself to use."

"History does not long entrust the care of freedom to the weak or timid."

"Those who take the extreme positions in American political and economic life are always wrong."

"The time has passed for dilly-dallying. We must demand satisfactory performance."

"Wars are stupid and they can start stupidly."

"I don't like the idea of something where you have to depend upon the integrity of the man and not the integrity of the institution."

"Statesmanship is developed in the hard knocks of general experience, private and public."

"Freedom has been defined as the opportunity for self-discipline."

"Things are more like they are now than they ever were before."

"We are ready in short, to dedicate our strength to serving the needs, rather than the fears, of the world."

"If you are waging peace, you can't be too particular sometimes about the special attitudes that different countries take. We were a young country once, and our whole policy for the first 150 years was, we were neutral. We must not be parsimonious, as long as we are not shooting, we are not spending one tenth as much."

This world in arms is not spending money alone.

It is spending the sweat of its laborers, the genius of its scientists, the hopes of its children.

The cost of one modern heavy bomber is this: a modern brick school in more than 30 cities.

It is two electric power plants, each serving a town of 60,000 population. It is two fine, fully equipped hospitals.

It is some fifty miles of concrete pavement.

We pay for a single fighter plane with a half million bushels of wheat.

We pay for a single destroyer with new homes that could have housed more than 8,000 people.

This is, I repeat, the best way of life to be found on the road the world has been taking.

This is not a way of life at all, in any true sense. Under the cloud of threatening war, it is humanity hanging from a cross of iron. These plain and cruel truths define the peril and point the hope that come with this spring of 1953."

"War is mankind's most tragic and stupid folly; to seek or advise its deliberate provocation is a black crime against all men."

"Our form of government has no sense unless it is founded in a deeply felt religious faith, and I don't care what it is."

"If any blame or fault attaches to the attempt, it is mine alone."

"Every gun that is made, every warship launched, every rocket fired signifies, in the final sense, a theft from those who hunger and are not fed, those who are cold and are not clothed.

This world in arms is not spending money alone. It is spending the sweat of its laborers, the genius of its scientists, the hopes of its children. The cost of one modern heavy bomber is this: a modern brick school in more than 30 cities. It is two electric power plants, each serving a town of 60,000 population. It is two fine, fully equipped hospitals. It is some fifty miles of concrete pavement. We pay for a single fighter with a half-million bushels of wheat. We pay for a single destroyer with new homes that could have housed more than 8,000 people. . . This is not a way of life at all, in any true sense. Under the cloud of threatening war, it is humanity hanging from a cross of iron."

"In the councils of government, we must guard against the acquisition of unwarranted influence, whether sought or unsought, by the military-industrial complex. The potential for the disastrous rise of misplaced power exists and will persist."

"So, the world is again faced with the problem of armed aggression. Powerful dictatorships are attacking an exposed, but free, area. What should we do? Shall we take the position that, submitting to threat, it is better to surrender pieces of free territory in the hope that this will satisfy the appetite of the aggressor and we shall have peace?"

"To pause there would be to confirm the hopeless finality of a belief that two atomic colossi are doomed malevolently to eye each other indefinitely across a trembling world. To stop there would be to accept helplessly the probability of civilization destroyed, the annihilation of the irreplaceable heritage of mankind handed down to us from generation to generation, and the condemnation of mankind to begin all over again the age-old struggle upward from savagery towards decency, and right, and justice. Surely no sane member of the human race could discover victory in such desolation."

"Through knowledge and understanding we will drive from the temple of freedom all those who seek to establish over us thought control, whether they be agents of a foreign state or demagogues thirsty for personal power and public notice."

"If a political party does not have its foundation in the determination to advance a cause that is right and that is moral, then it is not a political party; it is merely a conspiracy to seize power."

"Though force can protect in emergency, only justice, fairness, consideration and cooperation can finally lead men to the dawn of eternal peace."

(Source: 102 Dwight D. Eisenhower Quotes – BrainyQuote https://www.brainyquote.com/authors/dwight-d-eisenhower-quotes)

How many Republicans presently serving in governmental positions would mark these "like" if they came across them on Facebook?

In 1956, As I weighed which candidate I would vote for, I didn't feel that the candidate I did not choose to support was a scoundrel and needed to be horse whipped. I didn't believe that had the candidate I didn't support won; the nation was doomed. No, it was just that more voters suggested the other fellow was the better person for the job. It was the duty of all Americans to wish him well and give him time to prove himself. Such was the case with the Democrat nominee in 1956, Adlai Stevenson, a decent, intelligent man, with much charm and humor. Oh, how I wish it were still possible to match two decent Americans one for each major party making it difficult to decide for whom to vote.

ADLAI STEVENSON II QUOTES

Let's hear from Stevenson as well. I certainly listened to what he had to say. I actually met him once in Bloomington, Illinois, when he was visiting his sister who lived in a house across the street from my family's resident. In my mind, if he won, he would do a good job because he was a good man. What follows are some of his most famous quotations. *(Sources: https://www.brainyquote.com/authors/adlai-stevenson-i-quotes; https://www.azquotes.com/author/14116-Adlai_E_Stevenson, "Adlai's Almanac: The Wit and Wisdom of Stevenson of Illinois" by Adlai Ewing Stevenson, (p. 20), 1952.)*

"There was a time when a fool and his money were soon parted, but now it happens to everybody."

"If the Republicans will stop telling lies about the Democrats, we will stop telling the truth about them."

"I'm not an old, experienced hand at politics. But I am now seasoned enough to have learned that the hardest thing about any political campaign is how to win without proving that you are unworthy of winning."

"I believe in the forgiveness of sin and the redemption of ignorance."

"An editor is someone who separates the wheat from the chaff and then prints the chaff."

"Man is a strange animal. He generally cannot read the handwriting on the wall until his back is up against it."

"To act coolly, intelligently and prudently in perilous circumstances is the test of a man - and also a nation."

"It will be helpful in our mutual objective to allow every man in America to look his neighbor in the face and see a man-not a color."

"I don't want to send them to jail. I want to send them to school."
"We must recover the element of quality in our traditional pursuit of equality. We must not, in opening our schools to everyone, confuse the idea that all should have equal chance with the notion that all have equal endowments."

"All progress has resulted from people who took unpopular positions."

"Accuracy to a newspaper is what virtue is to a lady; but a newspaper can always print a retraction."

"An Independent is someone who wants to take the politics out of politics."

"I believe that if we really want human brotherhood to spread and increase until it makes life safe and sane, we must also be certain that there is no one true faith or path by which it may spread."

"A hungry man is not a free man."

"Nothing so dates a man as to decry the younger generation."

"We mean by 'politics' the people's business - the most important business there is."
present."

"Laws are never as effective as habits."

"Ignorance is stubborn and prejudice is hard."

"Freedom rings where opinions clash."

"Public confidence in the integrity of the Government is indispensable to faith in democracy; and when we lose faith in the system, we have lost faith in everything we fight and spend for."

"As citizens of this democracy, you are the rulers and the ruled, the law-givers and the law-abiding, the beginning and the end."

"Flattery is all right so long as you don't inhale."
"As citizens of this democracy, you are the rulers and the ruled, the law-givers and the law-abiding, the beginning and the end."

"Communism is the corruption of a dream of justice."

"You will find that the truth is often unpopular and the contest between agreeable fancy and disagreeable fact is unequal. For, in the vernacular, we Americans are suckers for good news."

"When an American says that he loves his country, he means not only that he loves the New England hills, the prairies glistening in the sun, the wide and rising plains, the great mountains, and the sea. He means that he loves an inner air, an inner light in which freedom lives and in which a man can draw the breath of self-respect."

"The idea that you can merchandise candidates for high office like breakfast cereal - that you can gather votes like box tops - is, I think, the ultimate indignity to the democratic process."

"That which seems the height of absurdity in one generation often becomes the height of wisdom in another."

"On this shrunken globe, men can no longer live as strangers."

"Nature is neutral. Man has wrested from nature the power to make the world a desert or make the deserts bloom. There is no evil in the atom; only in men's souls."

"We can chart our future clearly and wisely only when we know the path which has led to the present."

"To act coolly, intelligently and prudently in perilous circumstances is the test of a man - and also a nation."

"Freedom rings where opinions clash."

"Some people approach every problem with an open mouth."

"We have confused the free with the free and easy."

"Nothing so dates a man as to decry the younger generation."

"Freedom is not an ideal, it is not even a protection, if it means nothing more than freedom to stagnate, to live without dreams, to have no greater aim than a second car and another television set."

"Someone asked me...how it felt and I was reminded of a story that a fellow townsman of ours used to tell--Abraham Lincoln. They asked him how he felt once after an unsuccessful election. He said he felt like a little boy who had stubbed his toe in the dark. He said that he was too old to cry, but it hurt too much to laugh." (When Adlai was asked about losing the election)

"Journalists do not live by words alone, although sometimes they have to eat them."

"Peace is the one condition of survival in this nuclear age."

"Law is not a profession at all, but rather a business service station and repair shop."

"A beauty is a woman you notice; a charmer is one who notices you."

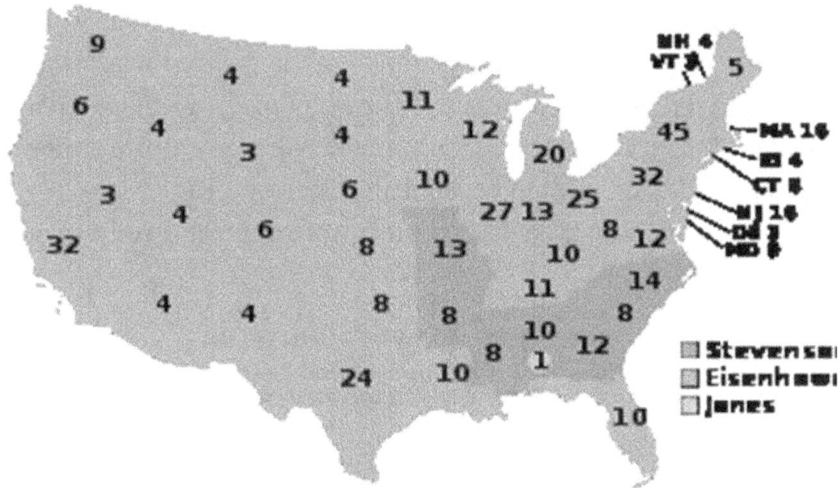

In the 1956 Presidential election, faithless elector W. F. Turner cast his vote for Jones, who was a circuit court judge in Turner's home town, for President of the United States and Herman E. Talmadge for Vice President, instead of voting for Adlai Stevenson and Estes Kefauver. (Our Campaigns.com-A.F. Turner)

My decision for whom to give my vote in 1956 was difficult. I eventually chose to vote for the incumbent, Eisenhower, as did the majority of other Americans. I believe part of the reason, was a lot of people considered Stevenson an intellectual, and Americans had long been anti-intellectual. The fifties was a rather sober time, and Stevenson, finding so much humor in things and making jokes, may have caused many voters to believe he wasn't serious enough to be president. He was also divorced.

"His ex-wife Ellen Borden was married to Adlai E. Stevenson in 1928, when she was 19, and they were divorced in 1949, when Mr. Stevenson was Governor of Illinois. The divorce was considered a liability during his campaign for President in 1952 and 1956, but Mr. Stevenson would say only that it was due to 'the mutual incompatibility of our lives.' (https://www.nytimes.com/1972/07/29/archives/mrs-ellen-istevenson-exwife-0-of-presldenhal-candzdate-dzes.html)

In 1956, while Adlai weighed a second race for the Presidency, his ex-wife said he was "a Hamlet who can't make up his mind" and added that he "loves to be dramatic" (Ibid)

Adlai never re-married, but was in relationships with Rita Gam (1964 - 1967), Shelley Winters (1961 - 1962), Marietta Tree (1952), Katherine Graham, Dorothy Malone, Joan Fontaine and Myrna Loy

A little-known fact about Stevenson is that he shot and killed 16-year-old Ruth Merwin, a guest and close friend of his sister, when he was a boy of 12. The incident haunted him forever.

" Some accounts state that Adlai was mimicking the manual of arms when an undetected round was dislodged by the handling of the gun and was discharged when a rusty spring moved it into the chamber. Other accounts had Adlai aiming the gun (which he believed to be empty and safe) from the balcony. A formal inquest was held. The jury found the incident to be a horrible accident. Ruth Merwin's mother responded in a gracious, compassionate manner, insisting that two lives not be lost.

KILLED IN STEVENSON HOME.

Girl Shot Accidentally by Former Vice President's Grandson.

BLOOMINGTON, Ill., Dec. 30.—Adlai Stevenson, grandson of former Vice President Stevenson, accidentally shot and killed Miss Ruth Merwin in the Stevenson home here to-night.

Miss Merwin was 16 years old.

Young Stevenson was overcome with grief when he learned the accident had resulted fatally.

Boys at a party in the home of young Stevenson's father, L. G. Stevenson, were students at a military academy, and in the evening they decided to give part of their drill. They found an old repeating rifle and, they thought, took out all the cartridges. In the drill the weapon, when in the hands of young Stevenson, was discharged. The bullet struck Miss Merwin in the forehead and caused instant death.

What effect did Adlai Stevenson shooting Ruth Merwin have on his personality and his psychological development? The question is tantalizing. Because he almost never spoke of it, it is hard to determine a conclusive answer. When William Glascow, a reporter for Time Magazine, asked Stevenson about it some forty years later, Stevenson reported: 'You know, you are the first person who has ever asked me about that since it happened-and this is the first time I have ever spoken of it to anyone.'

Stevenson spent a lifetime consumed with feelings of unworthiness, was known to be self-deprecating to a fault, was extremely cautious and did all he could to avoid violence or bloodshed." (http://barrybradford.com/adlai-stevenson-and-the-killing-of-ruth-merwin/)

I wish I had a similar dilemma in choosing who to vote for in future presidential elections. The best I could do in some elections then was to vote for the least undesirable. Sometimes that was too difficult, so I voted for the candidate of a third party. Over the years I noticed haw the two major parties changed and abandoned some long-time planks in their platforms. In my opinion, the most offensive changes and truly troublesome has taken part in the Republican Party in 2016 and since. In studying the history of the Republican Party, I developed some opinions about each of the Republican Presidential Candidates.

ABRAHAM LINCOLN

I rate Abraham Lincoln as the greatest president of the United States. I believe by both words and actions he has earned the distinction. Historically, Abraham Lincoln is one of the most effective and influential United States presidents. Of course, most every Americans are aware of declaring the Southern Confederate States couldn't secede from the Union and lead the North in putting down the Southern insurrection. One instrument used in this conflict was signing The Emancipation Proclamation, freeing the slaves. However, are you aware of the following accomplishments.

Abraham Lincoln was a strong supporter of the Thirteenth Amendment that formally ended slavery in the United States.

Abraham Lincoln's foreign policy was successful in preventing other countries from intervening in America's Civil War.

He Lay The Stepping Stone For Reconstruction of the Union

Lincoln Is The Only President Of The United States To Hold A Patent
He Established The United States Department Of Agriculture

Opening Settlement of the West through Homesteading

Authorizing The First Railroad Connecting the Atlantic and Pacific Coasts

He Signed The Morrill Land-Grant Act Which Led To Creation Of Numerous Universities

Coining the American Greenback dollar

Collecting the First Income Tax and Founding the IRS

Beginning the Secret Service

Instituting the first official Thanksgiving Day

Lincoln Established The US National Banking System

Abraham Lincoln set an example of strong character, leadership, and honesty which succeeding presidents tried to emulate.

Abraham Lincoln gave a series of great speeches before and during his presidency including the House Divided Speech, the Cooper Union Address, the First Inaugural Address, the Gettysburg Address, and the Second Inaugural Address.

Abraham Lincoln wrote a series of famous letters including the letters to Grace Bedell, Horace Greeley, Fanny McCullough, and Lydia Bixby.

Abraham Lincoln's quotes are among the most famous in the world. He understood that the President had the responsibility to the people to inform them about their government and laws. (Source: Collected Works of Abraham Lincoln, edited by Roy P. Basler et al)

There is no grievance that is a fit object of redress by mob law. January 27, 1838 Lyceum Address

Plainly, the central idea of secession, is the essence of anarchy. --March 4, 1861 Inaugural Address

Don't interfere with anything in the Constitution. That must be maintained, for it is the only safeguard of our liberties. And not to Democrats alone do I make this appeal, but to all who love these great and true principles. --August 27, 1856 Speech at Kalamazoo, Michigan

Let us then turn this government back into the channel in which the framers of the Constitution originally placed it. --July 10, 1858 Speech at Chicago

I have borne a laborious, and, in some respects to myself, a painful part in the contest. Through all, I have neither assailed, nor wrestled with any part of the constitution. --October 30, 1858 Speech at Springfield

The people -- the people -- are the rightful masters of both congresses, and courts -- not to overthrow the constitution, but to overthrow the men who pervert it. -- September 16 and 17, 1859 Notes for Speeches at Columbus and Cincinnati

I am exceedingly anxious that this Union, the Constitution, and the liberties of the people shall be perpetuated in accordance with the original idea for which that struggle was made, and I shall be most happy indeed if I shall be an humble instrument in the hands of the Almighty, and of this, his almost chosen people, for perpetuating the object of that great struggle. --February 21, 1861 Speech to the New Jersey Senate

At what point then is the approach of danger to be expected? I answer, if it ever reach us, it must spring up amongst us. It cannot come from abroad. If destruction be our lot, we must ourselves be its author and finisher. As a nation of freemen, we must live through all time, or die by suicide. --January 27, 1838 Lyceum Address

I think to lose Kentucky is nearly the same as to lose the whole game. Kentucky gone, we cannot hold Missouri, nor, as I think, Maryland. These all against us, and the job on our hands is too large for us. -September 22, 1861 Letter to Orville Browning

The dogmas of the quiet past, are inadequate to the stormy present. The occasion is piled high with difficulty, and we must rise -- with the occasion. As our case is new, so we must think anew, and act anew. We must disenthrall ourselves, and then we shall save our country. --December 1, 1862 Message to Congress

The proportions of this rebellion were not for a long time understood. I saw that it involved the greatest difficulties, and would call forth all the powers of the whole country. --June 2, 1863 Reply to Members of the Presbyterian General Assembly

In a word, I would not take any risk of being entangled upon the river, like an ox jumped half over a fence, and liable to be torn by dogs, front and rear, without a fair chance to gore one way or kick the other. --June 5, 1863 Letter to Joseph Hooker

Of our political revolution of '76, we all are justly proud. It has given us a degree of political freedom, far exceeding that of any other nation of the earth. In it the world has found a solution of the long-mooted problem, as to the capability of man to govern himself. In it was the germ which has vegetated, and still is to grow and expand into the universal liberty of mankind. --February 22, 1842 Temperance Address

The legitimate object of government, is to do for a community of people, whatever they need to have done, but cannot do, at all, or cannot, so well do, for themselves -- in their separate, and individual capacities. --July 1, 1854 [?] Fragment on Government

Our government rests in public opinion. Whoever can change public opinion, can change the government, practically just so much. --December 10, 1856 Speech at Chicago

Welcome, or unwelcome, agreeable, or disagreeable, whether this shall be an entire slave nation, is the issue before us. --ca. May 18, 1858 Fragment of a Speech

As I would not be a slave, so I would not be a master. This expresses my idea of democracy. Whatever differs from this, to the extent of the difference, is no democracy. --ca. August 1, 1858 Fragment on Democracy

I think we have fairly entered upon a durable struggle as to whether this nation is to ultimately become all slave or all free, and though I fall early in the contest, it is nothing if I shall have contributed, in the least degree, to the final rightful result. -- December 8, 1858 Letter to H.D. Sharpe

Understanding the spirit of our institutions to aim at the elevation of men, I am opposed to whatever tends to degrade them. --May 17, 1859 Letter to Theodore Canisius

...I do not mean to say that this government is charged with the duty of redressing or preventing all the wrongs in the world; but I do think that it is charged with the duty of preventing and redressing all wrongs which are wrongs to itself. --September 17, 1859 Speech at Cincinnati, Ohio

This is essentially a People's contest. On the side of the Union, it is a struggle for maintaining in the world, that form, and substance of government, whose leading object is, to elevate the condition of men -- to lift artificial weights from all shoulders -- to clear the paths of laudable pursuit for all -- to afford all, an unfettered start, and a fair chance, in the race of life. --July 4, 1861 Message to Congress

May our children and our children's children to a thousand generations, continue to enjoy the benefits conferred upon us by a united country, and have cause yet to rejoice under those glorious institutions bequeathed us by Washington and his compeers. --October 4, 1862 Speech at Frederick, Maryland

The restoration of the Rebel States to the Union must rest upon the principle of civil and political equality of both races; and it must be sealed by general amnesty.-- January 1864, Letter to James S. Wadsworth

While we must, by all available means, prevent the overthrow of the government, we should avoid planting and cultivating too many thorns in the bosom of society. -- March 18, 1864 Letter to Edwin M. Stanton

In this great struggle, this form of Government and every form of human right is endangered if our enemies succeed. There is more involved in this contest than is realized by everyone. --August 18, 1864 Speech to the 164th Ohio Regiment

It is not merely for to-day, but for all time to come that we should perpetuate for our children's children this great and free government, which we have enjoyed all our lives. --August 22, 1864 Speech to the One Hundred Sixty-sixth Ohio Regiment

Nowhere in the world is presented a government of so much liberty and equality. To the humblest and poorest amongst us are held out the highest privileges and positions. The present moment finds me at the White House, yet there is as good a chance for your children as there was for my father's. --August 31, 1864 Speech to 148th Ohio Regiment

Thoughtful men must feel that the fate of civilization upon this continent is involved in the issue of our contest. --December 27, 1864 Letter to John Maclean

When it comes to this, I should prefer emigrating to some country where they make no pretense of loving liberty -- to Russia, for instance, where despotism can be taken pure, and without the base alloy of hypocrisy. --From the August 24, 1855 Letter to Joshua Speed

That is the issue that will continue in this country when these poor tongues of Judge Douglas and myself shall be silent. It is the eternal struggle between these two principles -- right and wrong -- throughout the world. They are the two principles that have stood face to face from the beginning of time, and will ever continue to struggle. The one is the common right of humanity and the other the divine right of kings. --October 15, 1858 Debate at Alton, Illinois

If you are resolutely determined to make a lawyer of yourself, the thing is more than half done already. --November 5, 1855 Letter to Isham Reavis

Always bear in mind that your own resolution to succeed, is more important than any other one thing. --November 5, 1855 Letter to Isham Reavis

I know not how to aid you, save in the assurance of one of mature age, and much severe experience, that you cannot fail, if you resolutely determine, that you will not. --July 22, 1860 Letter to George Latham

And having thus chosen our course, without guile, and with pure purpose, let us renew our trust in God, and go forward without fear, and with manly hearts. --July 4, 1861 Message to Congress

Adhere to your purpose and you will soon feel as well as you ever did. On the contrary, if you falter, and give up, you will lose the power of keeping any resolution, and will regret it all your life. --June 28, 1862 Letter to Quintin Campbell

I expect to maintain this contest until successful, or till I die, or am conquered, or my term expires, or Congress or the country forsakes me... --June 28, 1862 Letter to William H. Seward

Upon the subject of education, not presuming to dictate any plan or system respecting it, I can only say that I view it as the most important subject which we as a people can be engaged in. --March 9, 1832 First Political Announcement

Mr. Clay's lack of a more perfect early education, however it may be regretted generally, teaches at least one profitable lesson; it teaches that in this country, one can scarcely be so poor, but that, if he will, he can acquire sufficient education to get through the world respectably. --July 6, 1852 Eulogy on Henry Clay

A capacity, and taste, for reading, gives access to whatever has already been discovered by others. It is the key, or one of the keys, to the already solved problems. And not only so. It gives a relish, and facility, for successfully pursuing the [yet] unsolved ones. --September 30, 1859 Address before the Wisconsin State Agricultural Society

The old general rule was that educated people did not perform manual labor. They managed to eat their bread, leaving the toil of producing it to the uneducated. This was not an insupportable evil to the working bees, so long as the class of drones remained very small. But now, especially in these free States, nearly all are educated--quite too nearly all, to leave the labor of the uneducated, in any wise adequate to the support of the whole. It follows from this that henceforth educated people must labor. Otherwise, education itself would become a positive and intolerable evil. No country can sustain, in idleness, more than a small percentage of its numbers. The great majority must labor at something productive. --September 30, 1859 Address before the Wisconsin State Agricultural Society

I am a little uneasy about the abolishment of slavery in this District, not but I would be glad to see it abolished, but as to the time and manner of doing it. --March 24, 1862 Letter to Horace Greeley

What I did, I did after very full deliberation, and under a heavy and solemn sense of responsibility. I can only trust in God that I have made no mistake. --September 24, 1862 Reply to Serenade in Honor of [Preliminary] Emancipation Proclamation

And by virtue of the power, and for the purpose aforesaid, I do order and declare that all persons held as slaves within said designated States, and parts of States, are, and henceforward shall be free; and that the Executive government of the United States, including the military and naval authorities thereof, will recognize and maintain the freedom of said persons. --January 1, 1863 Emancipation Proclamation

And upon this act, sincerely believed to be an act of justice, warranted by the Constitution, upon military necessity, I invoke the considerate judgment of mankind, and the gracious favor of Almighty God. --January 1, 1863 Emancipation Proclamation

Still, to use a coarse, but an expressive figure, broken eggs cannot be mended. I have issued the emancipation proclamation, and I cannot retract it. --January 8, 1863 Letter to John A. McClernand

I have very earnestly urged the slave-states to adopt emancipation; and it ought to be, and is an object with me not to overthrow, or thwart what any of them may in good faith do, to that end. --June 23, 1863 Letter to John M. Schofield

"The emancipation proclamation applies to Arkansas. I think it is valid in law, and will be so held by the courts. I think I shall not retract or repudiate it. Those who shall have tasted actual freedom I believe can never be slaves, or quasi slaves again." --July 31, 1863 Letter to Stephen A. Hurlburt

You dislike the emancipation proclamation; and, perhaps, would have it retracted. You say it is unconstitutional -- I think differently.--August 26, 1863 Letter to James Conkling

But the proclamation, as law, either is valid, or is not valid. If it is not valid, it needs no retraction. If it is valid, it cannot be retracted, any more than the dead can be brought to life. --August 26, 1863 Letter to James Conkling

On the question of liberty, as a principle, we are not what we have been. When we were the political slaves of King George, and wanted to be free, we called the maxim that "all men are created equal" a self-evident truth; but now when we have grown fat, and have lost all dread of being slaves ourselves, we have become so greedy to be masters that we call the same maxim "a self-evident lie." --August 15, 1855 Letter to George Robertson

I leave you, hoping that the lamp of liberty will burn in your bosoms until there shall no longer be a doubt that all men are created free and equal. --July 10, 1858 Speech at Chicago, Illinois

Our reliance is in the love of liberty which God has planted in our bosoms. Our defense is in the preservation of the spirit which prizes liberty as the heritage of all men, in all lands, everywhere. --September 11, 1858 Speech at Edwardsville, Illinois

This is a world of compensations; and he who would be no slave, must consent to have no slave. Those who deny freedom to others, deserve it not for themselves; and, under a just God, cannot long retain it. --April 6, 1859 Letter to Henry Pierce

I have never had a feeling politically that did not spring from the sentiments embodied in the Declaration of Independence. --February 22, 1861 Address in Independence Hall

I have here stated my purpose according to my view of official duty; and I intend no modification of my oft-expressed personal wish that all men everywhere could be free. --August 22, 1862 Letter to Horace Greeley

In giving freedom to the slave, we assure freedom to the free -- honorable alike in what we give, and what we preserve. We shall nobly save, or meanly lose, the last best, hope of earth. --December 1, 1862 Message to Congress

Four score and seven years ago our fathers brought forth on this continent, a new nation, conceived in Liberty, and dedicated to the proposition that all men are created equal. --November 19, 1863 Gettysburg Address

The world has never had a good definition of the word liberty, and the American people, just now, are much in want of one. We all declare for liberty; but in using the same word we do not all mean the same thing. --April 18, 1864 Address at Baltimore

"We have, as all will agree, a free Government, where every man has a right to be equal with every other man. In this great struggle, this form of Government and every form of human right is endangered if our enemies succeed." --August 22, 1864 Speech to the One Hundred Sixty-fourth Ohio Regiment

Every advocate of slavery naturally desires to see blasted, and crushed, the liberty promised the black man by the new constitution. --November 14, 1864 Letter to Stephen A. Hurlbut

In the untimely loss of your noble son, our affliction here, is scarcely less than your own. So much of promised usefulness to one's country, and of bright hopes for one's self and friends, have rarely been so suddenly dashed, as in his fall. --May 25, 1861 Letter to Ephraim D. and Phoebe Ellsworth

In this sad world of ours, sorrow comes to all; and, to the young, it comes with bitterest agony, because it takes them unawares. --December 23, 1862 Letter to Fanny McCullough

I pray that our Heavenly Father may assuage the anguish of your bereavement, and leave you only the cherished memory of the loved and lost, and the solemn pride that must be yours to have laid so costly a sacrifice upon the altar of freedom. --Nov. 21, 1864 Letter to Lydia Bixby

In very truth he was, the noblest work of God -- an honest man. --February 8, 1842 Eulogy of Benjamin Ferguson

I believe it is an established maxim in morals that he who makes an assertion without knowing whether it is true or false, is guilty of falsehood; and the accidental truth of the assertion, does not justify or excuse him. --August 11, 1846 Letter to Allen N. Ford

Let no young man choosing the law for a calling for a moment yield to the popular belief -- resolve to be honest at all events; and if in your own judgment you cannot be an honest lawyer, resolve to be honest without being a lawyer. --July 1, 1850 [?] Notes for a Law Lecture

Let every American, every lover of liberty, every well-wisher to his posterity, swear by the blood of the Revolution, never to violate in the least particular, the laws of the country; and never to tolerate their violation by others. --January 27, 1838 Lyceum Address

Let reverence for the laws, be breathed by every American mother, to the lisping babe, that prattles on her lap -- let it be taught in schools, in seminaries, and in colleges; let it be written in Primers, spelling books, and in Almanacs; -- let it be preached from the pulpit, proclaimed in legislative halls, and enforced in courts of justice. And, in short, let it become the political religion of the nation; and let the old and the young, the rich and the poor, the grave and the gay, of all sexes and tongues, and colors and conditions, sacrifice unceasingly upon its altars. --January 27, 1838 Lyceum Address

In law it is a good policy to never plead what you need not, lest you oblige yourself to prove what you cannot. --February 20, 1848 Letter to Usher Linder

The leading rule for the lawyer, as for the man of every other calling, is diligence. Leave nothing for to-morrow which can be done to-day. --July 1, 1850 [?] Notes for a Law Lecture

Discourage litigation. Persuade your neighbors to compromise whenever you can. Point out to them how the nominal winner is often a real loser -- in fees, expenses, and waste of time. As a peacemaker the lawyer has a superior opportunity of being a good man. There will still be business enough. --July 1, 1850 [?] Notes for a Law Lecture

Never stir up litigation. A worse man can scarcely be found than one who does this. Who can be more nearly a fiend than he who habitually overhauls the register of deeds in search of defects in titles, whereon to stir up strife, and put money in his pocket? --July 1, 1850 [?] Notes for a Law Lecture

Let no young man choosing the law for a calling for a moment yield to the popular belief -- resolve to be honest at all events; and if in your own judgment you cannot be an honest lawyer, resolve to be honest without being a lawyer. --July 1, 1850 [?] Notes for a Law Lecture

Let us at all times remember that all American citizens are brothers of a common country, and should dwell together in the bonds of fraternal feeling.--November 20, 1860 Remarks at Springfield, Illinois

The man does not live who is more devoted to peace than I am. None who would do more to preserve it. --February 21, 1861 Address to the New Jersey General Assembly

I have desired as sincerely as any man -- I sometimes think more than any other man -- that our present difficulties might be settled without the shedding of blood. --April 26, 1861 Address to the Frontier Guard

Engaged, as I am, in a great war, I fear it will be difficult for the world to understand how fully I appreciate the principles of peace, inculcated in this letter, and everywhere, by the Society of Friends. --March 19, 1862 Letter to Samuel B. Tobey

Peace does not appear so distant as it did. I hope it will come soon, and come to stay; and so, come as to be worth the keeping in all future time. --August 26, 1863 Letter to James Conkling

Much is being said about peace; and no man desires peace more ardently than I. Still I am yet unprepared to give up the Union for a peace which, so achieved, could not be of much duration. --September 12, 1864 Letter to Isaac Schermerhorn

In stating a single condition of peace, I mean simply to say that the war will cease on the part of the government, whenever it shall have ceased on the part of those who began it. --December 6, 1864 Annual Message to Congress

When the conduct of men is designed to be influenced, persuasion, kind, unassuming persuasion, should ever be adopted. It is an old and a true maxim, that a "drop of honey catches more flies than a gallon of gall." --February 22, 1842 Temperance Address

Being elected to Congress, though I am very grateful to our friends, for having done it, has not pleased me as much as I expected. --October 22, 1846 Letter to Joshua Speed

The Presidency, even to the most experienced politicians, is no bed of roses; and Gen. Taylor like others, found thorns within it. No human being can fill that station and escape censure. --July 25, 1850 Eulogy on Zachary Taylor

I am glad I made the late race. It gave me a hearing on the great and durable question of the age, which I could have had in no other way; and though I now sink out of view, and shall be forgotten, I believe I have made some marks which will tell for the cause of civil liberty long after I am gone. --November 19, 1858 Letter to Anson G. Henry

Always a Whig in politics, and generally on the Whig electoral tickets, making active canvasses--I was losing interest in politics, when the repeal of the Missouri Compromise aroused me again. --December 20, 1859 Autobiography

We have just carried an election on principles fairly stated to the people. Now we are told in advance, the government shall be broken up, unless we surrender to those we have beaten, before we take the offices. --January 11, 1861 Letter to James T. Hale

I have endured a great deal of ridicule without much malice; and have received a great deal of kindness, not quite free from ridicule. I am used to it. --November 2, 1863 Letter to James H. Hackett

I am thankful to God for this approval of the people. But while deeply grateful for this mark of their confidence in me, if I know my heart, my gratitude is free from any taint of personal triumph. I do not impugn the motives of any one opposed to me. It is no pleasure to me to triumph over any one; but I give thanks to the Almighty for this evidence of the people's resolution to stand by free government and the rights of humanity. --November 8, 1864 Response to a Serenade

Passion has helped us; but can do so no more. It will in future be our enemy. Reason, cold, calculating, unimpassioned reason, must furnish all the materials for our future support and defence. --January 27, 1838 Lyceum Address

Happy day, when, all appetites controlled, all poisons subdued, all matter subjected, mind, all conquering mind, shall live and move the monarch of the world. Glorious consummation! Hail fall of Fury! Reign of Reason, all hail! --February 22, 1842 Temperance Address

That I am not a member of any Christian Church, is true; but I have never denied the truth of the Scriptures; and I have never spoken with intentional disrespect of religion in general, or any denomination of Christians in particular. --July 31, 1846 Handbill Replying to Charges of Infidelity

I do not think I could myself, be brought to support a man for office, whom I knew to be an open enemy of, and scoffer at, religion. --July 31, 1846 Handbill Replying to Charges of Infidelity

In their enlightened belief, nothing stamped with the Divine image and likeness was sent into the world to be trodden on, and degraded, and imbruted by its fellows. --August 17, 1858 Speech at Lewistown, Illinois

To His care commending you, as I hope in your prayers you will commend me, I bid you an affectionate farewell. --February 11, 1861 Farewell Address

Intelligence, patriotism, Christianity, and a firm reliance on Him, who has never yet forsaken this favored land, are still competent to adjust, in the best way, all our present difficulty. --March 4, 1861 First Inaugural Address

The will of God prevails. In great contests each party claims to act in accordance with the will of God. Both may be, and one must be, wrong. --September 1862 Meditation on the Divine Will

If I had had my way, this war would never have been commenced; If I had been allowed my way this war would have ended before this, but we find it still continues; and we must believe that He permits it for some wise purpose of his own, mysterious and unknown to us; and though with our limited understandings we may not be able to comprehend it, yet we cannot but believe, that he who made the world still governs it. --October 26, 1862 Reply to Eliza Gurney

Nevertheless, amid the greatest difficulties of my Administration, when I could not see any other resort, I would place my whole reliance on God, knowing that all would go well, and that He would decide for the right. --October 24, 1863 Remarks to the Baltimore Presbyterian Synod

On principle I dislike an oath which requires a man to swear he has not done wrong. It rejects the Christian principle of forgiveness on terms of repentance. I think it is enough if the man does no wrong hereafter. --February 5, 1864 Memorandum to Secretary Stanton

If God now wills the removal of a great wrong, and wills also that we of the North as well as you of the South, shall pay fairly for our complicity in that wrong, impartial history will find therein new cause to attest and revere the justice and goodness of God. --April 4, 1864 Letter to Albert Hodges

To read in the Bible, as the word of God himself, that "In the sweat of thy face shalt thou eat bread," and to preach therefrom that, "In the sweat of other man's faces shalt thou eat bread," to my mind can scarcely be reconciled with honest sincerity. --May 30, 1864 Letter to George Ide and Others

I am very glad indeed to see you to-night, and yet I will not say I thank you for this call, but I do most sincerely thank Almighty God for the occasion on which you have called. --July 7, 1864 Response to a Serenade

Enough is known of Army operations within the last five days to claim our especial gratitude to God; while what remains undone demands our most sincere prayers to, and reliance upon, Him, without whom, all human effort is vain. --May 10, 1864 Telegram Press Release

We hoped for a happy termination of this terrible war long before this; but God knows best, and has ruled otherwise. We shall yet acknowledge His wisdom and our own error therein. --September 4, 1864 Letter to Eliza Gurney

I am much indebted to the good Christian people of the country for their constant prayers and consolations; and to no one of them, more than to yourself. --September 4, 1864 Letter to Eliza Gurney

All the good the Saviour gave to the world was communicated through this book. But for it we could not know right from wrong. All things most desirable for man's welfare, here and hereafter, are to be found portrayed in it. --September 7, 1864 Reply to Loyal Colored People of Baltimore upon Presentation of a Bible

Both read the same Bible, and pray to the same God; and each invokes His aid against the other. It may seem strange that any men should dare to ask a just God's assistance in wringing their bread from the sweat of other men's faces; but let us judge not that we be not judged. The prayers of both could not be answered; that of neither has been answered fully. --March 4, 1865 Inaugural Address

Men are not flattered by being shown that there has been a difference of purpose between the Almighty and them. To deny it, however, in this case, is to deny that there is a God governing the world. --March 15, 1865 Letter to Thurlow Weed

Neither let us be slandered from our duty by false accusations against us, nor frightened from it by menaces of destruction to the Government nor of dungeons to ourselves. LET US HAVE FAITH THAT RIGHT MAKES MIGHT, AND IN

THAT FAITH, LET US, TO THE END, DARE TO DO OUR DUTY AS WE
UNDERSTAND IT. --February 27, 1860 Cooper Union Address

May the Almighty grant that the cause of truth, justice, and humanity, shall in no
wise suffer at my hands. --May 21, 1860 Letter to Joshua Giddings

I am not at liberty to shift ground -- that is out of the question. If I thought a
repetition would do any good, I would make it. But my judgment is it would do
positive harm. The secessionists, per se believing they had alarmed me, would
clamor all the louder. --November 16, 1860 Letter to Nathaniel Paschall

I fully appreciate the present peril the country is in, and the weight of responsibility
on me. --December 22, 1860 Letter to Alexander Stephens

I appeal to you again to constantly bear in mind that with you, and not with
politicians, not with Presidents, not with office-seekers, but with you, is the question,
"Shall the Union and shall the liberties of this country be preserved to the latest
generation?" --February 11, 1861 Speech to Gov. Morton in Indianapolis

I am a patient man -- always willing to forgive on the Christian terms of repentance;
and also, to give ample time for repentance. Still I must save this government if
possible. --July 17, 1862 Letter to Reverdy Johnson

Fellow-citizens, we cannot escape history. We of this Congress and this
administration, will be remembered in spite of ourselves. No personal significance,
or insignificance, can spare one or another of us. The fiery trial through which we
pass, will light us down, in honor or dishonor, to the latest generation. --December 1,
1862 Message to Congress

In times like the present, men should utter nothing for which they would not
willingly be responsible through time and eternity. --December 1, 1862 Message to
Congress

I have understood well that the duty of self-preservation rests solely with the
American people. --January 19, 1863 Letter to the Workingmen of England

My purpose is to be, in my action, just and constitutional; and yet practical, in
performing the important duty, with which I am charged, of maintaining the unity,
and the free principles of our common country. --August 7, 1863 Letter to Horatio
Seymour

I freely acknowledge myself the servant of the people, according to the bond of
service -- the United States Constitution; and that, as such, I am responsible to them.
--August 26, 1863 Letter to James Conkling

With malice toward none; with charity for all; with firmness in the right, as God gives us to see the right, let us strive on to finish the work we are in; to bind up the nation's wounds; to care for him who shall have borne the battle, and for his widow, and his orphan...--March 4, 1865 Inaugural Address

If as the friends of colonization hope, the present and coming generations of our countrymen shall by any means, succeed in freeing our land from the dangerous presence of slavery; and, at the same time, in restoring a captive people to their long-lost father-land, with bright prospects for the future; and this too, so gradually, that neither races nor individuals shall have suffered by the change, it will indeed be a glorious consummation. --July 6, 1852 Eulogy on Henry Clay

Slavery is founded in the selfishness of man's nature -- opposition to it is in his love of justice. These principles are an eternal antagonism; and when brought into collision so fiercely, as slavery extension brings them, shocks, and throes, and convulsions must ceaselessly follow. Repeal the Missouri Compromise -- repeal all compromises -- repeal the declaration of independence -- repeal all past history, you still cannot repeal human nature. It still will be the abundance of man's heart, that slavery extension is wrong; and out of the abundance of his heart, his mouth will continue to speak. --October 16, 1854 Speech at Peoria

The Autocrat of all the Russias will resign his crown, and proclaim his subjects free republicans sooner than will our American masters voluntarily give up their slaves. --August 15, 1855 Letter to George Robertson

You know I dislike slavery; and you fully admit the abstract wrong of it. --August 24, 1855 Letter to Joshua Speed

The slave-breeders and slave-traders, are a small, odious and detested class, among you; and yet in politics, they dictate the course of all of you, and are as completely your masters, as you are the master of your own negroes. --August 24, 1855 Letter to Joshua Speed

I believe this Government cannot endure, permanently half slave and half free. I do not expect the Union to be dissolved -- I do not expect the house to fall -- but I do expect it will cease to be divided. --June 16, 1858 House Divided Speech

I have always hated slavery; I think as much as any Abolitionist. --July 10, 1858 Speech at Chicago

Now I confess myself as belonging to that class in the country who contemplate slavery as a moral, social and political evil... --October 7, 1858 Debate at Galesburg, Illinois

He [Stephen Douglas] is blowing out the moral lights around us, when he contends that whoever wants slaves has a right to hold them; that he is penetrating, so far as lies in his power, the human soul, and eradicating the light of reason and the love of liberty, when he is in every possible way preparing the public mind, by his vast influence, for making the institution of slavery perpetual and national. --October 7, 1858 Lincoln-Douglas Debate at Galesburg, Illinois

When Judge Douglas says that whoever, or whatever community, wants slaves, they have a right to have them, he is perfectly logical if there is nothing wrong in the institution; but if you admit that it is wrong, he cannot logically say that anybody has a right to do wrong. --October 13, 1858 Debate at Quincy, Illinois

This is a world of compensations; and he who would be no slave, must consent to have no slave. --April 6, 1859 Letter to Henry Pierce

Now what is Judge Douglas' Popular Sovereignty? It is, as a principle, no other than that, if one man chooses to make a slave of another man, neither that other man nor anybody else has a right to object. --September 16, 1859 Speech in Columbus, Ohio

An inspection of the Constitution will show that the right of property in a slave in not "distinctly and expressly affirmed" in it. --February 27, 1860 Speech at the Cooper Institute

We believe that the spreading out and perpetuity of the institution of slavery impairs the general welfare. We believe -- nay, we know, that that is the only thing that has ever threatened the perpetuity of the Union itself. --September 17, 1859 Speech in Cincinnati, Ohio

Let there be no compromise on the question of extending slavery. If there be, all our labor is lost, and, ere long, must be done again. --December 10, 1860 Letter to Lyman Trumbull

You think slavery is right and ought to be extended; while we think it is wrong and ought to be restricted. That I suppose is the rub. It certainly is the only substantial difference between us. --December 22, 1860 Letter to Alexander Stephens

I say now, however, as I have all the while said, that on the territorial question -- that is, the question of extending slavery under the national auspices, -- I am inflexible. I am for no compromise which assists or permits the extension of the institution on soil owned by the nation. --February 1, 1861 Letter to William H. Seward

One section of our country believes slavery is right, and ought to be extended, while the other believes it is wrong, and ought not to be extended. --March 4, 1861 Inaugural Address

I am naturally anti-slavery. If slavery is not wrong, nothing is wrong. I cannot remember when I did not so think, and feel. And yet I have never understood that the

Presidency conferred upon me an unrestricted right to act officially upon this judgment and feeling. --April 4, 1864 Letter to Albert Hodges

One eighth of the whole population were colored slaves, not distributed generally over the Union, but localized in the Southern part of it. These slaves constituted a peculiar and powerful interest. All knew that this interest was, somehow, the cause of the war. --March 4, 1865 Inaugural Address

Then came the Black-Hawk war; and I was elected a Captain of Volunteers -- a success which gave me more pleasure than any I have had since. --December 20, 1859 Autobiography

The colored population is the great available and yet unavailed of, force for restoring the Union. The bare sight of fifty thousand armed, and drilled black soldiers on the banks of the Mississippi, would end the rebellion at once. --March 26, 1863 Letter to Andrew Johnson

I would like to speak in terms of praise due to the many brave officers and soldiers who have fought in the cause of the war. --July 7, 1863 Response to a Serenade

We never should, and I am sure, never shall be niggard of gratitude and benefaction to the soldiers who have endured toil, privations and wounds, that the nation may live. --August 10, 1863 Letter to Mrs. Hunter et al

And then, there will be some black men who can remember that, with silent tongue, and clenched teeth, and steady eye, and well-poised bayonet, they have helped mankind on to this great consummation... --August 26, 1863 Letter to James Conkling

It is for us the living, rather, to be dedicated here to the unfinished work which they who fought here have thus far so nobly advanced. --November 19, 1863 Gettysburg Address

While we are grateful to all the brave men and officers for the events of the past few days, we should, above all, be very grateful to Almighty God, who gives us victory. --May 9, 1864 Response to a Serenade

I am greatly obliged to you, and to all who have come forward at the call of their country. --August 22, 1864 Speech to the One Hundred Sixty-fourth Ohio Regiment

All this talk about the dissolution of the Union is humbug -- nothing but folly. We WON'T dissolve the Union, and you SHAN'T. --July 23, 1856 Speech at Galena, Illinois

I do not expect the Union to be dissolved -- I do not expect the house to fall -- but I do expect it will cease to be divided. --June 16, 1858 House Divided Speech

To the best of my judgment I have labored for, and not against the Union. --October 29, 1858 Speech at Springfield, Illinois

...my opinion is that no state can, in any way lawfully, get out of the Union, without the consent of the others; and that it is the duty of the President, and other government functionaries to run the machine as it is. --December 17, 1860 Letter to Thurlow Weed

When the people rise in masses in behalf of the Union and the liberties of their country, truly may it be said, "The gates of hell shall not prevail against them." --February 11, 1861 Reply to Governor Morton

I hold, that in contemplation of universal law, and of the Constitution, the Union of these States is perpetual. Perpetuity is implied, if not expressed, in the fundamental law of all national governments. --March 4, 1861 Inaugural Address

I therefore consider that in view of the Constitution and the laws, the Union is unbroken; and to the extent of my ability I shall take care, as the Constitution itself expressly enjoins upon me, that the laws of the Union be faithfully executed in all the States. --March 4, 1861 Inaugural Address

The Union is much older than the Constitution. It was formed in fact, by the Articles of Association in 1774. It was matured and continued by the Declaration of Independence in 1776. --March 4, 1861 Inaugural Address

The mystic chords of memory, stretching from every battle-field, and patriot grave, to every living heart and hearth-stone, all over this broad land, will yet swell the chorus of the Union, when again touched, as surely, they will be, by the better angels of our nature. --March 4, 1861 Inaugural Address

I would save the Union. I would save it the shortest way under the Constitution. The sooner the national authority can be restored; the nearer the Union will be "the Union as it was." --August 22, 1862 Letter to Horace Greeley

We can scarcely dispense with the aid of West-Virginia in this struggle; much less can we afford to have her against us, in congress and in the field. Her brave and good men regard her admission into the Union as a matter of life and death. --December 31, 1862 Opinion on the Admission of West Virginia into the Union

He who does something at the head of one Regiment, will eclipse him who does nothing at the head of a hundred. --December 31, 1861 Letter to David Hunter

And now, beware of rashness. Beware of rashness, but with energy, and sleepless vigilance, go forward, and give us victories. --January 26, 1863 Letter to Joseph Hooker

Let your military measures be strong enough to repel the invader and keep the peace, and not so strong as to unnecessarily harass and persecute the people. --May 27, 1863 Letter to John M. Schofield

I was deeply mortified by the escape of Lee across the Potomac, because the substantial destruction of his army would have ended the war... --July 21, 1863 Letter to Oliver O. Howard

You say you will not fight to free negroes. Some of them seem willing to fight for you; but, no matter. Fight you, then exclusively to save the Union. --August 26, 1863 Letter to James Conkling

We are in civil war. In such cases there always is a main question; but in this case that question is a perplexing compound -- Union and Slavery. It thus becomes a question not of two sides merely, but of at least four sides, even among those who are for the Union, saying nothing of those who are against it. --October 5, 1863 Letter to Charles Drake et al

Now we are engaged in a great civil war, testing whether that nation, or any nation so conceived and so dedicated, can long endure. --November 19, 1863 Gettysburg Address

It is easy to see that, under the sharp discipline of civil war, the nation is beginning a new life. --December 8, 1863 Message to Congress

War at the best, is terrible, and this war of ours, in its magnitude and in its duration, is one of the most terrible. --June 16, 1864 Speech at Philadelphia

The true rule for the Military is to seize such property as is needed for Military uses and reasons, and let the rest alone. --January 20, 1865 Letter to Joseph J. Reynolds

Both parties deprecated war; but one of them would make war rather than let the nation survive; and the other would accept war rather than let it perish. And the war came .... Fondly do we hope -- fervently do we pray -- that this mighty scourge of war may speedily pass away. --March 4, 1865 Inaugural Address

Gen. Sheridan says "If the thing is pressed, I think that Lee will surrender." Let the thing be pressed. --April 7, 1865 Telegram to General Grant

We know, Southern men declare that their slaves are better off than hired laborers amongst us. How little they know, whereof they speak! There is no permanent class of hired laborers amongst us ... Free labor has the inspiration of hope; pure slavery has no hope. --ca. September 17, 1859 Fragment on Free Labor

Every man is proud of what he does well; and no man is proud of what he does not do well. With the former, his heart is in his work; and he will do twice as much of it with less fatigue. The latter performs a little imperfectly, looks at it in disgust, turns from it, and imagines himself exceedingly tired. The little he has done, comes to nothing, for want of finishing. --September 30, 1859 Address before the Wisconsin State Agricultural Society

By the "mud-sill" theory it is assumed that labor and education are incompatible; and any practical combination of them impossible. According to that theory, a blind horse upon a tread-mill, is a perfect illustration of what a laborer should be -- all the better for being blind, that he could not tread out of place, or kick understandingly. According to that theory, the education of laborers, is not only useless, but pernicious, and dangerous. In fact, it is, in some sort, deemed a misfortune that laborers should have heads at all. --September 30, 1859 Address before the Wisconsin State Agricultural Society

Every blade of grass is a study; and to produce two, where there was but one, is both a profit and a pleasure. --September 30, 1859 Address before the Wisconsin State Agricultural Society

This leads to the further reflection, that no other human occupation opens so wide a field for the profitable and agreeable combination of labor with cultivated thought, as agriculture. I know of nothing so pleasant to the mind, as the discovery of anything which is at once new and valuable -- nothing which so lightens and sweetens toil, as the hopeful pursuit of such discovery. And how vast, and how varied a field is agriculture, for such discovery. The mind, already trained to thought, in the country school, or higher school, cannot fail to find there an exhaustless source of profitable enjoyment. --September 30, 1859 Address before the Wisconsin State Agricultural Society

I don't believe in a law to prevent a man from getting rich; it would do more harm than good. So, while we do not propose any war upon capital, we do wish to allow the humblest man an equal chance to get rich with everybody else. --March 6, 1860 Speech at New Haven, Connecticut

The point you press -- the importance of thorough organization -- is felt, and appreciated by our friends everywhere. And yet it involves so much more of the dry, and irksome labor, that most of them shrink from it... --September 1, 1860 Letter to Henry Wilson

The lady -- bearer of this -- says she has two sons who want to work. Set them at it, if possible. Wanting to work is so rare a merit, that it should be encouraged. -- October 17, 1861 Letter to George Ramsay

Conservatives love to tout Abraham Lincoln as one of history's most celebrated Republicans — especially on Feb. 12, his birthday. But the present GOP has nothing to do with the party of Lincoln., and the 16th president would probably be horrified by the likes of Sen. Ted Cruz (R-Texas) and Donald Trump. (Alana Horowitz Satlin, https://www.huffpost.com/entry/lincoln-modern-gop-republicans_n_56bdea90e4b0b40245c61bb5)

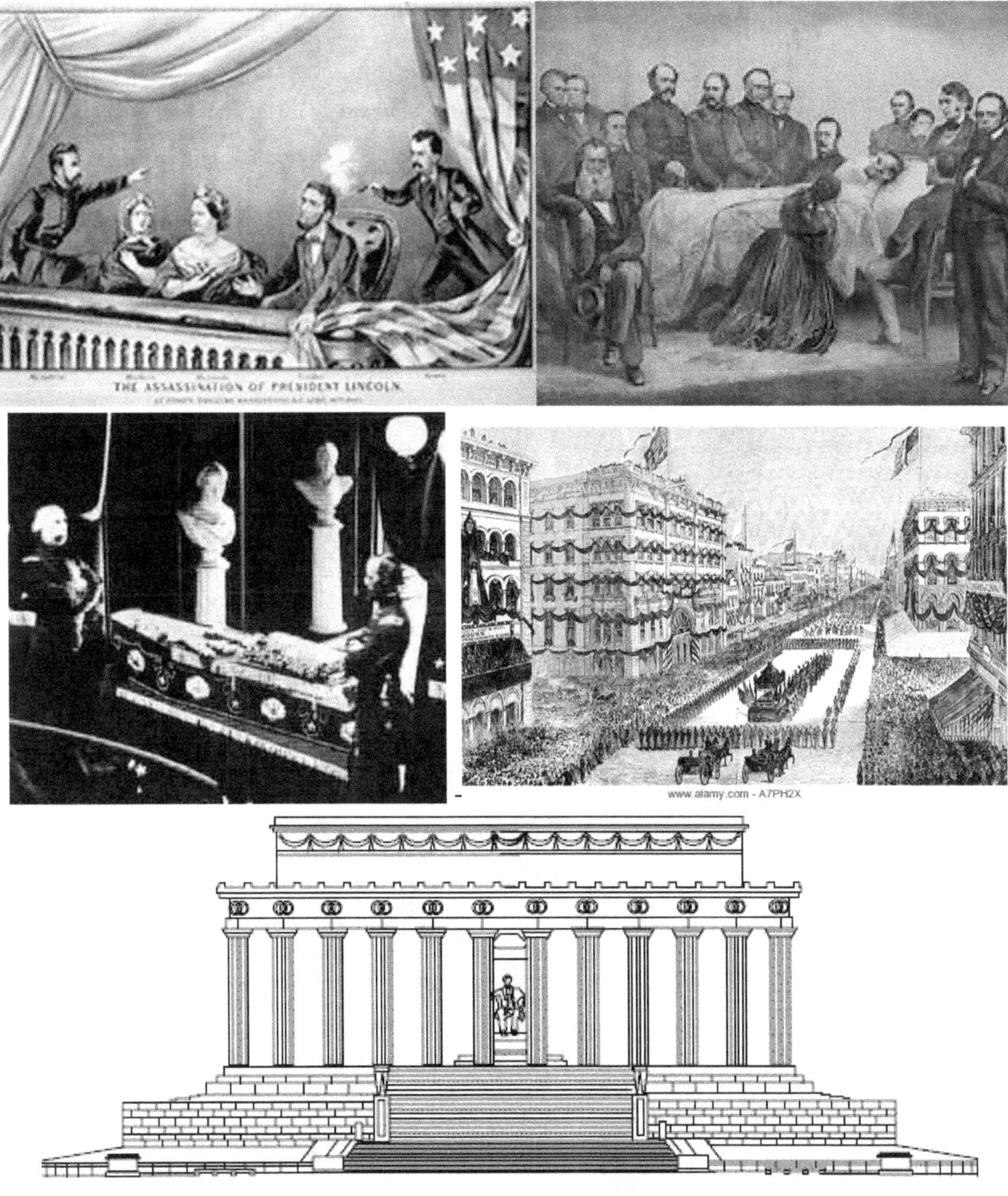

Can you imagine that illiterate moron Trump ever expressing his thoughts in a way that will be memorable for centuries? More thoughts about the Republican Party.

Conservatives love to tout Abraham Lincoln as one of history's most celebrated Republicans — especially on Feb. 12, his birthday. But the present GOP has nothing to do with the party of Lincoln., and the 16th president would probably be horrified by the likes of Sen. Ted Cruz (R-Texas) and Donald Trump. (Alana Horowitz Satlin, https://www.huffpost.com/entry/lincoln-modern-gop-republicans_n_56bdea90e4b0b40245c61bb5)

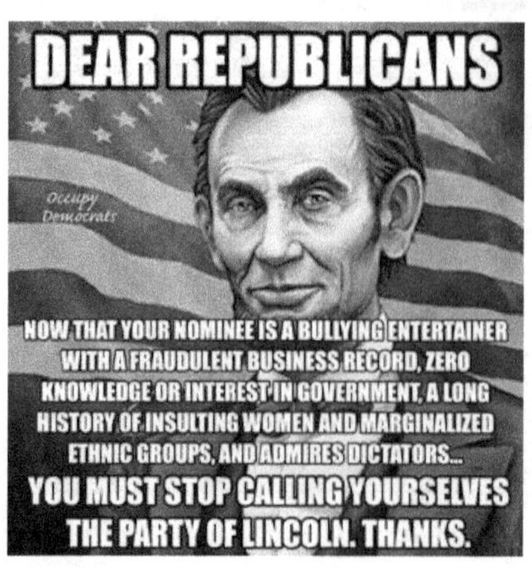

FREDERICK DOUGLASS AND BLACK REPUBLICANS

Republican like to remind Americans that Frederick Douglass was a Republican, but they seldom quote Douglass' reason for being a republican. Would Trump and today's GOP agree with his thoughts?

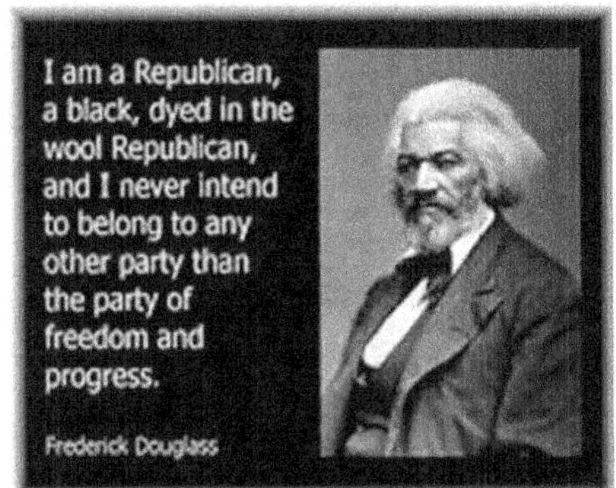

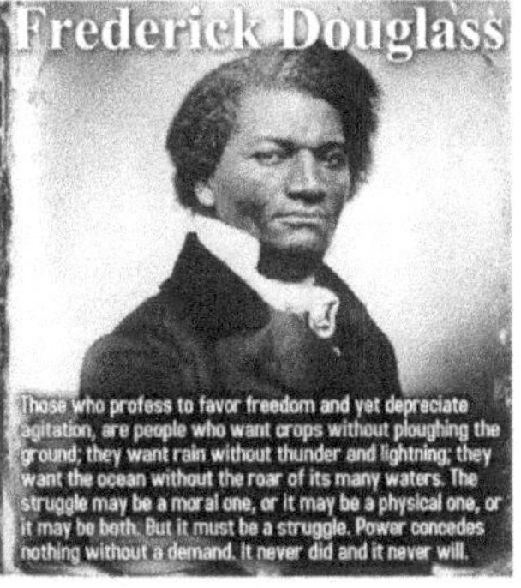

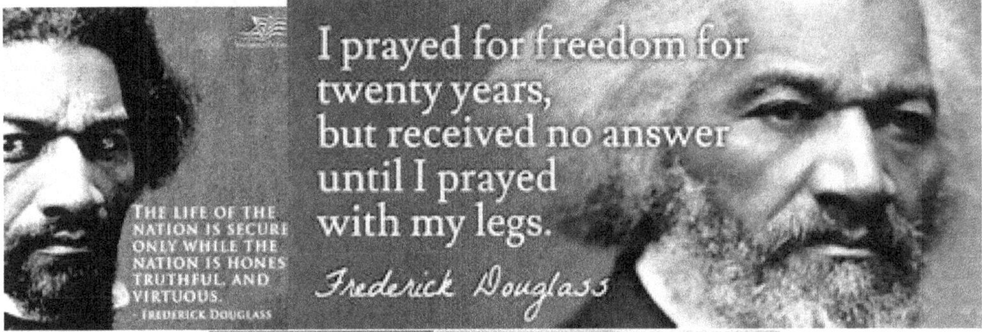

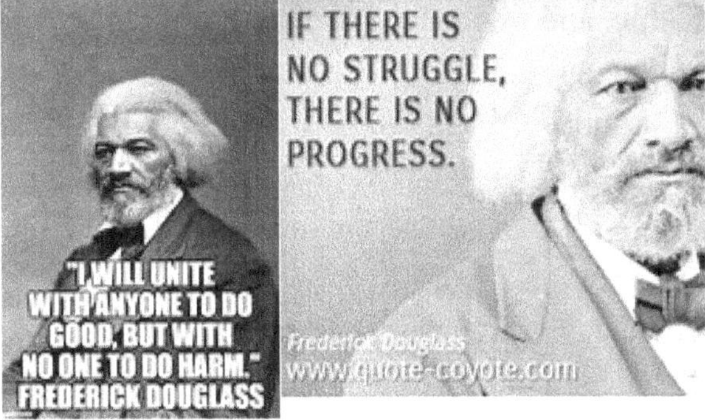

QUOTATIONS BY FREDERICK DOUGLASS

Power and those in control concede nothing ... without a demand. Hey never have and never will... Each and every one of us must keep demanding, must keep fighting, must keep thundering, must keep plowing, must keep on keeping things struggling, must speak out and speak up until justice is served because where there is no justice there is no peace.

There is no negro problem. The problem is whether the American people have loyalty enough, honor enough, patriotism enough, to live up to their own constitution.

In a composite Nation like ours, made up of almost every variety of the human family, there should be, as before the Law, no rich, no poor, no high, no low, no black, no white, but one country, one citizenship equal rights and a common destiny for all.

A government that cannot or does not protect the humblest citizen in his right to life, Liberty and the pursuit of happiness, should be reformed or overthrown, without delay.

Liberty is meaningless where the right to utter one's thoughts and opinions has ceased to exist. That, of all rights, is the dread of tyrants. It is the right which they first of all strike down.

Find out just what any people will quietly submit to and you have found out the exact measure of injustice and wrong which will be imposed upon them, and these will continue till they are resisted with either words or blows, or with both.

I love the pure, peaceable, and impartial Christianity of Christ; I therefore hate the corrupt, slaveholding, women-whipping, cradle-plundering, partial, and hypocritical Christianity of this land. Indeed, I can see no reason, but the most deceitful one, for calling the religion of this land Christianity. I look upon it as the climax of all misnomers, the boldest of all frauds, and the grossest of all libels.

One by one I have seen obstacles removed, errors corrected, prejudices softened, proscriptions relinquished, and my people advancing in all the elements that go to make up the sum of the general welfare. And I remember that God reigns in eternity, and that whatever delays, whatever disappointments and discouragements may come, truth, justice, liberty and humanity will ultimately prevail.

The church of this country is not only indifferent to the wrongs of the slave, it actually takes sides with the oppressors.... For my part, I would say, welcome infidelity! Welcome atheism! Welcome anything! in preference to the gospel, as preached by these Divines! They convert the very name of religion into an engine of tyranny and barbarous cruelty, and serve to confirm more infidels, in this age, than all the infidel writings of Thomas Paine, Voltaire, and Bolingbroke put together have done!

If we would reach a degree of civilization higher and grander than any yet attained, we should welcome to our ample continent all the nations, kindreds, tongues and peoples, and as fast as they learn our language and comprehend the duties of citizenship, we should incorporate them into the American body politic. The outspread wings of the American eagle are broad enough to shelter all who are likely to come.

[A] woman should have every honorable motive to exertion which is enjoyed by man, to the full extent of her capacities and endowments. The case is too plain for argument. Nature has given woman the same powers, and subjected her to the same earth, breathes the same air, subsists on the same food, physical, moral, mental and spiritual. She has, therefore, an equal right with man, in all efforts to obtain and maintain a perfect existence.

The relation between the white and colored people of this country is the great, paramount, imperative, and all-commanding question for this age and nation to solve.

Where justice is denied, where poverty is enforced, where ignorance prevails, and where any one class is made to feel that society is an organized conspiracy to oppress, rob and degrade them, neither persons nor property will be safe. (TOP 25 QUOTES BY FREDERICK DOUGLASS (of 232) | A-Z Quotes https://www.azquotes.com/author/4104-Frederick_Douglass)

(https://www.history.com/news/5-former-slaves-turned-statesmen)

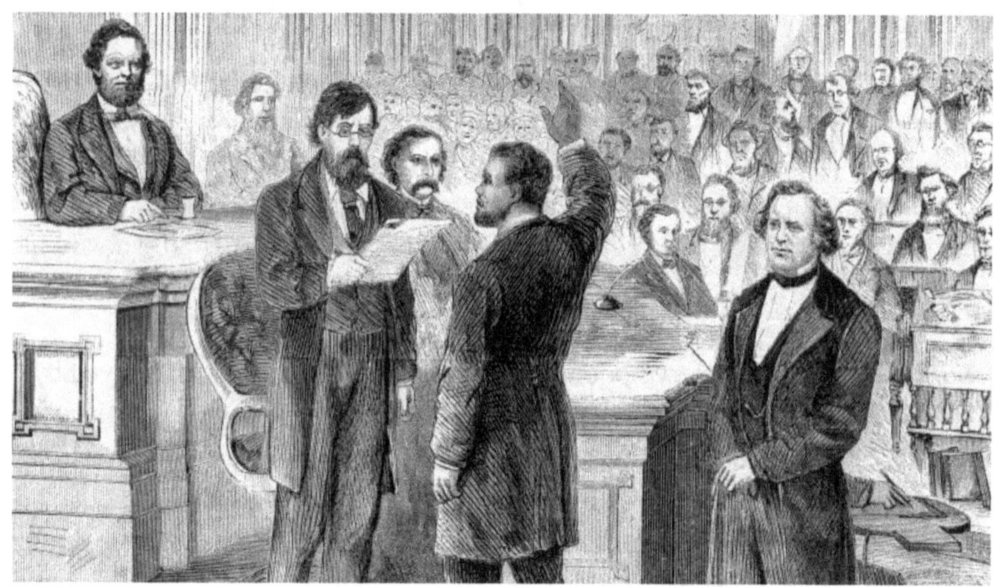

Hiram Revels
Mississippi Senator, Hiram Revels. (Credit: The Library of Congress)

"Hiram Rhodes Revels arrived on Capitol Hill to take his seat as the first black member of the U.S. Congress in 1870. But first, the Mississippi Republican faced Democrats determined to block him. The Constitution requires senators to hold citizenship for at least nine years, and they argued Revels had only recently become a citizen with the 1866 Civil Rights Act and the 14th Amendment. Before that, the Supreme Court had ruled in its 1857 Dred Scott decision that black people weren't U.S. citizens.

This technicality wasn't actually their main issue with Revels. At the time, the Democrats were the party of white southern men, and they simply didn't want any black men in Congress.

In any case, their bad faith legal argument didn't hold up. Revel's fellow Republicans argued he was born a free man in the United States and had lived there all his life. Dred Scott was a bad decision that should've never been made, which the Civil Rights Act and 14th Amendment had sought to redress, they argued. Just because the law had only recently recognized black men's citizenship didn't mean he was a "new" citizen.

"Mr. Revels, the colored Senator from Mississippi, was sworn in and admitted to his seat this afternoon," reported The New York Times on February 25, 1870. "Mr. Revels showed no embarrassment whatever, and his demeanor was as dignified as could be expected under the circumstances. The abuse which had been poured upon him and on his race during the last two days might well have shaken the nerves of anyone."

Revels took his oath only five years after the Civil War. Over the next decade, 15 more black men took their seats in the House and Senate, including men like South Carolina Congressman Robert Smalls who were previously enslaved.

"It really does reflect what a revolutionary period Reconstruction was," says Gregory Downs, a history professor at the University of California, Davis. Congress had ordered the Army to register black southern men to vote in 1867. "In a series of a few months, you had people…in South Carolina and other places who had been slaves as recently as two or three years before now participating, now voting and even being elected to serve to remake the Constitution."

The large population of formerly enslaved people meant that there were many more black voters in the south than the north (and actually, some northern states didn't enfranchise black men until after the southern states). Black men elected black representatives and white Republicans locally and at the state level, which led to representation at the federal level.

But the people who had objected to Revels joining the Senate were still mad, and it was only a matter of time before backlash struck. In the 1870s, organizations like the White League and the Red Shirts began terrorizing and intimidating black men so they wouldn't vote and participate in government.

Because of these tactics, "the height of statewide black power crests in the middle of the 1870s," Downs says. "But what does remain in place from the 1880s into the mid-1890s is an enormous amount of black local political power centered in the regions where black people are a sizable majority."

That too came under attack as Jim Crow laws, poll taxes and other racist measures spread throughout the south. "The 1890s and early 1900s is where you get the laws that aim to permanently exclude virtually all black voters from participating," Downs says. "The final black congressman from the south is George White who gives his farewell address, the phoenix speech, in 1901."

After White, there were no more black Congress members from the original 11 Confederate states until 1973, when Andrew Young, Jr., of Georgia and Barbara Jordan of Texas (both Democrats) took their seats. Jordan's election was particularly significant as she came just after New York's Shirley Chisholm became the first-ever

black Congresswoman in 1969—a full century after emancipation."
(https://www.history.com/news/first-black-congressman-hiram-revels)

"Leah Wright Rigueur is an Assistant Professor of Public Policy at the Harvard Kennedy School of Government. Her award-winning first book, The Loneliness of the Black Republican, looks at the tumultuous relationship between the GOP and racial minorities. Leah's research, writing, and commentary has been featured in numerous outlets including the New York Times, the Washington Post, the Root, CNN, MSNBC, NPR, PBS, the Atlantic, and the New Republic."

(The following are excerpts from The Loneliness of the Black Republican: Pragmatic Politics and the Pursuit of Power by Leah Wright Rigueur. Copyright © 2015 by Princeton University Press).

The GOP of today bears little resemblance to the "Party of Lincoln" to which black voters had been fiercely loyal since the era of Reconstruction. Instead, the modern Republican Party is indelibly associated with Herbert Hoover's "lily-white" movement, "Operation Dixie" of the 1950s, and Richard Nixon's "southern strategy."

Some black families never left the Republican fold, while other individuals have found their way back to the GOP. The past three decades alone have witnessed the rise of a number of prominent African American members of the Republican Party: Samuel Pierce, Clarence Thomas, Colin Powell, J. C. Watts, Condoleezza Rice, Michael Steele, Constance Berry Newman, Alan Keyes, Robert A. George, Herman Cain, Michael Powell, Lynn Swann, Allen West, and Tim Scott, to name a few.

To their critics, black Republicans are Booker T. Washington's successors, racial apologists whose affiliations and beliefs mark them as traitorous individuals, complicit in an age-old crusade to "delegitimize the black quest for racial and social justice."

In contrast, white Republicans often heap gratuitous public praise on African American members of the GOP, applauding them for having the gumption to leave the "plantation politics of the Democratic Party," as Pat Buchanan did on CNN in 2011, while defending Herman Cain. This line of thinking stems from the flawed and simplistic belief that African Americans have been brainwashed into voting for the Democratic Party and, as a result, ignore the benefits of belonging to the GOP.

Our assumptions about blacks in the Republican Party are teleological and ahistorical, informed by the Republican Party as it exists in the present; thus, our views are often flat, lacking historical depth.

Our implicit views of black Republicans—either as strange alien creatures or as noble exceptions among their duped Democratic brethren—reject the notion of political choice; too often we assume that blacks in America are Democrats by default. In this scenario, black Republicans are simultaneously invisible and hypervisible: isolated political misfits who provoke extreme reactions

Most of these black party members joined the Republican Party (or never left it) out of a belief in what they called "traditional" conservatism: anticommunism, free market enterprise and capitalism, self-help and personal responsibility, limited government intervention, and a respect for authority, history, and precedent, along with Western institutions and traditions.

Black Republicans' brand of conservatism was an ideology rooted in nineteenth-century middle-class mores of respectability, built upon a faith in the Protestant work ethic and the lodestones of self-help, personal responsibility, morality, and political involvement. This was a model propagated by the black elite, as many scholars have convincingly argued, and was an imperfect challenge to white supremacy in an era of second-class citizenship; it was reflected in the economic and business ethos embodied by Booker T. Washington and the class privilege inherent in W.E.B. Du Bois's theory of a talented tenth uplifting the "best" of the race.

Moreover, in spite of conservatism's association with the right wing of the modern GOP, black Republicans have long seen the ideology as a legitimate solution, one that should be considered seriously in the struggle for racial equality. Thus, African Americans attempted to influence the direction of conservatism—not to destroy it but rather to expand the boundaries of the ideology in order to include black needs and interests. This interpretation of conservatism has been flexible, by both definition and necessity, since issues of race, representation, and power guided black Republicans' actions.

There were three different waves of national black Republican thought and activity, a period that begins in 1936—significant not only for the major political realignment of African American voters but also for the remarkable voting fluidity of the black electorate; in fact, through 1962, nearly a third of black voters pulled the lever for Republican candidates in midterm and presidential elections. The decision to nominate Barry Goldwater as the GOP presidential nominee in 1964 marks the beginning of the next wave of black party activity, as the Arizona senator's right-wing agenda sent shock- waves through black Republicans' ranks, motivating them to organize on a national scale in pursuit of intraparty reform. Many began to look to state and local politics, hoping to duplicate the electoral success of Massachusetts's Edward W. Brooke; and, as we will see, the black senator reinvigorated the idea of pragmatic politics for black Republicans, or, rather, the pursuit of power through party hierarchies in a way that could reconcile conservatism with African American needs. Likewise, they also looked to the Republican-led White House in the late 1960s, where a small band of black appointees was able to introduce an economic civil rights agenda.

The third and final wave reflects the confusion and chaos of the 1970s, a period in which black Republicans, ousted from the White House, turned to the Republican National Committee (RNC) to push party reform, still invested in a pragmatic approach to achieving power. Though their solidarity movement found moments of success, black Republicans also experienced colossal failures. Just as significant, the second and third wave of activity coincided with the passage of the major federal civil rights laws of the 1960s and a society-wide shift from explicit forms of racism to implicit and institutional forms of discrimination. The enactment and the enforcement of this legislation gave black Republicans a kind of freedom, or the leeway, to become more conservative, and adhere to mainstream party ideas about racial equality, if they so choose. This distinct outlook enabled black party members to concurrently embrace new types of nonpartisan strategies for wooing black voters and partisan techniques for nullifying the black vote.

What do some of today's Prominent Black Republicans have to say about Trump and his Party? Who are Trump black supporters in 2016, and likely will do so in 2020? Part of the answer is found in what follows.

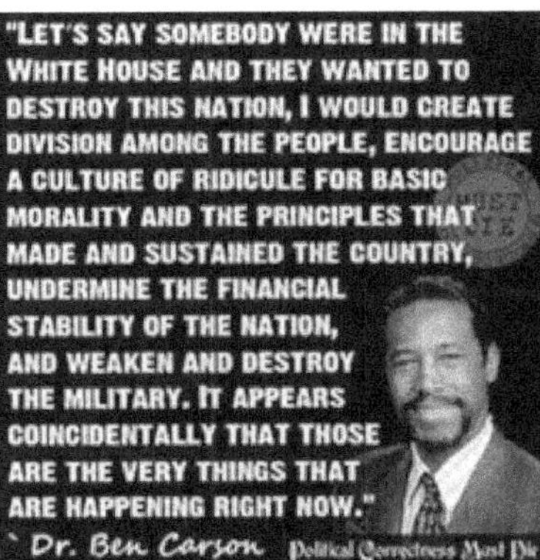

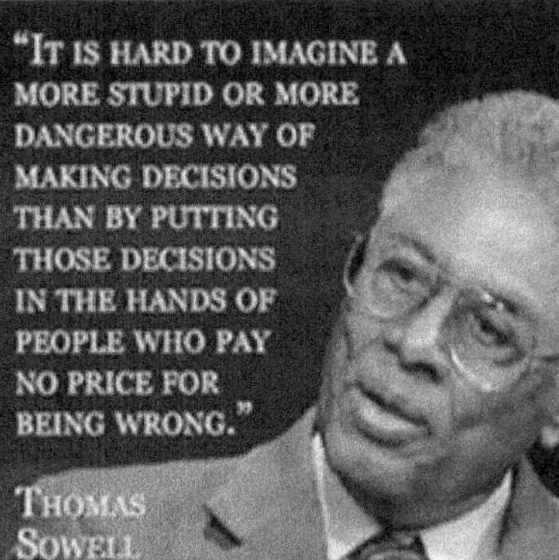

If you are taught bitterness and anger, then you will believe you are a victim. You will feel aggrieved and the twin brother of aggrievement is entitlement. So now you think you are owed something and you don't have to work for it and now you're on a really bad road to nowhere because there are people who will play to that sense of victimhood, aggrievement and entitlement, and you still won't have a job.
— Dr. Condoleezza Rice

"For the party that says they support diversity, I wish they supported diversity of thought."
-Tim Scott

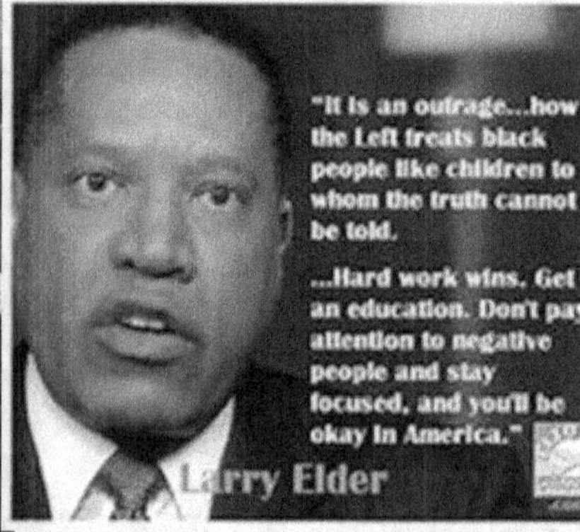
"It is an outrage...how the Left treats black people like children to whom the truth cannot be told.
...Hard work wins. Get an education. Don't pay attention to negative people and stay focused, and you'll be okay In America."
Larry Elder

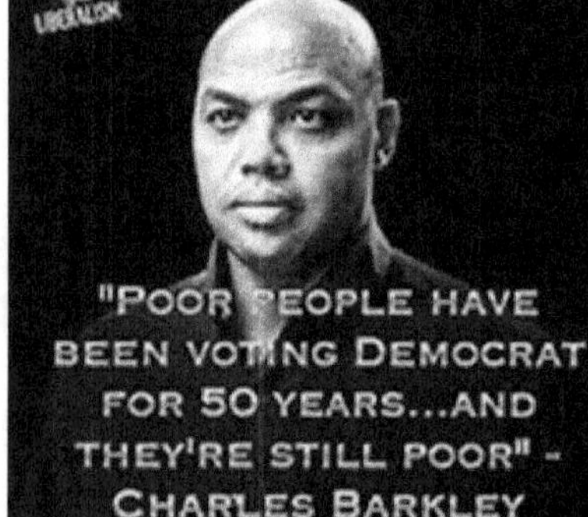
"POOR PEOPLE HAVE BEEN VOTING DEMOCRAT FOR 50 YEARS...AND THEY'RE STILL POOR" - CHARLES BARKLEY

"It is not surprising that lazy, shiftless politicians who have an abysmal record for their community would want to diffuse the issue of what they are doing for their communities by dropping the race card."
Niger Innis

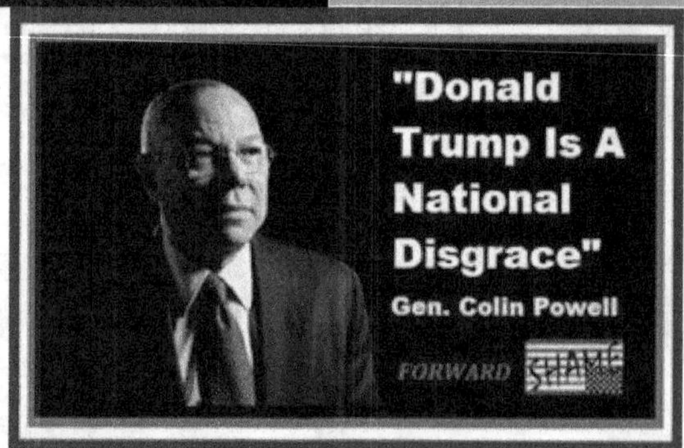
"Donald Trump Is A National Disgrace"
Gen. Colin Powell
FORWARD

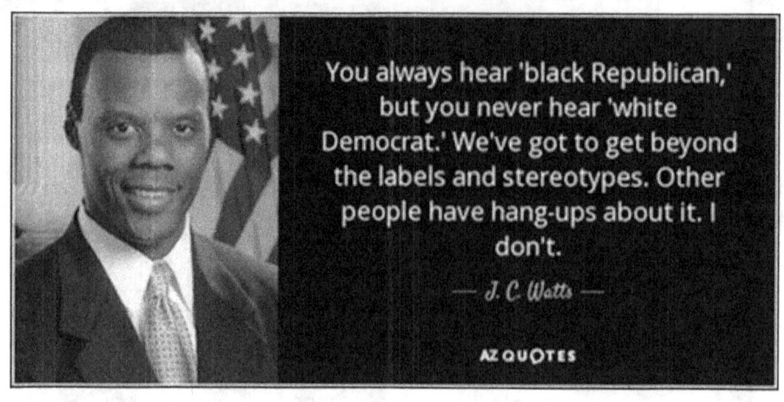
You always hear 'black Republican,' but you never hear 'white Democrat.' We've got to get beyond the labels and stereotypes. Other people have hang-ups about it. I don't.
— J. C. Watts —
AZ QUOTES

PLEASE
STOP
HELPING
US
How Liberals Make
It Harder for
Blacks to Succeed
JASON L. RILEY
CONGRESSMAN
WILL
HURD
Fighting for
Bipartisan Solutions

Among the cancers devouring the
American body politic, one of the
most virulent involves liberals who
play the race card as carelessly as
children playing 52 Pickup.

— Deroy Murdock —

AZ QUOTES

I frankly don't care if you
agree with my stand on
abortion. I take that stand
because no other stand is
consistent with decent
principles, and no other
standard is consistent with
the will of God.

-- Alan Keyes

"History is not going to be kind to liberals.
With their mindless programs, they've
managed to do to Black Americans what
slavery, Reconstruction, and rank racism
found impossible: destroy their family and
work ethic."
- Dr. Walter Williams

Obama Illustrated / * Facebook * Twitter * YouTube

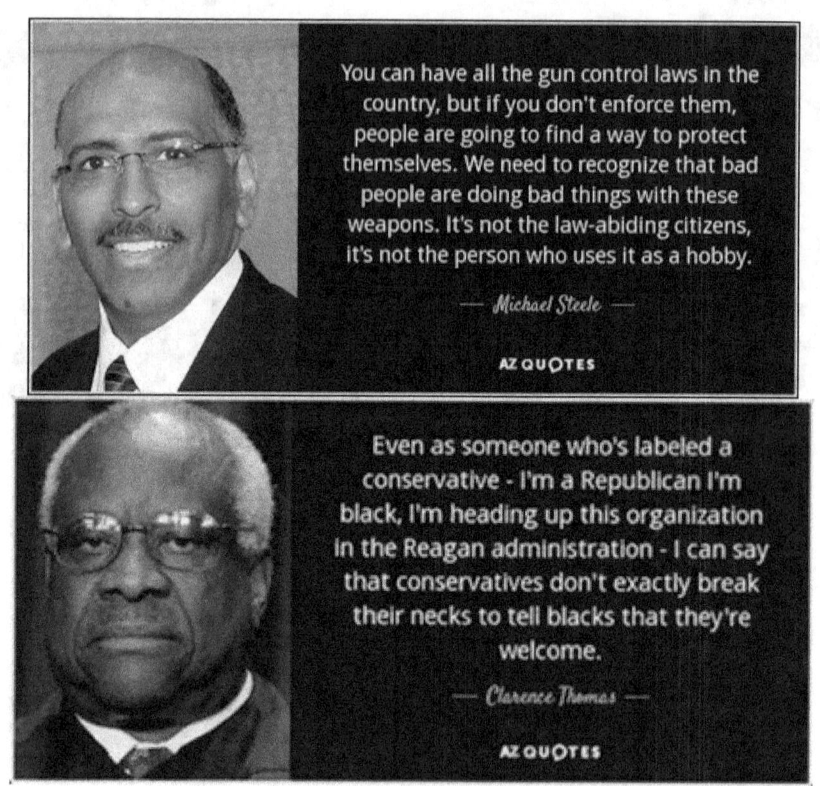

Friday, January 22, 2016
National Black Republican Association Endorses Donald J. Trump

The National Black Republican Association was founded in 2005 by Frances Rice, a retired Lieutenant Colonel and attorney of the U.S. Army. Rice is currently the Chairman of the NBRA.

NBRA Endorses Donald J. Trump
By Frances Rice

We, the grassroots activists of the National Black Republican Association, are pleased to announce our endorsement of Donald J. Trump for President of the United States of America.

As citizens who happen to be black, we support Mr. Trump because he shares our values. We, like Mr. Trump, are fiscally conservative, steadfastly pro-life and believers in a small government that fosters freedom for individuals and businesses, so they can grow and become prosperous.

We are deeply concerned about illegal immigration, a major cause of high black unemployment, especially among black youth.

Black Americans across America are beginning to wake up and see clearly the reality of what is happening in black neighborhoods. Democrats have run black communities for the past 60 years and the socialist policies of the Democrats have turned those communities into economic and social wastelands, witness Detroit, Baltimore and South Chicago.

We believe that Mr. Trump has demonstrated that he can push back against the mainstream media, end political correctness and free black communities from the destructive grip of socialist Democrats.

We urge our fellow black Americans to seize control over their own destiny and leverage their vote the way other groups do. It is way past time black Americans stop having their vote taken for granted by Democrats, hold politicians accountable for the content of their policies and not vote merely based on the label of their party.

Here's What Trump's Black Male Supporters Say They See in Him

Desmond Grant, who enthusiastically voted for Barack Obama in 2008 and 2012, sees Donald Trump as a racist. However, that did not stop Grant, a 40-year-old black man, from voting for Trump in 2016.

"Well, I mean I work here with a lot of racist people," says Grant, who owns a small trucking company in Houston, Texas, where he has lived his entire life. "That's America. You can't help it, they're everywhere. And you know, as long as they don't disrespect me in my face, they ain't gonna have no problems. But when we leave here, they can go raising the KKKs and do whatever they wanna do. But as long as we're on the job, we're gonna respect each other."

That outlook doesn't account for what could happen on a job through a racist coworker's neighborhood, but Grant says that the climate for small businesses matters more to him than what lives in the president's heart and mind on race and that his trucking company has thrived in the Trump era. The president, he says, presents an aura of strength that's more important than the shortcomings his critics focus on.

"He does know how to make money," says Grant. "He's not an honest man and he's not too bright, but he don't give a fuck. You know what I'm saying? He's not the most well-spoken but he stands his ground—and that's part of being a man. He can do that very well."

  A black man speaks favorably about Trump. He certainly must be ready for a scolding from Joe Biden, who proclaimed on The Breakfast Club Friday morning that "if you have trouble figuring out whether you are for me or Trump, then you ain't black."

Memo to Biden, who apologized hours later for a remark he said was made "in jest": Trump won 8 percent of the black vote in 2016—4 percent of the black female vote and 13 percent of the black male vote.

"There's certainly enough indications in the data to say that African-American men approve of Trump at higher rates than African-American women," says John Della Volpe, director of polling at Harvard's Kennedy School of Government's Institute of Politics. "Biden does better among black women than he does with black men, especially among younger men… Democrats have done a better job of holding onto to black male voters over 50 than they have with younger men."

In the most recent Harvard Institute of Politics poll of voters aged 18 to 30, 15 percent of black male voters support Trump over Biden compared to only 3 percent of black female voters. "Trump's presentation of outsider bootstrap success is more inclined to resonate with black men than black women," says Corey Fields, a professor of sociology at Georgetown University and the author of Black Elephants in the Room. Black women, he says, are less likely to be deceived by Trump as "they see him and his actions through both the prisms of race and gender—not just race."

Democrats should be worried and avoid falling back into the trap of taking the black vote for granted, according to Charles Cherry, Publisher of The Florida Courier, a statewide newspaper covering black communities across the state. "I mean these are quiet Trump supporters. And when you talk to them, you hear them say 'You know, I don't like the guy but…' or 'he stands with his faith' or 'you know where he's coming from.' They perceive him as being a strong guy who doesn't give a damn. And from a black male mindset, that's something that some guys like."

Marcelis Turner, 27, a Detroit native who is now an RNC field director in Wayne County, sees an opening for the president in the Harvard Institute of Politics poll, which also showed black men were more likely to say that the economy is their greatest concern. Turner, who voted for Obama in 2012 and sat out 2016, says there are many voters like him—who didn't vote in 2016—now drawn to Trump for what the president has done on criminal justice reform and what he can do on the economy.

"We're looking at this differently than many other generations," says Turner. "We care about building the economy for ourselves and our communities. I know that is what drew me to Trump."

The idea that Trump is strong on the economy and projects an image of strength kept coming up in my conversations with black men who are supporting him. "I like Trump because he's an alpha male's alpha male," says Wilfred Rucker, a 60-year-old black Republican voter and Trump supporter in Charlotte, North Carolina. "On the left, it's more about consensus and compromise. On our side, it's about winning or losing. Conflict is not to be avoided. The only thing that is to be avoided is losing."

Rucker says black conservatives consider themselves to be "Americans first, conservatives second, and black third. We just happen to be black. It's just not important, it's as important in seeing someone who's fat, seeing someone who's tall, seeing someone who wears glasses. It's an undeniable physical characteristic."

Rucker broke with his party in 2008 and voted for Barack Obama, and a big hole appears in Rucker's perspective when he berates 44 for failing to do enough for black people as president: "I thought I voted for the first black president, but I ended up voting for the first half-white president."

So why does someone who sees black identity as a mere physical characteristic like height expect the first black president to place race at the helm of his agenda? Why does Rucker criticize Obama for failing to do things that his heroic Trump has not done either, like appointing a black Supreme Court justice?

"You're getting things twisted," Rucker replies when I raise those questions.

Death or the Democratic Party: For so many elections since 1964, the black partisan mindset has been reduced to that choice.

What was so refreshing about 2008 was the opportunity to finally vote for something—the brilliance of Barack Obama—and not against a Republican like, say, Ronald Reagan, who, in his debate with Jimmy Carter in 1980, said he wanted to return to the racial climate of the '50s, when there wasn't a race problem. Of course, Obama's Republican opponent, John McCain, seemed to at least know that the 1950s was not a decade without a race problem. Rather than try to Willie Horton his way to the White House like the handlers of the elder Bush, McCain stood up to one of his supporters at a rally as he corrected her for insulting the true identity of his opponent, Barack Obama. In 2008, I didn't feel the need to vote against John McCain. I voted for Barack Obama.

Now, Biden's comment carries us back to that old model—You're black and safe (or stuck) with Biden versus Facing the End of the World with Trump. In doing so, Biden gives license to those black Trump men to claim a false space of individuality and bravery in living beyond the limits of racial orthodoxy as if they must know something that is unknown to the rest of black America: "Black millennial men have a familiarity with the president that precedes his time in office," says Paris Denard, 37, a senior communications adviser for black media affairs at the RNC and an advisory board member for Black Voices for Trump.

"We know him from The Apprentice… We know him from NeNe Leakes talking about cashing Trump checks on Real Housewives Atlanta. We know him from being the subject, in a positive way, in many hip-hop songs. We see him throughout the years with black community leaders and athletes, hip-hop stars and music people. He's a provider: He is a good father. As a young black man, you admire people who are great fathers… It goes with the type of person and the type of alpha male that he is."

Denard accuses the liberal news media, in sympathy with the Democratic Party, of deliberately plotting to portray Trump in ways that make him repulsive to black female voters, one of the Democrats' strongest voting blocks. "The real reason why the media is so hellbent on portraying President Trump as a racist is because they know that it's going to drive down his popularity with women voters if they focus on his tone and his policies about children in ways that are just flat-out false."

Yet black men, Denard argues, are able to see the true Trump as "not only inspirational but aspirational," a view that inherently hinges on gender stereotypes bestowing the quality of compassion to black women and rugged wisdom to black men who can see the truths behind those false media portrayals that trick the women. When I raise this point with him, along with how much he sounds like a Bernie supporter talking about how The media was against us, and In the pocket of the Party Establishment, he raises his voice:

"Look, when you turn on the television, you hear and you see a false narrative about the president—about his tone, and about him being racist."

Black conservatives like Reginald Grant, 32, have a less romanticized view of Trump and the GOP's campaign to appeal to black voters. Grant, like his first cousin, Desmond Grant, voted for Trump in 2016. Even though he was troubled by some of the president's behavior during the campaign, Reginald Grant thought he was not "evil" like Hillary Clinton.

"So, I kept saying, maybe when he gets to office, he'll become more of what you think of when you hear the term presidential," says Grant, a geography teacher in Houston. "I don't see any type of evolution to him or change in that regard."

Instead, the president's "racist response" to the NFL protests was Grant's breaking point, and, he says, Trump's poor handling of the pandemic has further highlighted his shortcomings.

Republicans would be doing better with black voters if not for Trump, says Grant, noting that polls consistently show strong threads of conservatism among African-Americans. After all, whoever passes a test with a score of 15 percent? True, but unfortunately for Democrats, Republicans are on a steep curve when it comes to how many black votes, they need to shave off of a key Democratic voting block to win in some swing states. (https://www.thedailybeast.com/heres-what-trumps-black-male-supporters-say-they-see-in-him?ref=scroll)

THEODORE ROOSEVELT

"Theodore Roosevelt, bynames Teddy Roosevelt and TR, (born October 27, 1858, New York, New York, U.S.—died January 6, 1919, Oyster Bay, New York), 26th president of the United States (1901–09) and a writer, naturalist, and soldier. He expanded the powers of the presidency and of the federal government in support of the public interest in conflicts between big business and labour and steered the nation toward an active role in world politics, particularly in Europe and Asia. He won the Nobel Prize for Peace in 1906 for mediating an end to the Russo-Japanese War (1904–05), and he secured the route and began construction of the Panama Canal (1904–14). (Key events in the life of Theodore Roosevelt. Encyclopædia Britannica, Inc.)

QUOTATIONS BY THEODORE ROOSEVELT

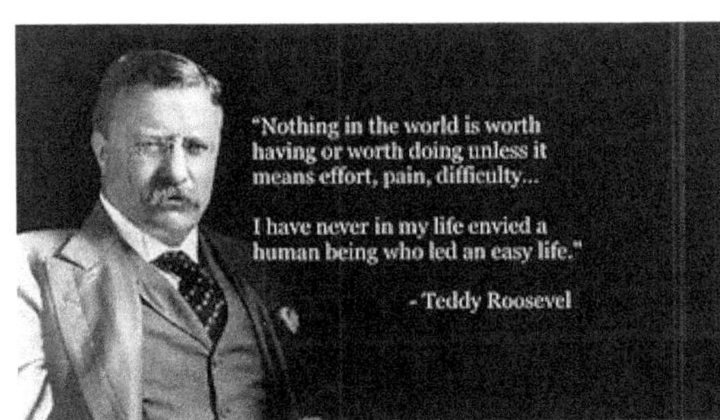

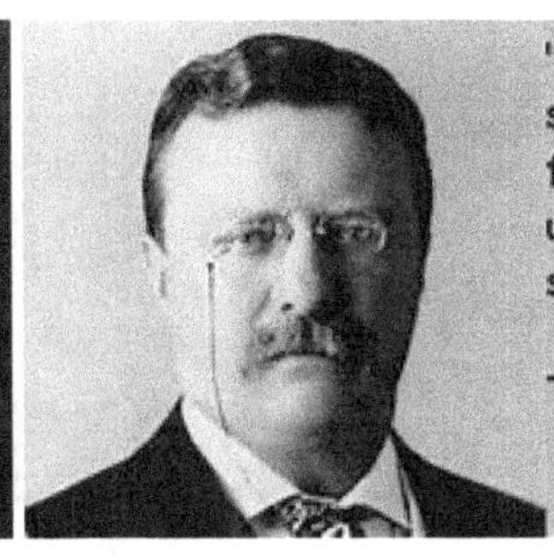

We must dare to
be great; and we
must realize that
greatness is the
fruit of toil and
sacrifice and high
courage."
TEDDY
ROOSEVELT
1901-1909
Leader.org

Complaining about a
problem without
proposing a solution is
called whining.
- Teddy Roosevelt

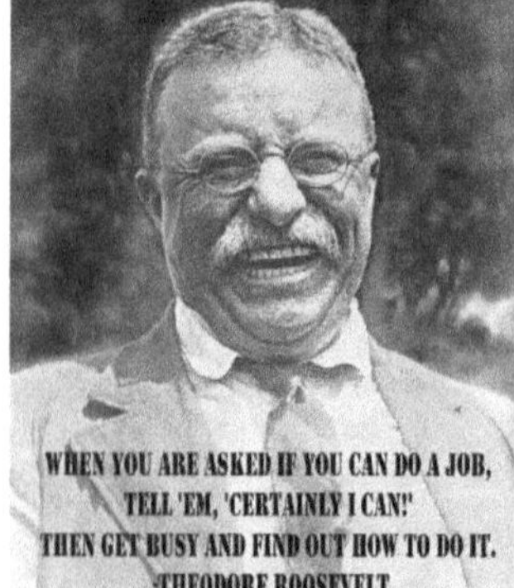
WHEN YOU ARE ASKED IF YOU CAN DO A JOB,
TELL 'EM, 'CERTAINLY I CAN!'
THEN GET BUSY AND FIND OUT HOW TO DO IT.
-THEODORE ROOSEVELT

In any moment of decision, the best thing you
can do is the right thing, the next best thing is
the wrong thing, and the worst thing you can
do is nothing.

(Theodore Roosevelt)

izquotes.com

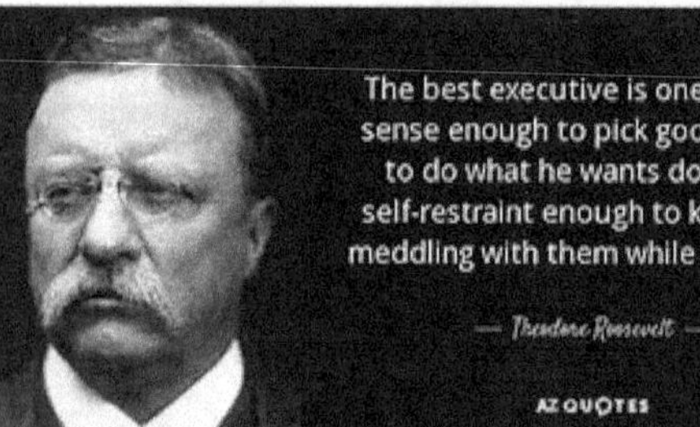
The best executive is one who has
sense enough to pick good people
to do what he wants done, and
self-restraint enough to keep from
meddling with them while they do it.

— Theodore Roosevelt —

AZ QUOTES

"The greatest doer
must also be a
great dreamer"

Theodore Roosevelt - www.azquotes.com

If you could kick the person
in the pants responsible
for most of your trouble,
you wouldn't sit for a month.

— Theodore Roosevelt

QTES

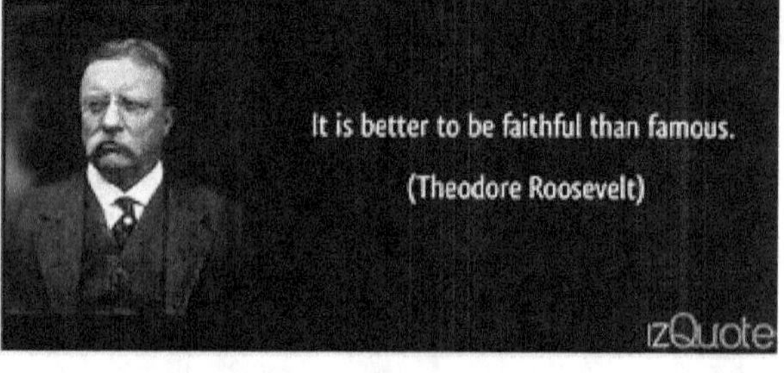
It is better to be faithful than famous.

(Theodore Roosevelt)

izQuotes

The only man who makes
no mistakes is the man
who never does anything.
Do not be afraid to make
mistakes providing you
do not make the same
one twice.

THEODORE ROOSEVELT

It is NECESSARY that
laws should be passed
to prohibit the use of
CORPORATE FUNDS
directly or indirectly
for political purposes;
— it is still more —
NECESSARY that such
LAWS should be
thoroughly enforced.
Theodore
Roosevelt

"To announce that there must be no criticism of the President, or that we are to stand by the President, right or wrong, is not only unpatriotic and servile, but is morally treasonable to the American Public."
President Theodore Roosevelt

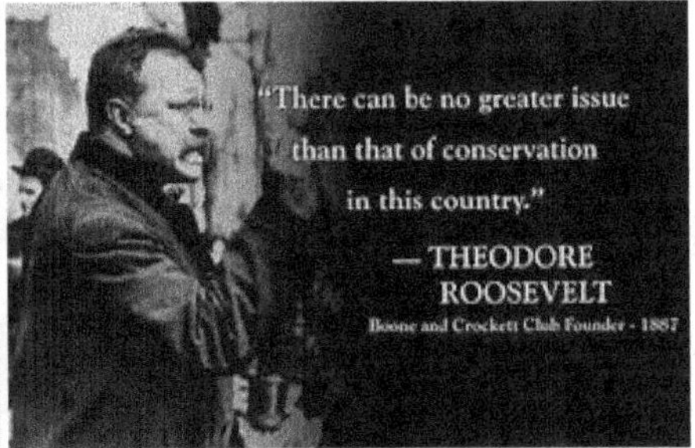
"There can be no greater issue than that of conservation in this country."
— THEODORE ROOSEVELT
Boone and Crockett Club Founder - 1887

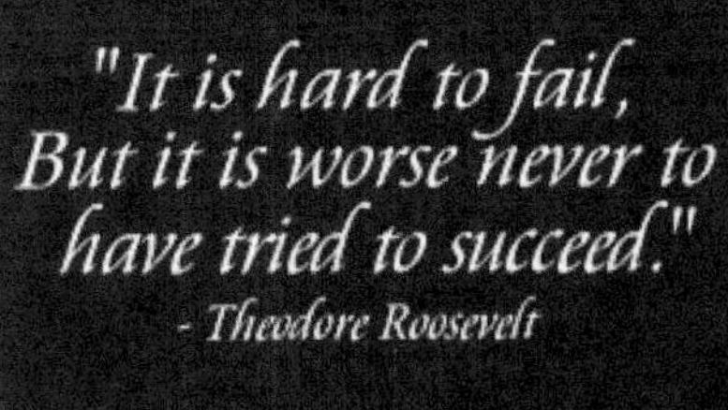
"It is hard to fail, But it is worse never to have tried to succeed."
- Theodore Roosevelt
popularquotesbyfamouspeople.blogspot.com

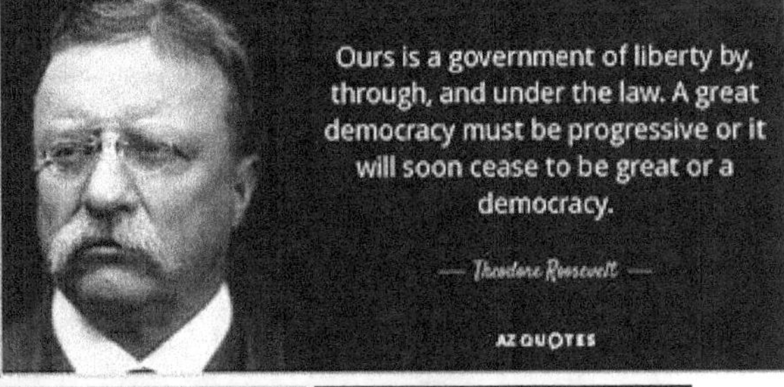
Ours is a government of liberty by, through, and under the law. A great democracy must be progressive or it will soon cease to be great or a democracy.
— Theodore Roosevelt —
AZ QUOTES

Here is your country. Cherish these natural wonders, cherish the natural resources, cherish the history and romance as a sacred heritage, for your children and your children's children. Do not let selfish men or greedy interests skin your country of its beauty, its riches or its romance.
— Theodore Roosevelt —
AZ QUOTES

The great corporations which we have grown to speak of rather loosely as trusts are the creatures of the State, and the State not only has the right to control them, but it is in duty bound to control them wherever the need of such control is shown. There is clearly need of supervision need to possess the power of regulation of these great corporations through the representatives of the public.
Theodore "Teddy" Roosevelt
Facebook.com/BeingLiberal.org

We are not attacking the corporations, but endeavoring to do away with any evil in them. We are not hostile to them; we are merely determined that they shall be so handled as to subserve the public good. We draw the line against misconduct, not against wealth.
Theodore Roosevelt
State of the Union, 1902

LEARN HOW TO FIGHT
BECAUSE MOST BULLIES DON'T BOTHER TO

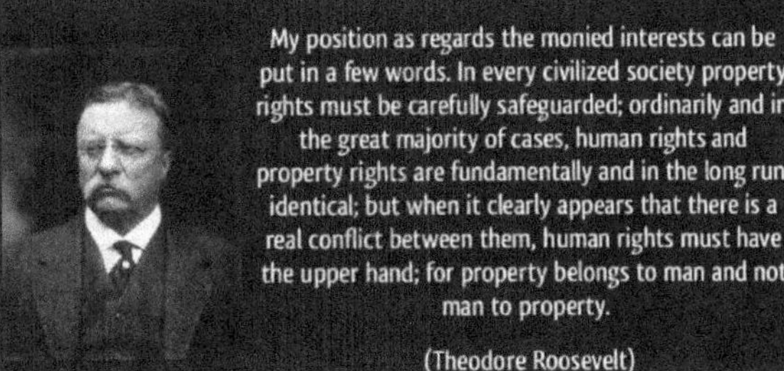
My position as regards the monied interests can be put in a few words. In every civilized society property rights must be carefully safeguarded; ordinarily and in the great majority of cases, human rights and property rights are fundamentally and in the long run, identical; but when it clearly appears that there is a real conflict between them, human rights must have the upper hand; for property belongs to man and not man to property.
(Theodore Roosevelt)

"There once was a time in history when the limitation of governmental power meant increasing liberty for the people.

In the present day the limitation of governmental power, of governmental action, means the enslavement of the people by the great corporations,

who can only be held in check through the extension of governmental power."

- Theodore Roosevelt
San Francisco - Sept. 14, 1912

APATHY
"To sit home, read one's favorite paper, and scoff at the misdeeds of the men who do things is easy, but it is markedly ineffective. It is what evil men count upon the good men doing."

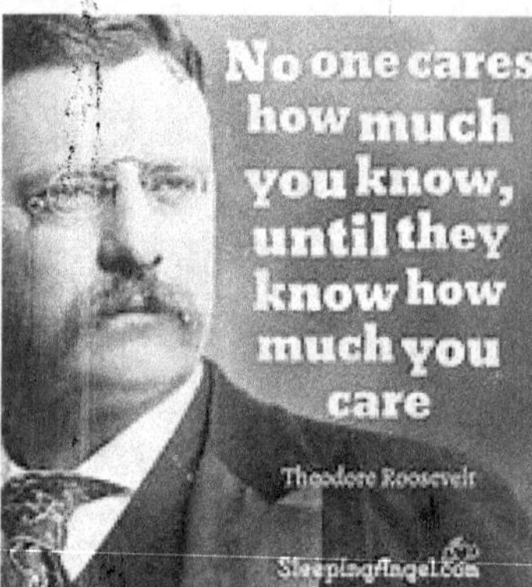

No one cares how much you know, until they know how much you care

Theodore Roosevelt

SleepingAngel.com

DUTY
"The performance of duty, and not an indulgence in vapid ease and vapid pleasure, is all that makes life worth while."

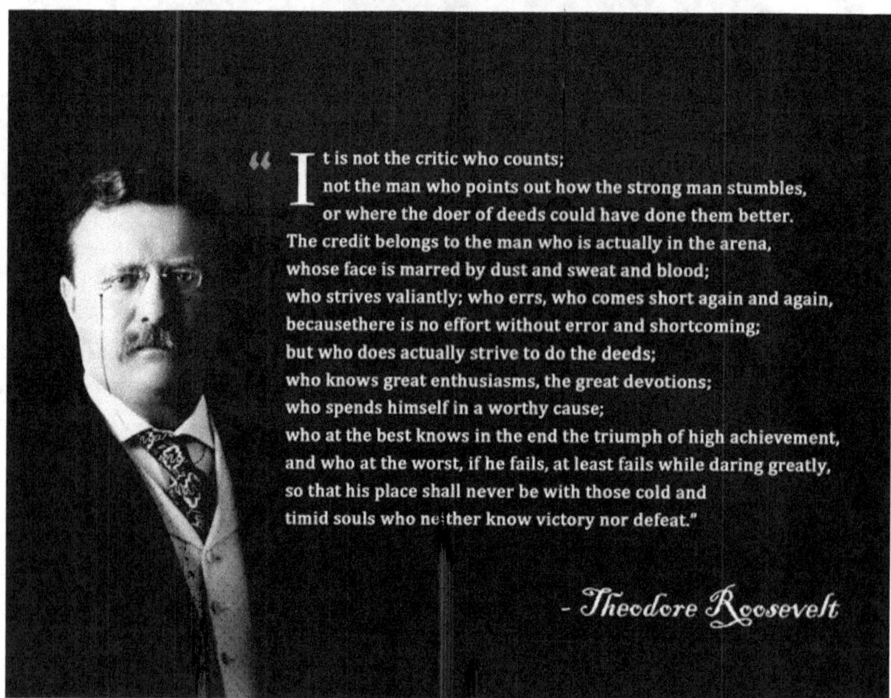

It is not the critic who counts;
not the man who points out how the strong man stumbles,
or where the doer of deeds could have done them better.
The credit belongs to the man who is actually in the arena,
whose face is marred by dust and sweat and blood;
who strives valiantly; who errs, who comes short again and again,
because there is no effort without error and shortcoming;
but who does actually strive to do the deeds;
who knows great enthusiasms, the great devotions;
who spends himself in a worthy cause;
who at the best knows in the end the triumph of high achievement,
and who at the worst, if he fails, at least fails while daring greatly,
so that his place shall never be with those cold and
timid souls who neither know victory nor defeat."

- Theodore Roosevelt

RONALD REAGAN

I certainly disagreed with Ronald Reagan on a lot of points, but I never disliked the man as I do the current President. He shot some zingers at those who didn't agree with them, but they were not mean or cruel as are the ravings of the current moron in the White House. Like many other recent Republican Presidents, Reagan didn't seceding in reigning in spending, and up went the National Debt. Still considered to the orange monster, he was a saint.

QUOTATIONS BY RONALD REAGAN

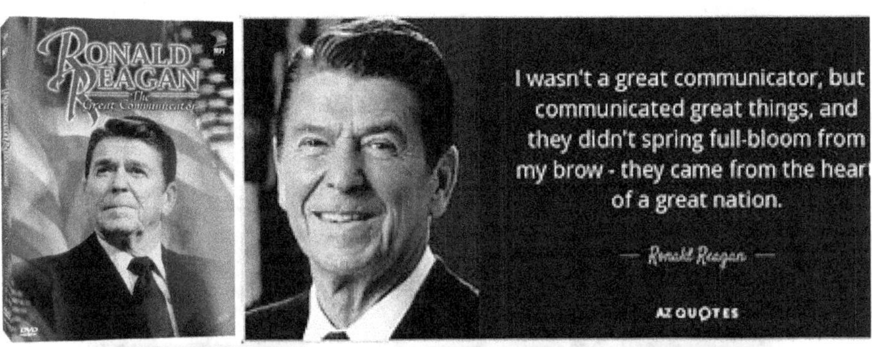

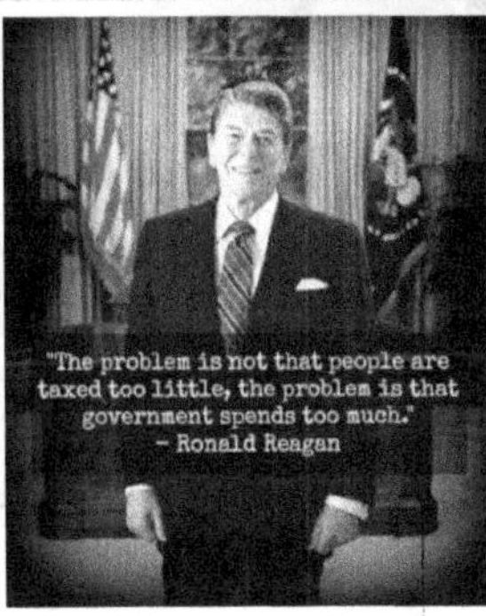

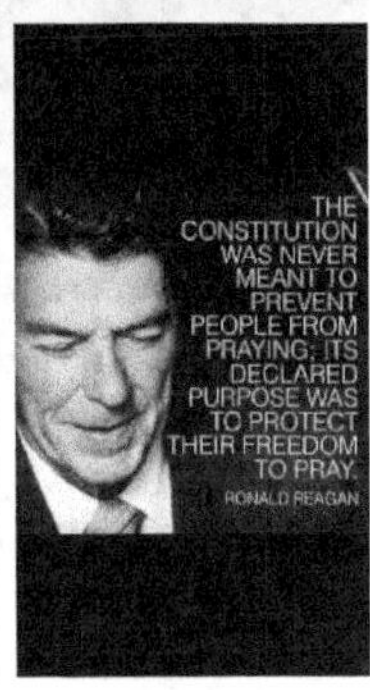

"We establish no religion in this country. We command no worship. We mandate no belief, nor will we ever. Church and state are and must remain separate."

Ronald Reagan

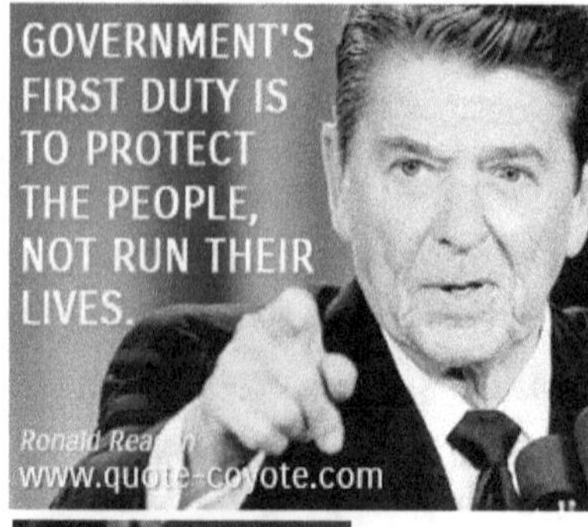

GOVERNMENT'S FIRST DUTY IS TO PROTECT THE PEOPLE, NOT RUN THEIR LIVES.
Ronald Reagan
www.quote-coyote.com

@GOPLabs
"Government does not tax to get the money it needs; government always finds a need for the money it gets."
— Ronald Reagan

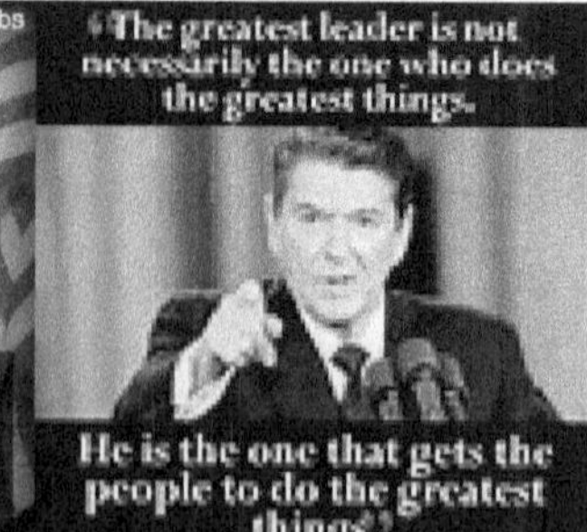

"The greatest leader is not necessarily the one who does the greatest things.
He is the one that gets the people to do the greatest things."

" General Secretary Gorbachev, if you seek peace, if you seek prosperity for the Soviet Union and eastern Europe, if you seek liberalization, come here to this gate. Mr. Gorbachev, open this gate. Mr. Gorbachev, tear down this wall."
Ronald Reagan
June 12, 1987

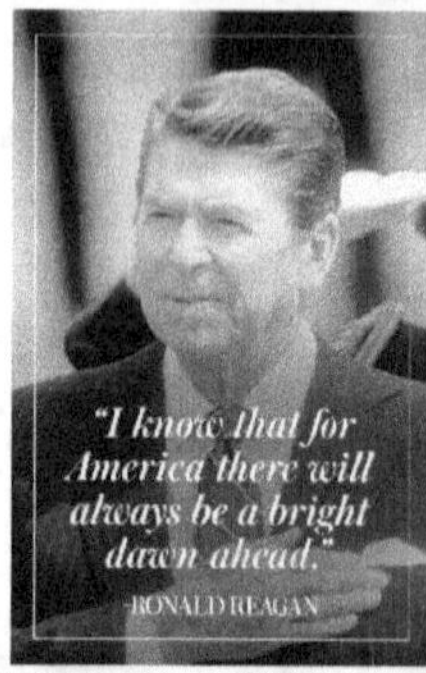

"I know that for America there will always be a bright dawn ahead."
-RONALD REAGAN

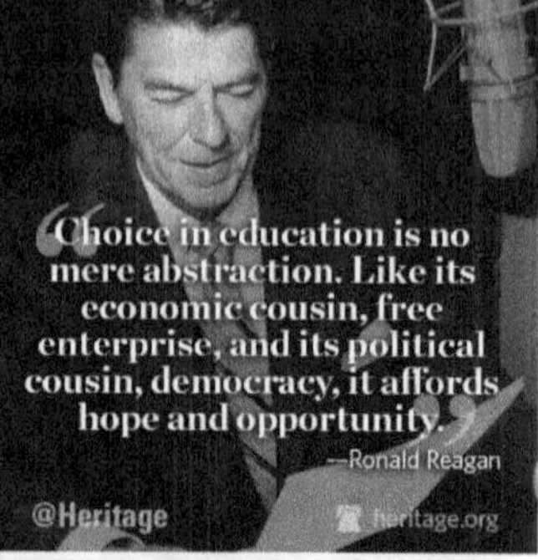

Choice in education is no mere abstraction. Like its economic cousin, free enterprise, and its political cousin, democracy, it affords hope and opportunity.
—Ronald Reagan
@Heritage
heritage.org

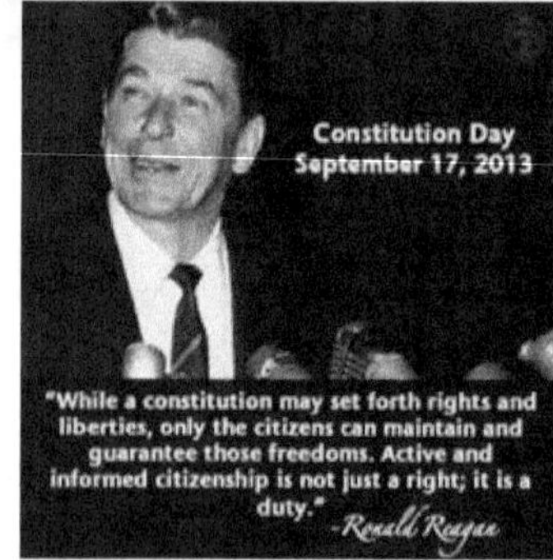

Constitution Day September 17, 2013
"While a constitution may set forth rights and liberties, only the citizens can maintain and guarantee those freedoms. Active and informed citizenship is not just a right; it is a duty."
-Ronald Reagan

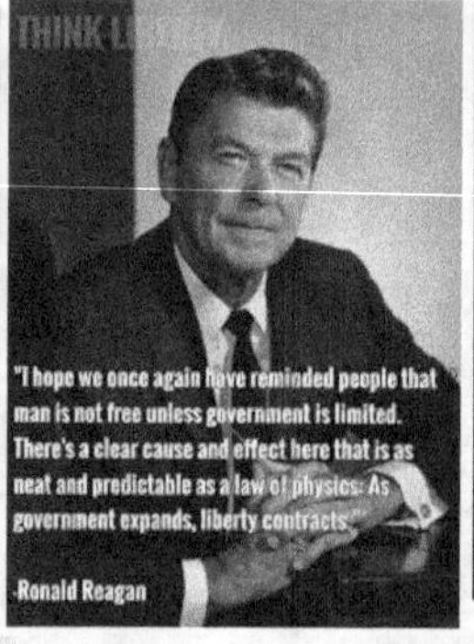

THINK LIBERTY
"I hope we once again have reminded people that man is not free unless government is limited. There's a clear cause and effect here that is as neat and predictable as a law of physics: As government expands, liberty contracts."
-Ronald Reagan

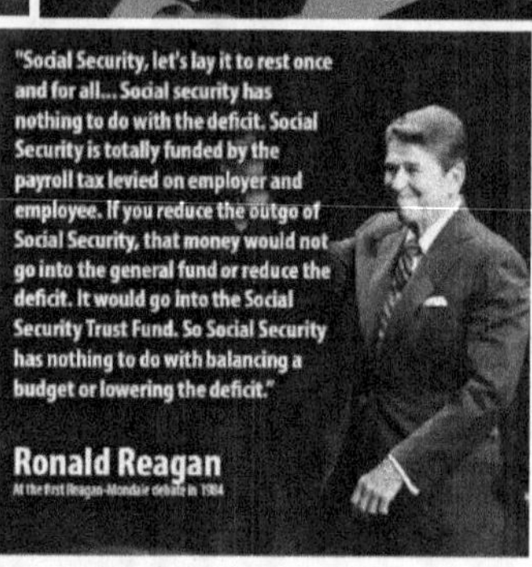

"Social Security, let's lay it to rest once and for all... Social security has nothing to do with the deficit. Social Security is totally funded by the payroll tax levied on employer and employee. If you reduce the outgo of Social Security, that money would not go into the general fund or reduce the deficit. It would go into the Social Security Trust Fund. So Social Security has nothing to do with balancing a budget or lowering the deficit."
Ronald Reagan
At the first Reagan-Mondale debate in 1984

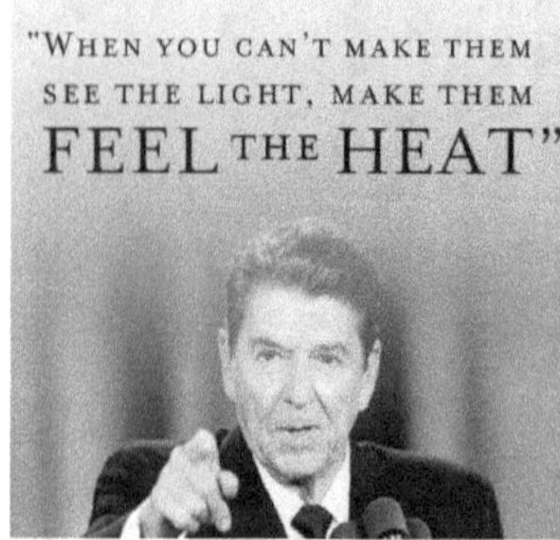

"WHEN YOU CAN'T MAKE THEM SEE THE LIGHT, MAKE THEM FEEL THE HEAT"

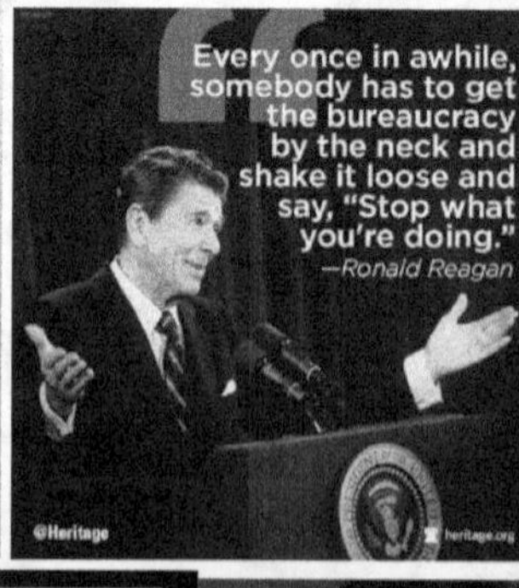

Every once in awhile, somebody has to get the bureaucracy by the neck and shake it loose and say, "Stop what you're doing."
—Ronald Reagan
@Heritage
heritage.org

Pssssst! Republicans? Listen up: Your Lord is speaking:
There is "no reason why on the street today a citizen should be carrying loaded weapons."
Guns are a "ridiculous way to solve problems that have to be solved among people of good will."

RONALD REAGAN
"I believe the best social program is a job..."

"EVIL IS POWERLESS IF THE GOOD ARE UNAFRAID."
RONALD REAGAN

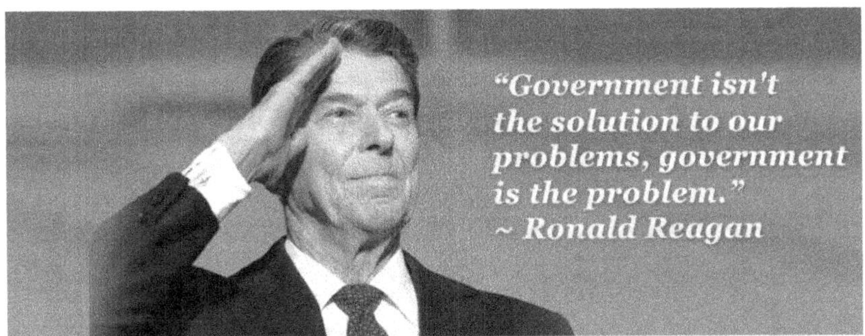

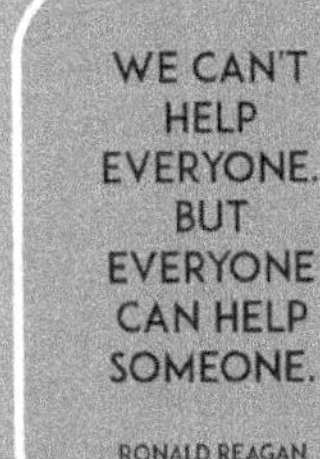

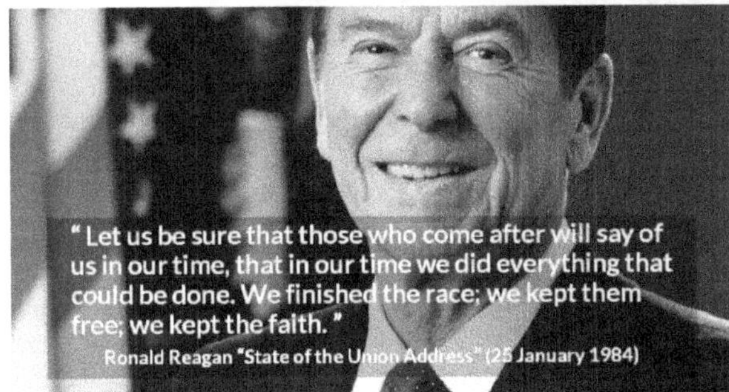

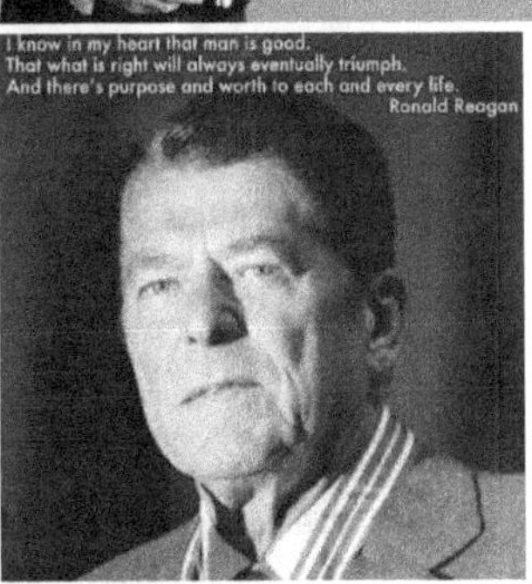

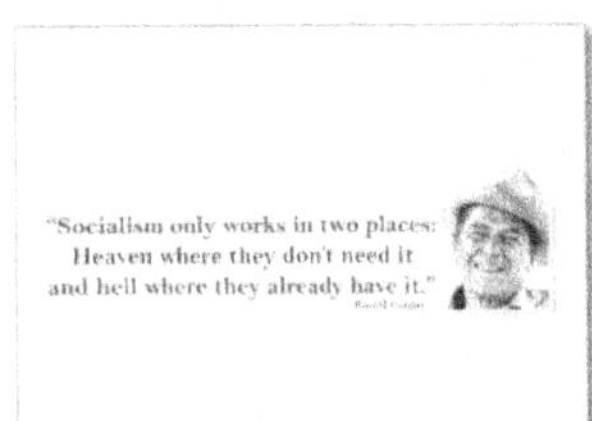

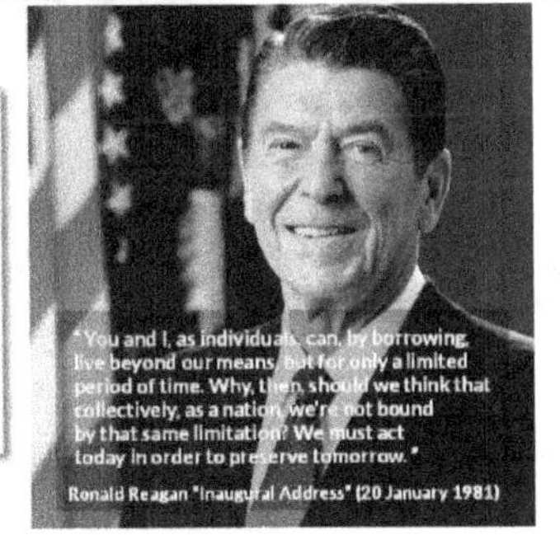

And the following is where I found fault with Ronnie.

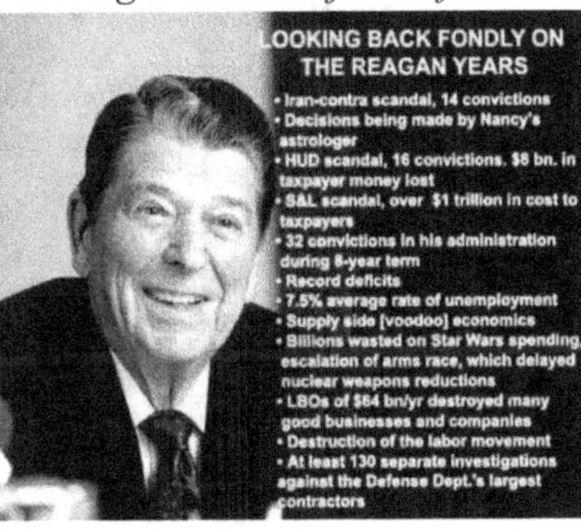

THE OTHER REPUBLICAN PRESIDENTS QUOTATIONS

ULYSSES GRANT

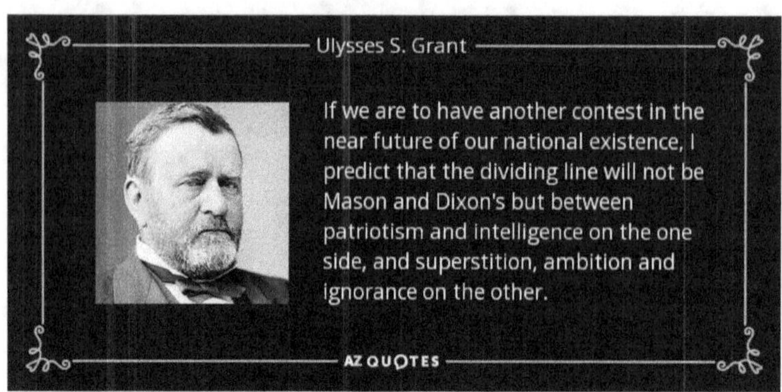

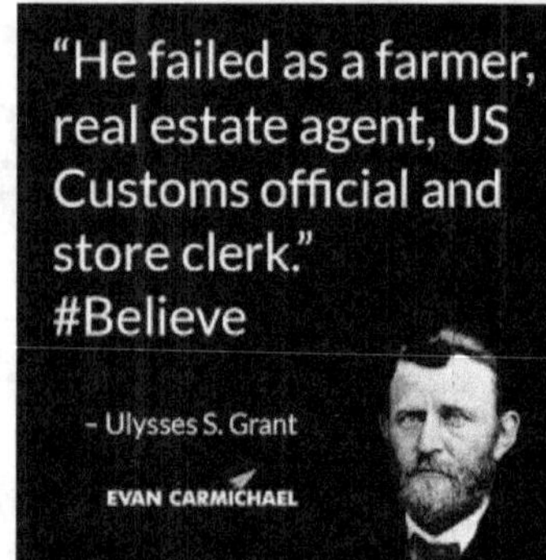

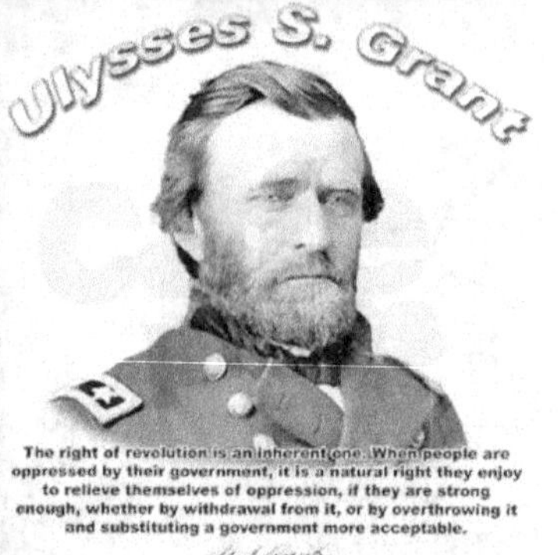

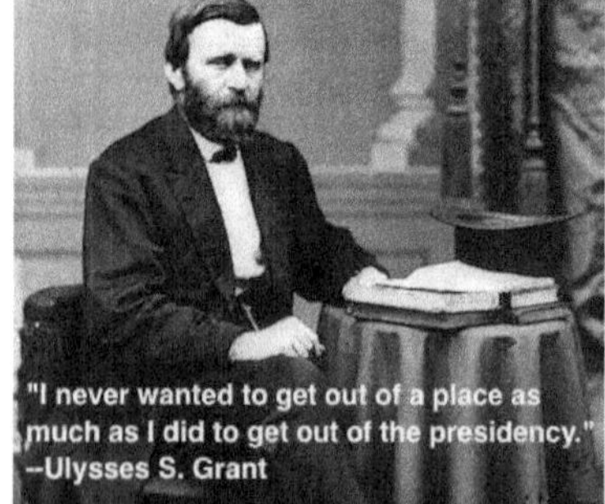

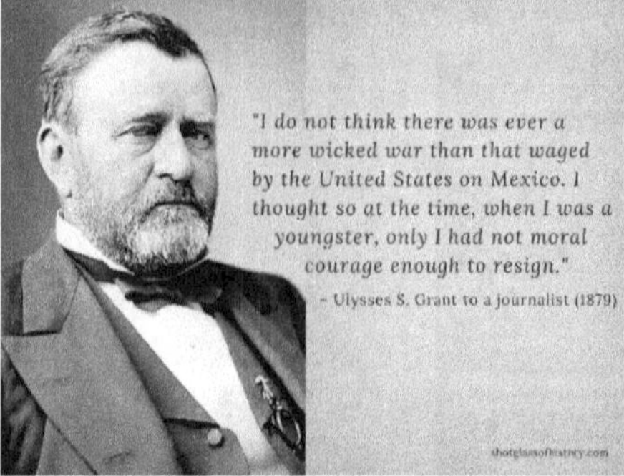

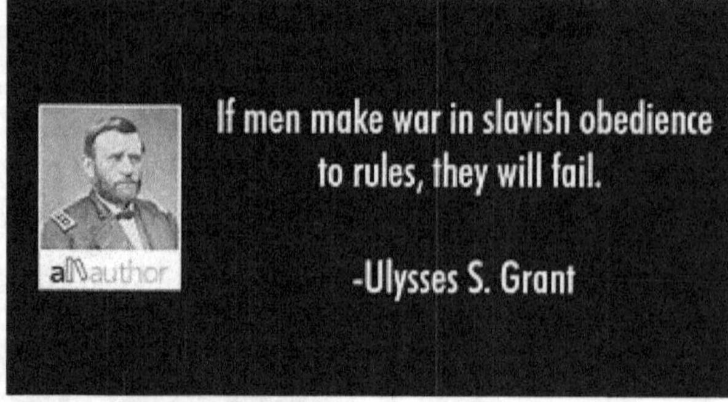

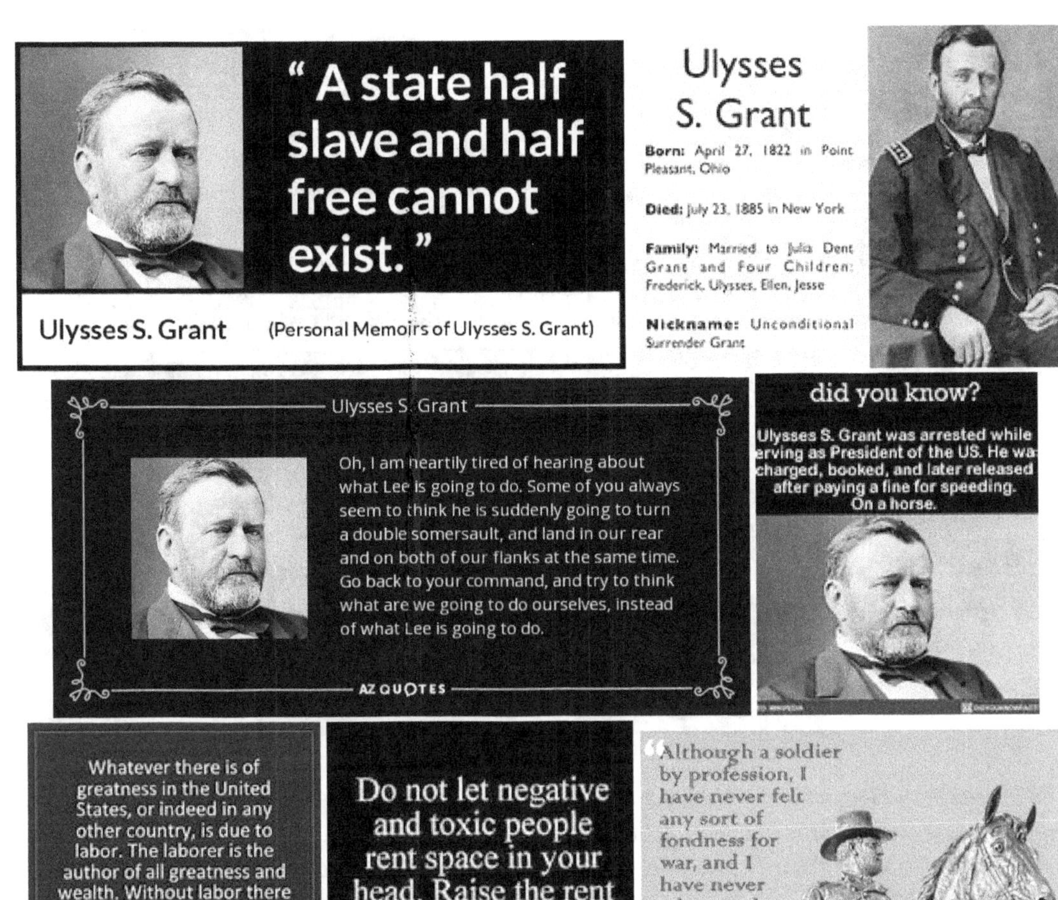

RUTHERFORD B. HAYES

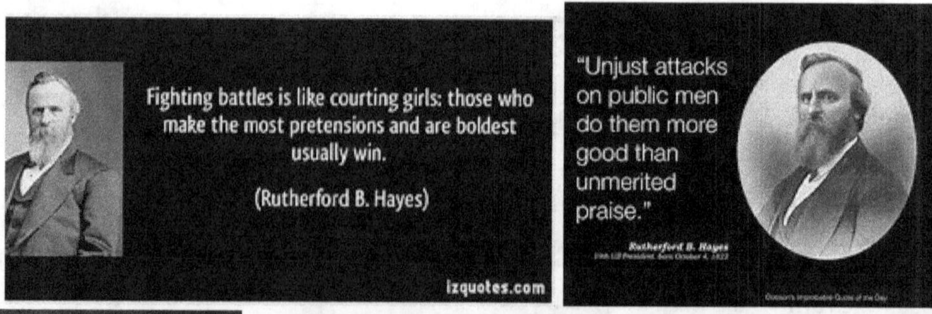

The Presidential Election In 1876 Almost Led To A Constitutional Crisis. To Learn The Story Behind The Following Images, May I Suggest As A Source My Book: The American Presidents From Polk To Hayes: What They Did, What They Said & What Was Said About Them, Chapter Nine, Outskirts Press January 29, 2016)

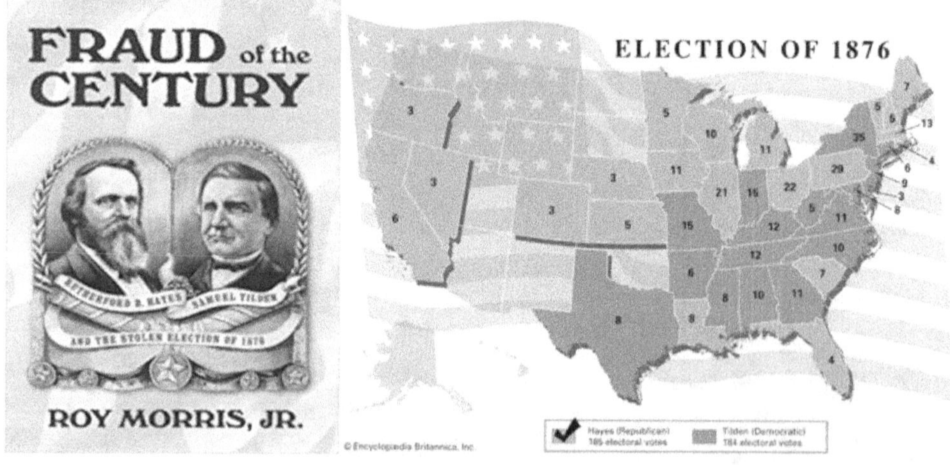

Section 3
The End of Reconstruction

- The Compromise of 1877
    - Republican Hayes Elected President
    - Federal Troops Leave the South
    - A Southerner Is Given a Powerful Cabinet Position
    - Federal Subsidies to Help the South Build
      Railroads and Improve Ports

JAMES A. GARFIELD

James A. Garfield's tenure as president was brief as a result of an assassin's bullet, assisted by physicians who proved his wound looking for the bullet with the bare hands, causing infections and a painful 80 days before he mercifully died.

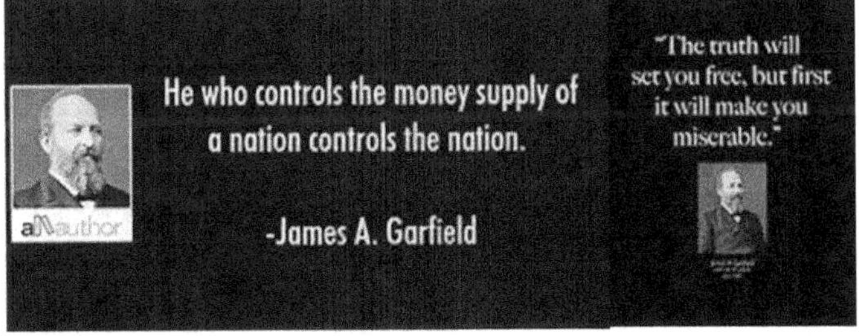

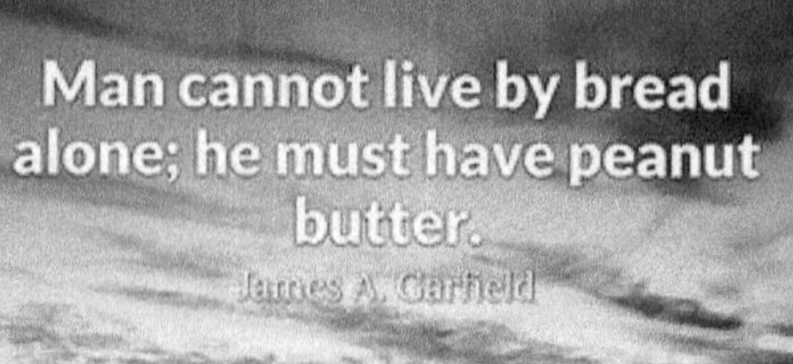

Man cannot live by bread alone; he must have peanut butter.
James A. Garfield
BrainyQuote

I am trying to do two things: dare to be a radical and not a fool, which is a matter of no small difficulty. ~James A. Garfield
topfamousquotes.com

THE IDEAL COLLEGE IS MARK HOPKINS ON ONE END OF A LOG AND A STUDENT ON THE OTHER.
QUOTEHD.COM
James A. Garfield
American President

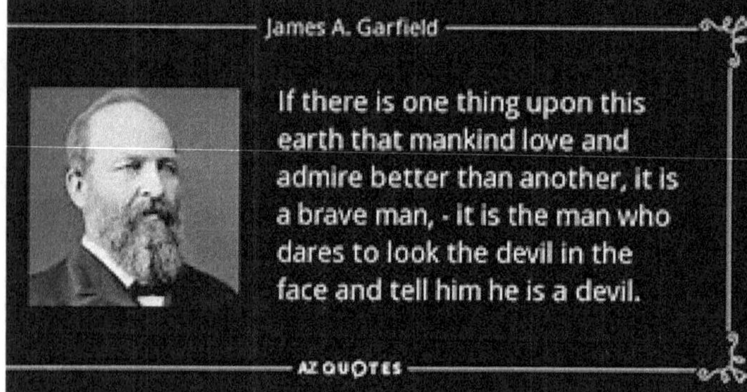

FB-antitheists
"The divorce between Church and State ought to be absolute. It ought to be so absolute that no Church property anywhere, in any state or in the nation, should be exempt from equal taxation; for if you exempt the property of any church organization (school), to that extent you impose a tax upon the whole community."
President James Garfield

The President is the last person in the world to know what the people really want and think.
QUOTEHD.COM
James A. Garfield
American President

James A. Garfield
If there is one thing upon this earth that mankind love and admire better than another, it is a brave man, - it is the man who dares to look the devil in the face and tell him he is a devil.
AZ QUOTES

"Be fit for more than the thing you are now doing. Let everyone know that you have a reserve in yourself — that you have more power than you are now using. If you are not too large for the place you occupy, you are too small for it."

Trivia about James Garfield
• Height: 6 feet
• He was raised on a poor farm
• He was a Civil War hero
• James Garfield was the poorest man ever to have become President
• He was the first left-handed president
www.facts-about.org.uk

ALL FREE GOVERNMENTS ARE MANAGED BY THE COMBINED WISDOM AND FOLLY OF THE PEOPLE.
QUOTEHD.COM
James A. Garfield
American President

James A. Garfield
Now more than ever the people are responsible for the character of their Congress. If that body be ignorant, reckless, and corrupt, it is because the people tolerate ignorance, recklessness, and corruption.
AZ QUOTES

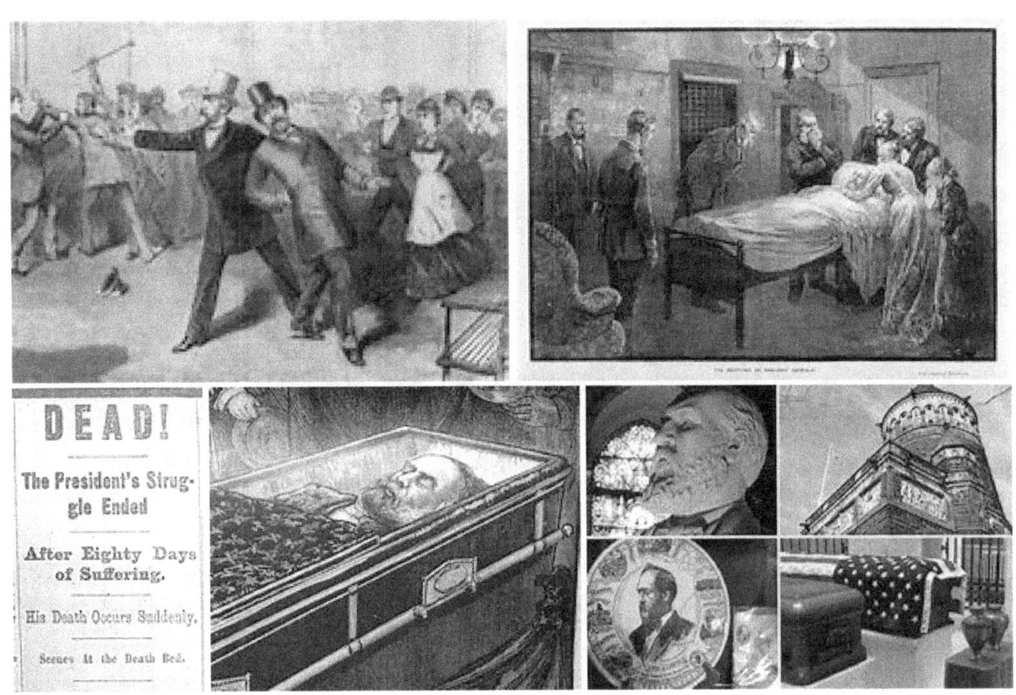

CHESTER A. ARTHUR

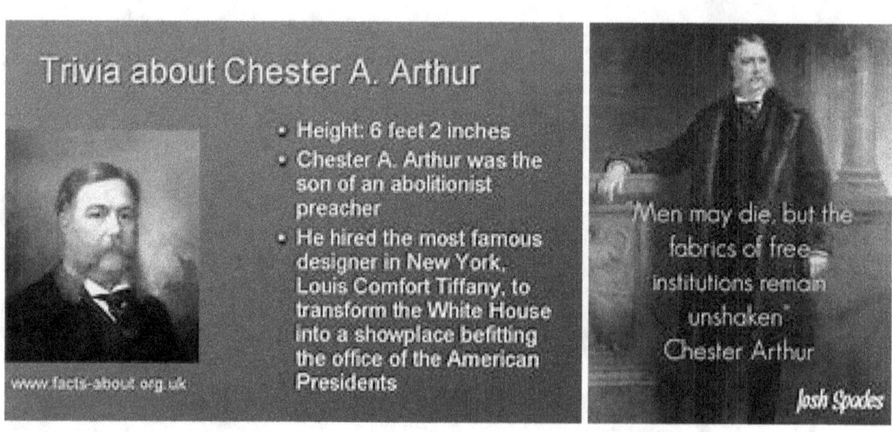

Chester A. Arthur

21st U.S. President (1829 – 1886)

Chester Alan Arthur was a graduate of Union College, a Republican who worked as a lawyer before becoming the 20th vice president under James Garfield. While Garfield was mortally wounded by Charles J. Guiteau on July 2, 1881, he did not die until September 19, at the Buffalo home of JOHN G. MILBURN. Arthur was then sworn in as President, serving until March 4, 1885.

Before entering elected politics, Arthur was the Collector of Customs for the Port of New York, a position to which he was appointed by President Ulysses S. Grant. He was then removed by the succeeding President, Rutherford B. Hayes, who was intent on rooting out patronage, even though Arthur had proved to be a prudent administrator.

As President, he became a champion of civil service reform. Arthur's primary achievement was the passage of the Pendleton Civil Service Reform Act. The passage of this legislation earned Arthur the moniker "The Father of Civil Service." Publisher Alexander K. McClure wrote, "No man ever entered the Presidency so profoundly and widely distrusted, and no one ever retired... more generally respected." Mark Twain, deeply cynical about politicians, conceded, "It would be hard indeed to better President Arthur's administration."

With the secret knowledge that he was dying, Arthur declined to campaign in 1885 and on the fourth ballot lost the Republican nomination to James Blaine, his former Secretary of State. Blaine was defeated by GROVER CLEVELAND. Arthur died of Brights Disease in November 1886, six years after his wife succumbed to pneumonia. Arthur was described by one admirer as "the greatest social lion we have had in many years," but historians generally give mediocre marks to his abbreviated presidency.

The bust of Arthur by AUGUSTUS SAINT GAUDENS, is in the U.S. Senate gallery. Arthur selected the sculptor, who took the $800 commission after Arthur's death.

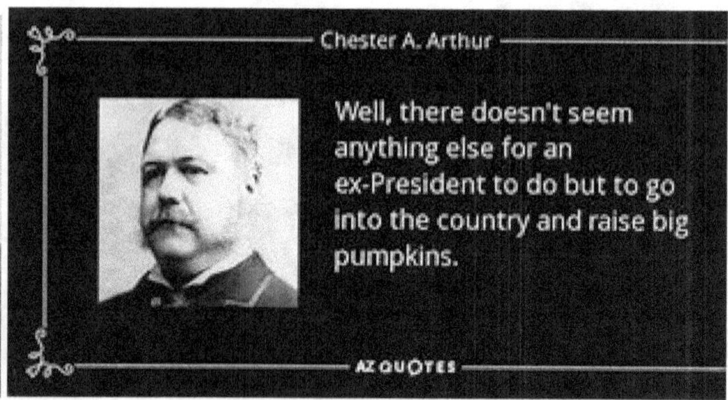

BENJAMIN HARRISON

"Harrison may not be the most memorable chief executive in American history, but he did, in fact, embody the end of an era: He was the last president to have a beard."

(Brien Cormac wrote this of the president in his 2004 book Secret Lives of the U.S. Presidents: What Your Teachers Never Told You About the Men of the White House)

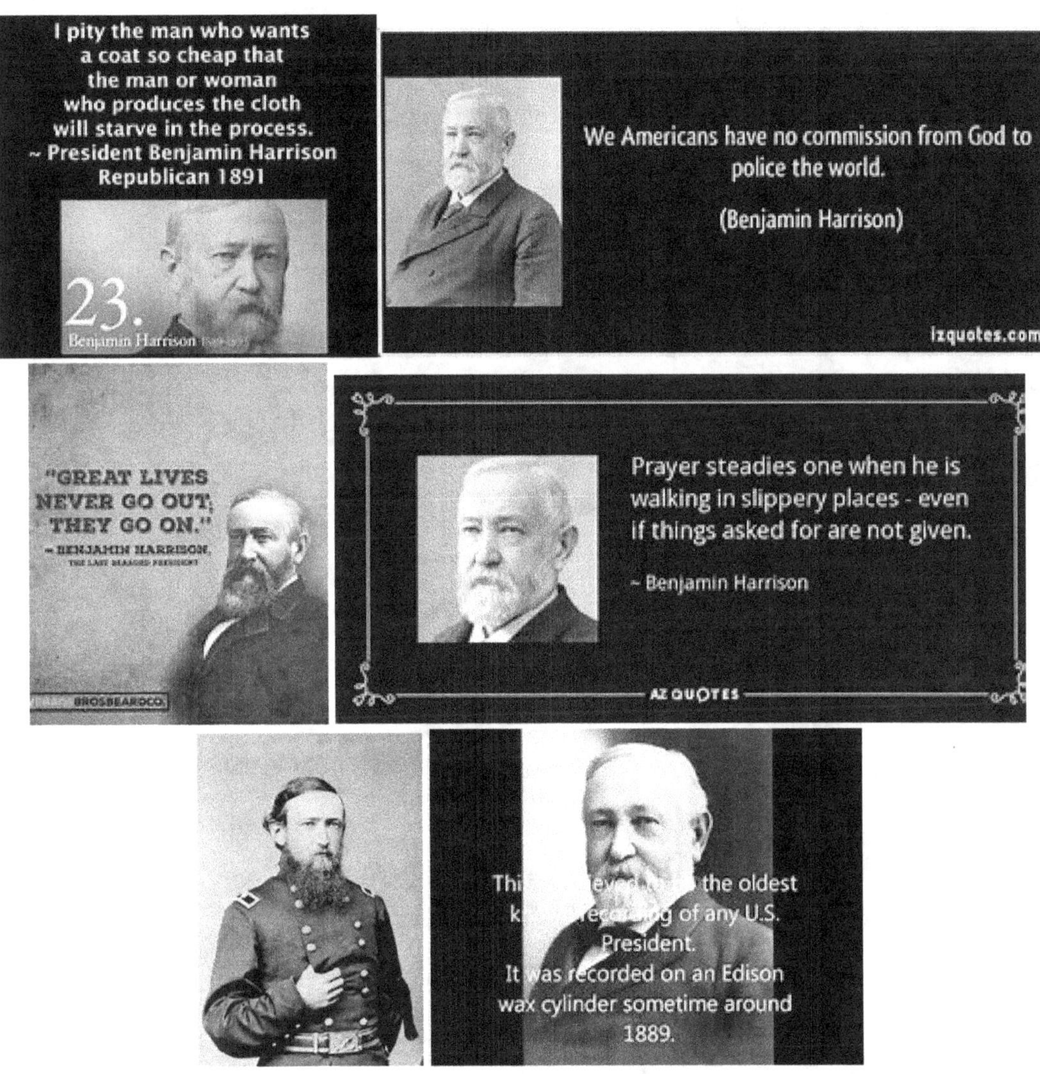

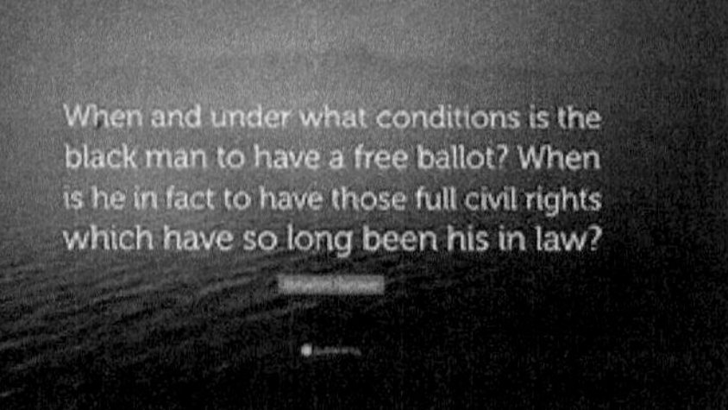

William McKinley

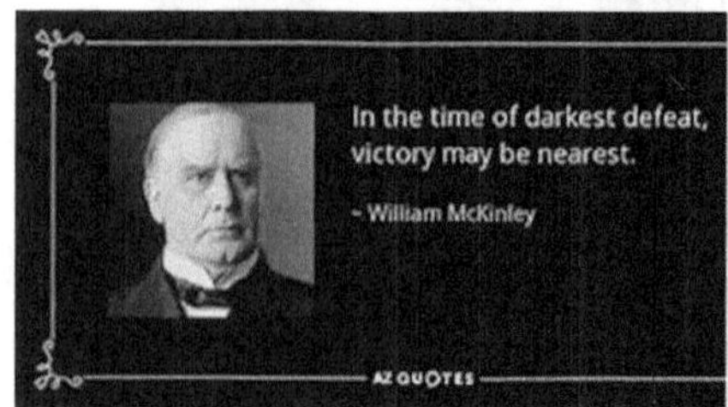

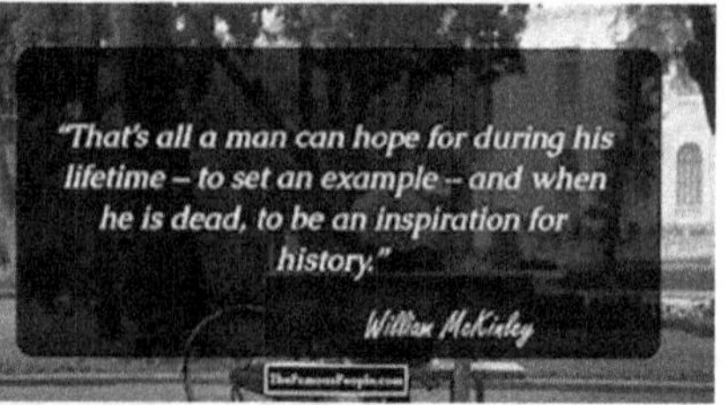

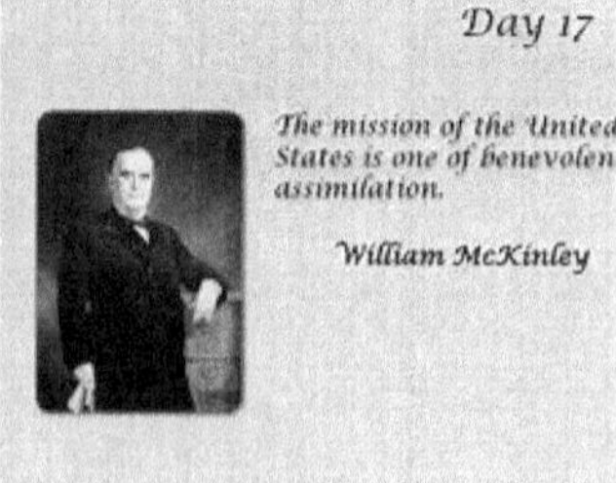

"I have never been in doubt since I was old enough to think intelligently that I would someday be made President." William McKinley

Half-heartedness
never won a battle.
William McKinley

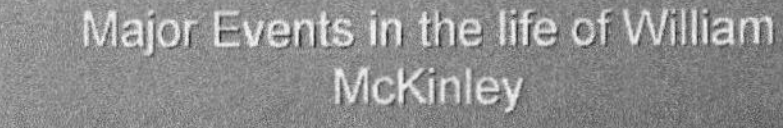

Major Events in the life of William McKinley
• Spanish-American War (1898)
• Annexation of Hawaii (1898)
• Open Door Policy/Boxer Rebellion (1899-1900)
• Gold Standard Act (1900)
www.facts-about.org.uk

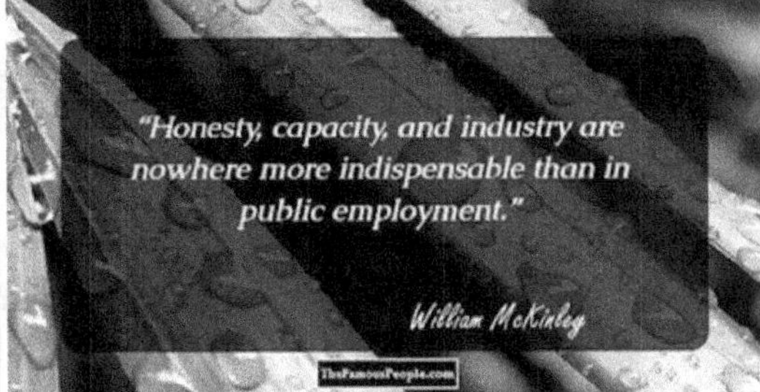

"Honesty, capacity, and industry are nowhere more indispensable than in public employment."
William McKinley
ThePamousPeople.com

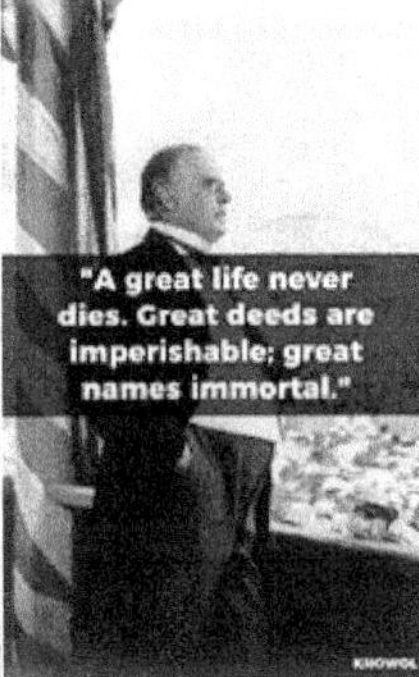

Let us ever remember that our interest is in concord, not in conflict; and that our real eminence rests in the victories of peace, not those of war.
William McKinley
American President
"A great life never dies. Great deeds are imperishable; great names immortal."
KNOWOL

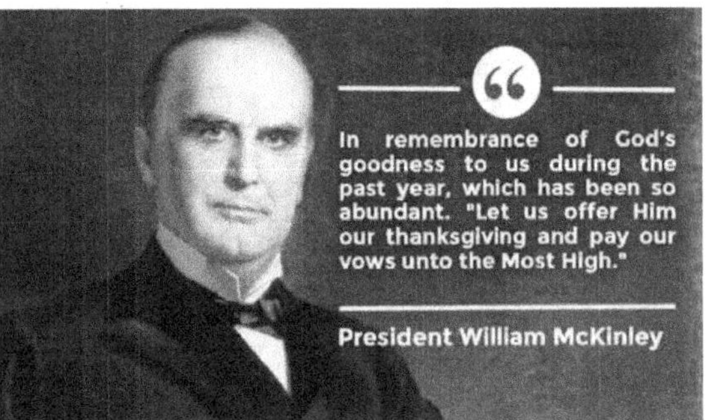

In remembrance of God's goodness to us during the past year, which has been so abundant. "Let us offer Him our thanksgiving and pay our vows unto the Most High."
President William McKinley

Good-bye -- good bye, all. It is God's way. His will, not ours, be done. Nearer my God to Thee, nearer to Thee.
William McKinley
American Politician
QUOTEHD.COM

CHICAGO AMERICAN
THE PRESIDENT IS DEAD

William Howard Taft

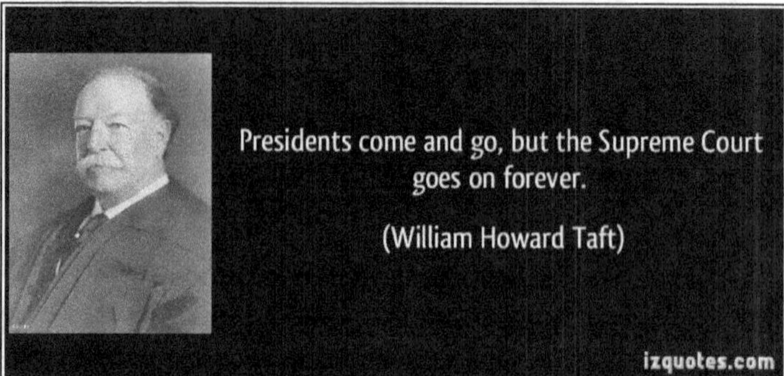

We are all imperfect.
We can not expect
perfect government.

-William Howard
Taft

The President cannot make clouds to rain and cannot make the corn to grow. He cannot make business good, although when these things occur, political parties do claim some credit for the good things that have happened in this way
~ William Howard Taft

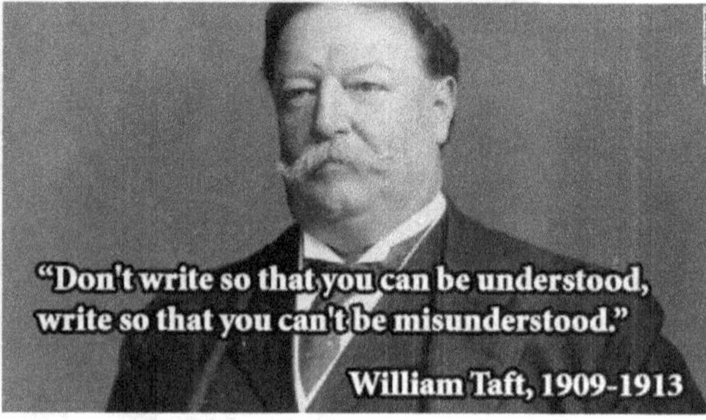

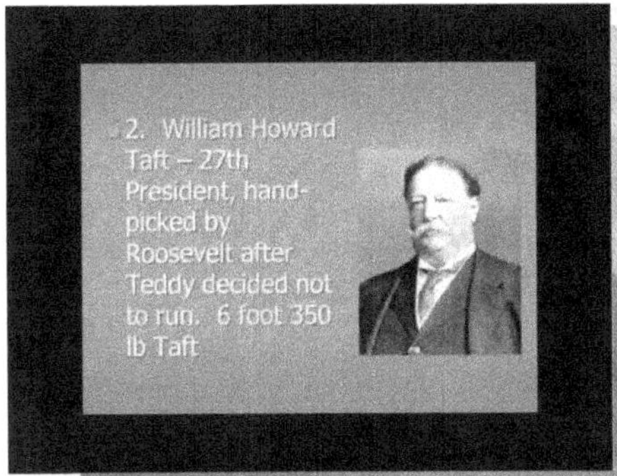

Taft's Progressive Reforms

1. **Children's Bureau**
   * It made sure companies were not hiring children too young or over working the ones that were already employed there.
2. **Conservation**
   * He expanded the National Forests and protected our country's wildlife.
3. **Bureau of Mines**
   * This was set up to monitor mining companies and making sure the employees were getting treated fairly.

As the Republican platforms says, the welfare of the farmer is vital to that of the whole country.

(William Howard Taft)

POLITICS, WHEN I AM IN IT, IT MAKES ME SICK.

William Howard Taft
American President

"Don't write so that you can be understood, write so that you can't be misunderstood."

William Taft, 1909-1913

Too many people don't care what happens so long as it doesn't happen to them.

— William Howard Taft —

AZ QUOTES

"THE WORLD IS NOT GOING TO BE SAVED BY LEGISLATION."

WILLIAM HOWARD TAFT

Anti-Semitism is a noxious weed that should be cut out. It has no place in America.

(William Howard Taft)

izquotes.c

We must dare to be great; and we must realize that greatness is the fruit of toil and sacrifice and high courage.

www.philippine-history.org

WARREN G. HARDING

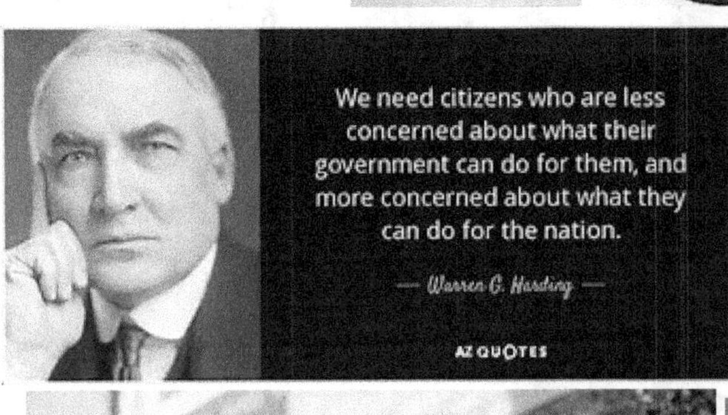

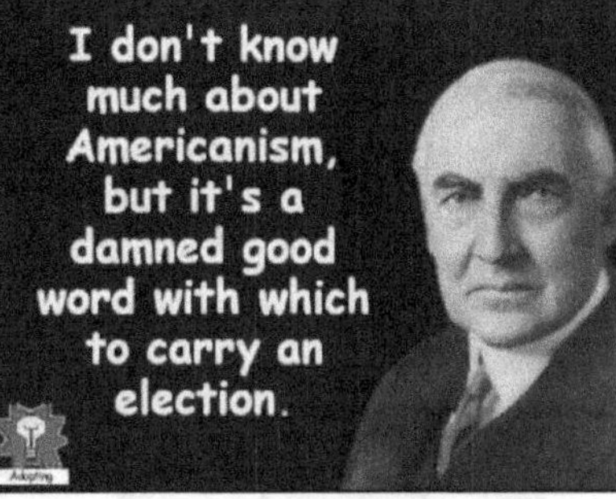

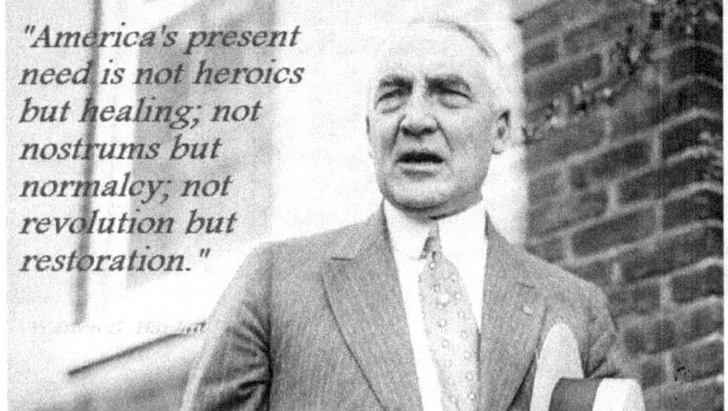

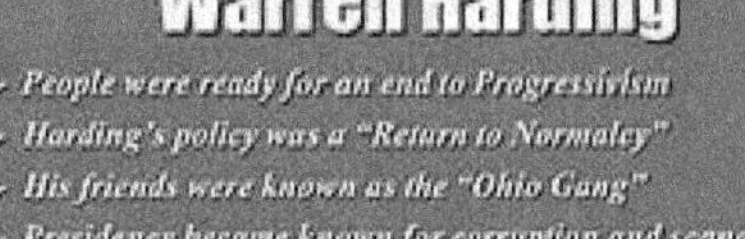

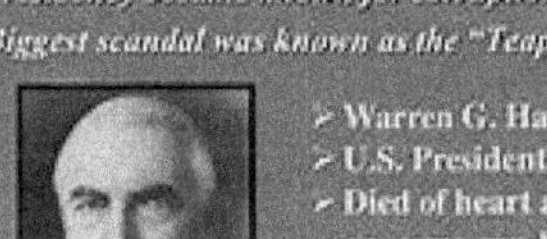

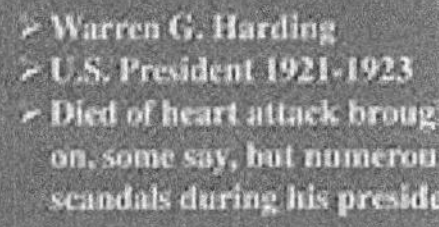

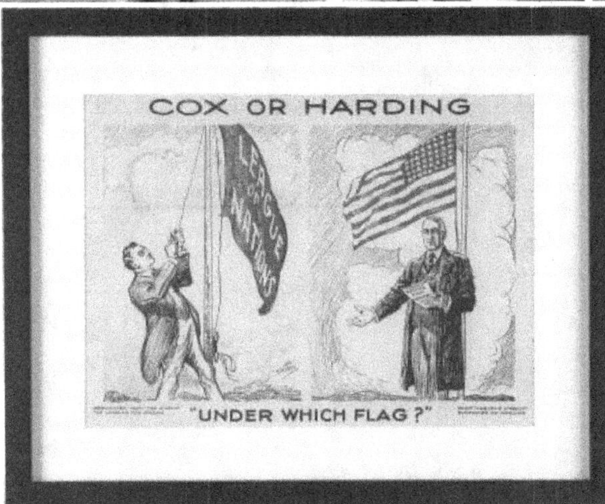

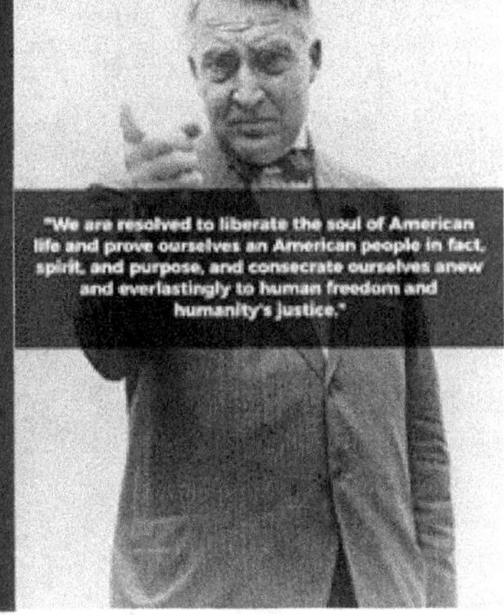

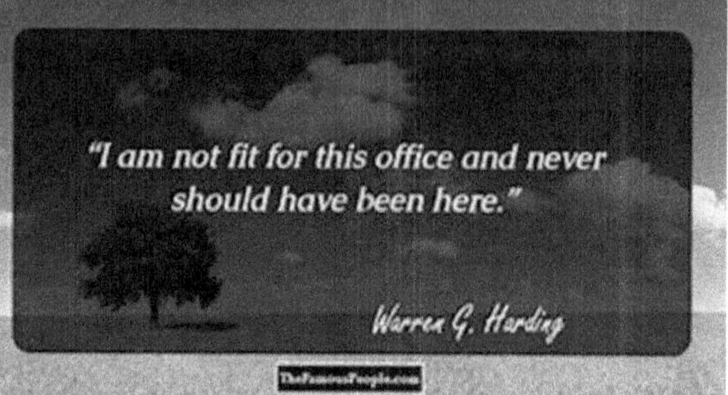

Interior View President Harding Memorial - Marion, Ohio

Calvin Coolidge

Patriotism Is Easy To Understand In America. It Means Looking Out For Yourself By Looking Out For Your Country.

- Calvin Coolidge

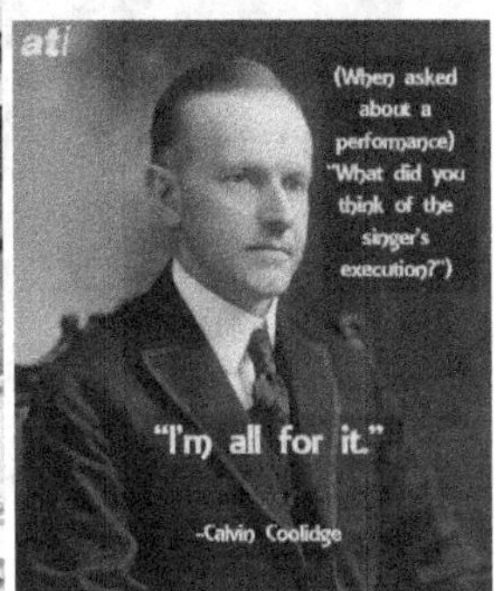

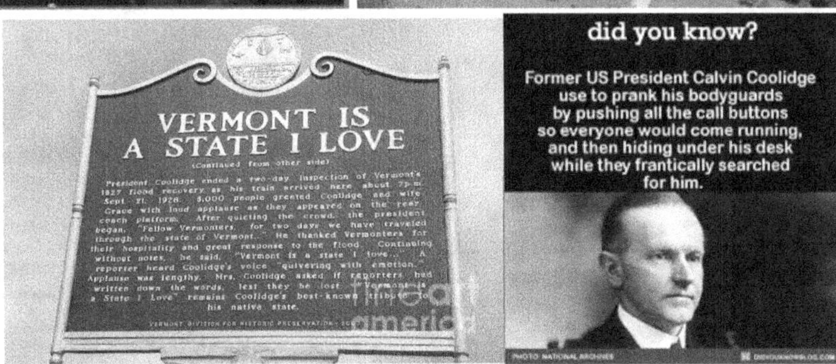

VERMONT IS A STATE I LOVE

(Continued from other side)

President Coolidge ended a two-day inspection of Vermont's 1927 flood recovery as his train arrived here about 7p.m. Sept. 21, 1928. 8,000 people greeted Coolidge and wife Grace with loud applause as they appeared on the rear coach platform. After quieting the crowd, the president began, "Fellow Vermonters, for two days we have traveled through the state of Vermont." He thanked Vermonters for their hospitality and great response to the flood. Continuing without notes, he said, "Vermont is a state I love... A reporter heard Coolidge's voice quivering with emotion. Applause was lengthy. Mrs. Coolidge asked if reporters had written down the words, lest they be lost. "Vermont is a State I Love" remains Coolidge's best-known tribute to his native state.

VERMONT DIVISION FOR HISTORIC PRESERVATION

did you know?

Former US President Calvin Coolidge use to prank his bodyguards by pushing all the call buttons so everyone would come running, and then hiding under his desk while they frantically searched for him.

PHOTO NATIONAL ARCHIVES

"Christmas is not a time nor a season, but a state of mind. To cherish peace and goodwill, to be plenteous in mercy, is to have the real spirit of Christmas

-Calvin Coolidge

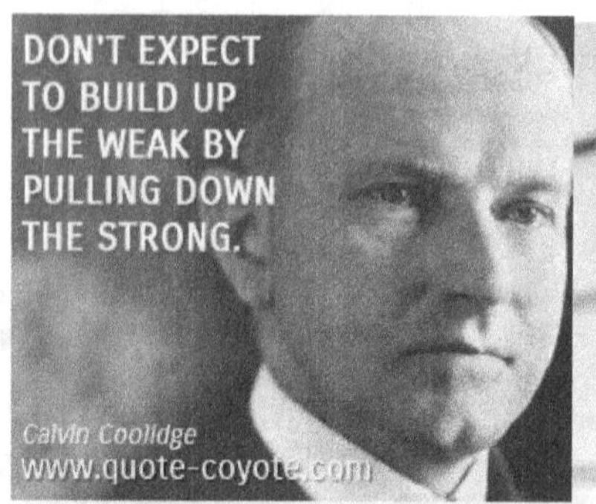
DON'T EXPECT
TO BUILD UP
THE WEAK BY
PULLING DOWN
THE STRONG.
Calvin Coolidge
www.quote-coyote.com

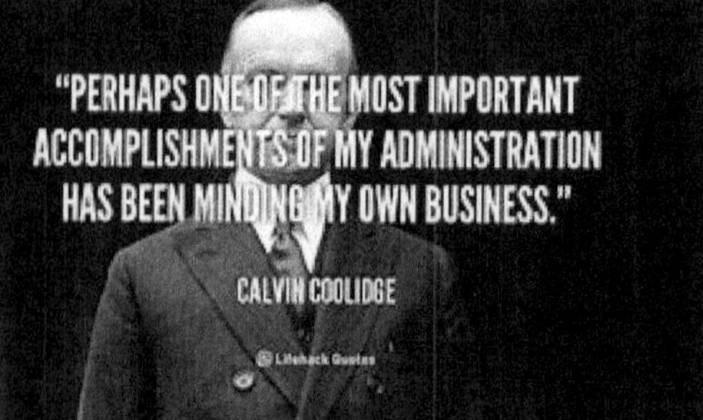
"PERHAPS ONE OF THE MOST IMPORTANT
ACCOMPLISHMENTS OF MY ADMINISTRATION
HAS BEEN MINDING MY OWN BUSINESS."
CALVIN COOLIDGE
Lifehack Quotes

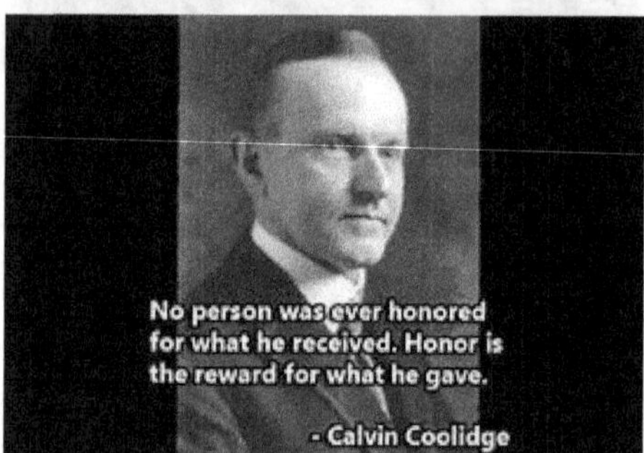
Four-fifths Of All
Our Troubles Would
Disappear, If We
Would Only Sit Down
And Keep Still.
- Calvin Coolidge
LinesQuotes.

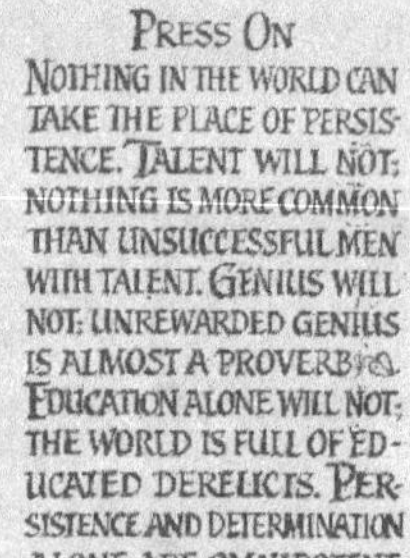
Trivia about Calvin Coolidge
• Height: 5 feet 10 inches
• Calvin Coolidge was known
  to be frugal and stoic. A
  man of simple tastes
• Nickname - "Silent Cal"
• Coolidge secured
  reductions in taxes for
  wealthy Americans referred
  to as the "Coolidge
  Prosperity"
www.facts-about.org.uk

No person was ever honored
for what he received. Honor is
the reward for what he gave.
- Calvin Coolidge

PRESS ON
NOTHING IN THE WORLD CAN
TAKE THE PLACE OF PERSIS-
TENCE. TALENT WILL NOT;
NOTHING IS MORE COMMON
THAN UNSUCCESSFUL MEN
WITH TALENT. GENIUS WILL
NOT; UNREWARDED GENIUS
IS ALMOST A PROVERB.
EDUCATION ALONE WILL NOT;
THE WORLD IS FULL OF ED-
UCATED DERELICTS. PER-
SISTENCE AND DETERMINATION
ALONE ARE OMNIPOTENT.

VETO
CAL

"The nation which forgets its
defenders will be itself forgotten."
~ Calvin Coolidge

"To live under the
American Constitution is
the greatest political
privilege that was ever
accorded to the
human race."
www.thefederalistpapers.org
Calvin Coolidge

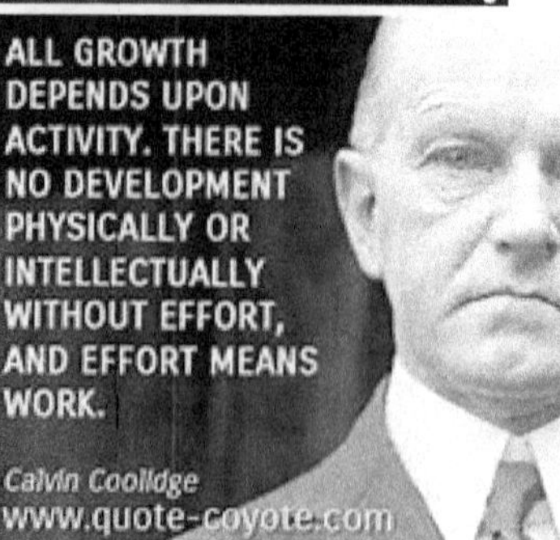
"There is no dignity
quite so impressive,
and no one independence
quite so important, as
living within
your means."
www.thefederalistpapers.org
Calvin Coolidge

KEEP COOLIDGE
"[America's] preservation is
worth all the effort and all the
sacrifice that it may cost."
~Calvin Coolidge

ALL GROWTH
DEPENDS UPON
ACTIVITY. THERE IS
NO DEVELOPMENT
PHYSICALLY OR
INTELLECTUALLY
WITHOUT EFFORT,
AND EFFORT MEANS
WORK.
Calvin Coolidge
www.quote-coyote.com

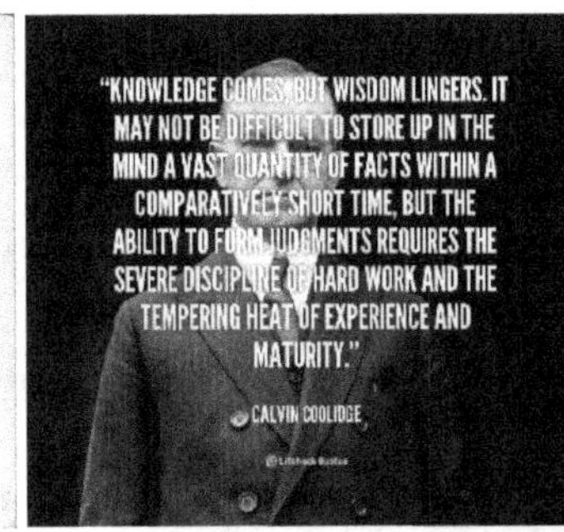

Herbert Hoover

Had Herbert Hoover never been elected president, he would be remembered as one of history's greatest humanitarians. Instead, he is most remembered for being accused of mishandling the Great Depression.

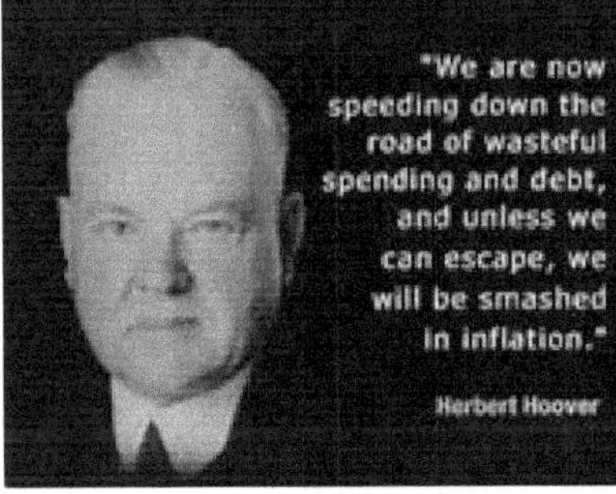

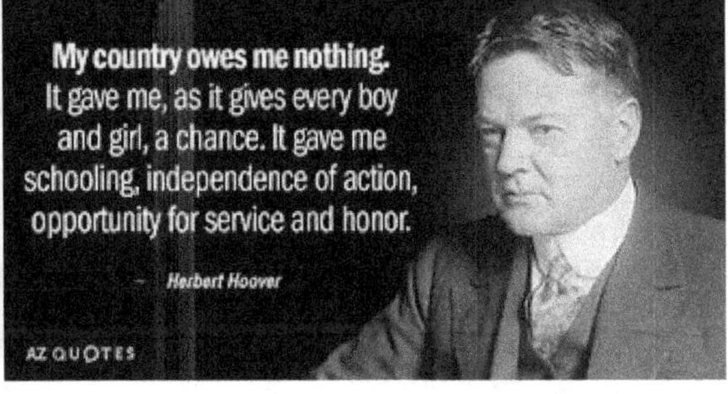

Metallica cont.

- A young American named Herbert C. Hoover and his wife, L.H. Hoover, translated Agricola's work into English.
- The translation was published in 1912
- Hoover graduated from Stanford in 1891 as a Mining Engineer
- Hoover served as the 31st president of the US (1929 – 1933)

America - a great social and economic experiment, noble in motive and far-reaching in purpose.

Herbert Hoover
American President

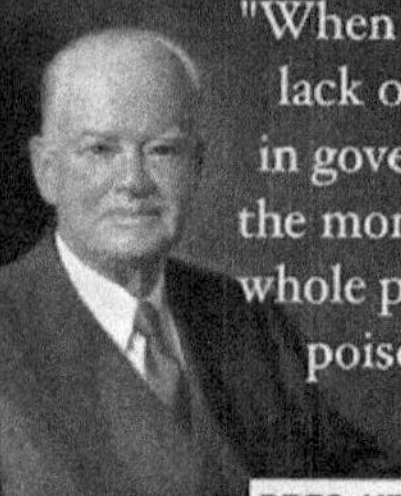

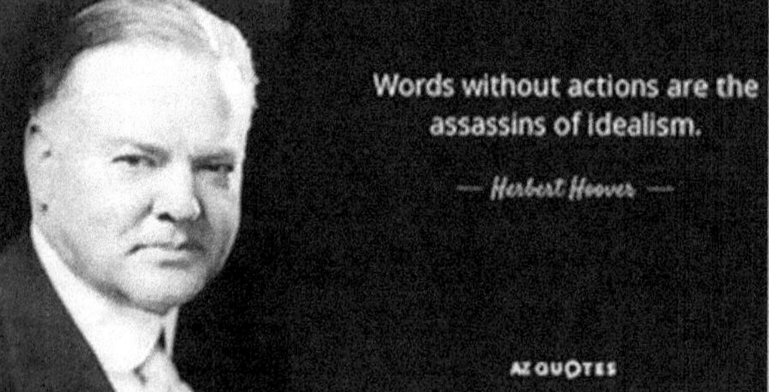

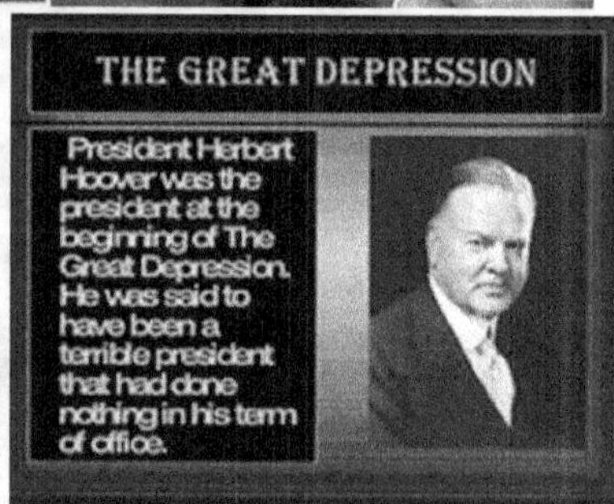

Herbert Hoover was President from 1928-1932.

Herbert Hoover believed in a laissez – faire government. He started some programs to help the US get out of the Great Depression, but they did not apply to the masses of people who were unemployed.

Most people did not believe Hoover was doing enough, so the shacks that the poor people lived in were called Hoovervilles and the newspapers that people covered up with were called Hoover blankets.

By Warren, in the Philadelphia Public Ledger
RAIL-SPLITTING

BUSINESS BOULEVARD
DETOUR
SPECULATION STREET

TRUST ME! PROSPERITY IS NOT AROUND THE CORNER.
WALL ST
YOU'RE RUINED!
...WELL, MAYBE NOT THIS ONE...

360.00
340.00
320.00
300.00
280.00
260.00
240.00
220.00
Compare to March 21, 2016
Compare to Feb. 11, 2016
1929 Crash
Dow Jones Industrials
J J A S O N D 30

THE WORLD AND NATION IN THE MOST DISTRESSING ECONOMIC SITUATION EVER KNOWN

HOOVERVILLE
"IT SEEMS THERE WASN'T ANY DEPRESSION AT ALL!"
Source: Daniel Fitzpatrick, St. Louis Post-Dispatch, December 18, 1935 (adapted)

FREE
P COFFEE & DO
OR THE UNEMPLOYED
HORAN

WE DEMAND WORK OR WAGES
CITY OF WHITE AND NEGRO

Hoover's Response to the Great Depression

Hoover's core beliefs—that government should not provide direct aid, but find ways to help people help themselves—shaped his presidency.

Ideas and Beliefs	Direct Action
• Before the market crash, Hoover tried to help farmers by strengthening farm cooperatives.	• Businesses cut jobs and wages, and state and local governments cut programs and laid off workers.
• Cooperative: an organization owned and controlled by its members, who work together for a common goal.	• The crisis persuaded Hoover to go against his beliefs and establish the Reconstruction Finance Corporation in 1932, a program that provided $2 billion in direct government aid to banks and institutions.
• After the crash, Hoover continued to believe in voluntary action, and he urged business and government leaders not to lay off workers, hoping that their cooperation would help the economic crisis pass.	• Later that year he asked Congress to pass the Federal Home Loan Bank, a program to encourage home building.

HOLT, RINEHART AND WINSTON. All Rights Reserved.

HOOVER'S PHILOSOPHY

- Hoover was not quick to react to the depression
- He believed in "rugged individualism" – the idea that people succeed through their own efforts
- People should take care of themselves, not depend on governmental hand-outs
- He said people should "pull themselves up by their bootstraps"

Herbert Hoover

- ❖ Blamed the Great Depression on world-wide economic conditions beyond US's control
- ❖ Believed in limited government action
- ❖ less government is better
- ❖ Restore American's confidence by saying "Hang in there! Prosperity is just around the corner!"
- ❖ Creates the Restoration Finance Corporation (RFC) to give credit to large industries, railroads, and insurance companies
- ❖ Promoted federal programs to help businesses because once they recovered, it would trickle down to consumers
- ❖ To help create jobs, Hoover proposed spending money on new public buildings, roads, parks, and dams
- ❖ Despite these steps, Hoover's refusal to provide direct help to Americans badly damaged his image as the nation's leader

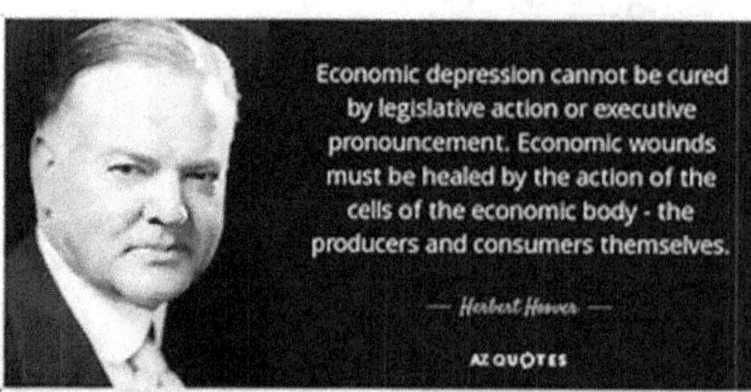

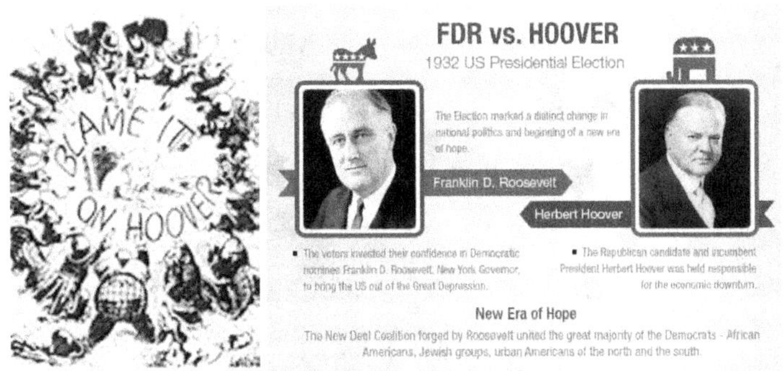

There are some parallels between the time of the Great Depression and President Hoover, and the Great Pandemic Covid 19 and President. Neither caused the disaster, but neither successfully confronted it. In Hoover's case, he tried to leave solving the depression to the "Rugged Individualism" of the people. In 2020, Trump first declared the pandemic to be a Democrat hoax, they he claimed it would disappear when it got warmer, followed by "It's what it is" attitude as the number of new cases grew and grew as did the deaths. Neither Hoover or Trump used the power of the president's office to develop a nation-wide plan to deal with the crisis. One difference – Hoover had some redeeming traits and successes, Trump has none.

Richard M. Nixon

"Tricky Dick" can thank Trump for wrestling away the title of most corrupt president of all time. Also, before Nixon went rogue and considered himself above the law, as does Trump now, he had some significant advances, in particular, opening relations with China.

https://www.azquotes.com/picturequotes

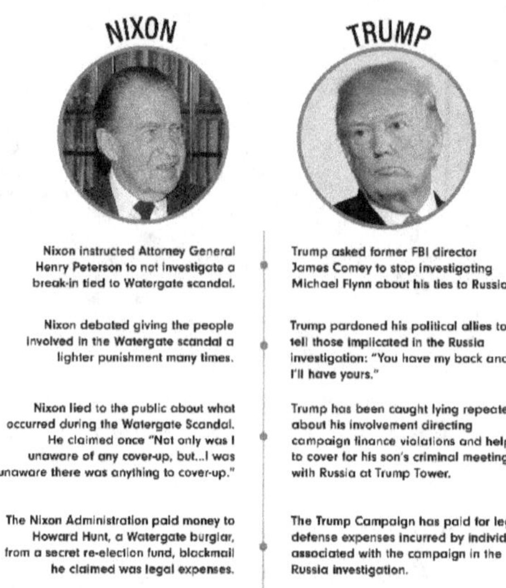

(Source of the following fifty Quotations: https://www.azquotes.com/picturequotes)

1. When the President does it, that means that it's not illegal.
2. Never forget, the press is the enemy. The establishment is the enemy. The professors are the enemy. Professors are the enemy. Write that on a blackboard 100 times and never forget it.

3. Nothing would please the Kremlin more than to have the people of this country choose a second rate president.

4. I was not lying. I said things that later on seemed to be untrue.

5. **I know you heard what you thought I said, but what I said isn't what I meant.**

6. Only if you have been in the deepest valley, can you ever know how magnificent it is to be on the highest mountain.

7. I didn't do anything wrong and I promise to never do it again.

8. Capitalism works better than it sounds, while socialism sounds better than it works.

9. We cannot learn from one another until we stop shouting at one another - until we speak quietly enough so that our words can be heard as well as our voices.

10. Defeat doesn't finish a man, quit does. A man is not finished when he's defeated. He's finished when he quits.

11. The important thing is that we maintain plausible deniability.

12. Remember, always give your best. Never get discouraged. Never be petty. Always remember, others may hate you. But those who hate you don't win unless you hate them. And then you destroy yourself.

13. Politics would be a helluva good business if it weren't for the goddamned people.

14. Well, I screwed it up real good, didn't I?

15. Any nation that decides the only way to achieve peace is through peaceful means is a nation that will soon be a piece of another nation.

16. Idealism without realism is impotent. Realism without idealism is immoral.

17. The three most difficult words to speak are, "I was wrong."
18. I would have made a good pope.

19. Being trustworthy is something you are, something you stand for and a core value you live by. It isn't something you can train for nor is it something you can manipulate. You either have those values or you don't.

20. If you take no risks, you will suffer no defeats. But if you take no risks, you win no victories.

21. When the strongest nation in the world can be tied up for years in a war with no end in sight, when the richest nation in the world can't manage its own economy, when the nation with the greatest tradition of the rule of law is

plagued by unprecedented lawlessness, and when the President of the United States cannot travel abroad or to any major city at home without fear of a hostile demonstration - then it's time for new leadership for the United States of America.

22. We will establish a new system that makes high-quality health care available to every American in a dignified manner and at a price he can afford.

23. No event in American history is more misunderstood than the Vietnam War. It was misreported then, and it is misremembered now.

24. Honesty may not be the best policy, but it is worth trying once in a while.

25. I think Congress has spent enough time on ethics. I think it's time they moved on to something else.

26. You don't know how to lie. If you can't lie, you'll never go anywhere.

27. A public man must never forget that he loses his usefulness when he as an individual, rather than his policy, becomes the issue.

28. You can't depend on the man who made the mess to clean it up.

29. With all the power that a president has, the most important thing to bear in mind is this: You must not give power to a man unless, above everything else, he has character. Character is the most important qualification the president of the United States can have.

30. What we have done with the American Indian is its way as bad as what we imposed on the Negroes. We took a proud and independent race and virtually destroyed them. We have to find ways to bring them back into decent lives in this country.

31. My strong point, if I have a strong point, is performance. I always do more than I say. I always produce more than I promise.

32. Before we become too arrogant with the most deadly of the seven deadly sins, the sin of pride, let us remember that the two great wars of this century, wars which cost twenty million dead, were fought between Christian nations praying to the same God.

33. The peace we seek in the world is not the flimsy peace which is merely an
interlude between wars, but a peace which can endure for generations to
come. It is important that we understand both the necessity and the
limitations of America's role in maintaining that peace. Unless we in America
work to preserve the peace, there will be no peace. Unless we in America
work to preserve freedom, there will be no freedom.

34. You find out who your true friends are not when you are on top of the world,
but when the world is on top of you.

35. I refuse to make a decision that somebody else can make. The first rule of
leadership is to save yourself for the big decision. Don't allow your mind to
become cluttered.

36. My own view is that taping of conversations for historical purposes was a bad
decision on the part of all the presidents. I don't think Kennedy should have
done it. I don't think Johnson should have done it, and I don't think we should
have done it.

37. History is a pathetic junkyard of broken treaties.

38. Millions who endure poverty and bad government can now know what they
are missing. To see how the other half lives all they have to do is switch on
their television sets.

39. If some of my judgments were wrong - and some were wrong - they were
made in what I believed at the time to be the best interest of the nation.

40. The Constitution supposes what the history of all governments demonstrates,
that the executive is the branch of power most interested in war and most
prone to it. It has accordingly with studied care, vested the question of war in
the legislature. [If a president is successful in bypassing the Congress] it is
evident that the people are cheated out of the best ingredients in the
government, the safeguards of peace which is the greatest of their blessings.

41. With all our differences, whenever we are confronted with a threat to our
security we are not then Republicans or Democrats but Americans; we are
not then the fifty states but the United States.

42. The Soviet Union began by banishing God. The United States began as a
community of people who wanted to worship God as they chose. . . Man does
not live by bread alone. Those in the United States whose desire to create a
strictly secular society is as strong as Lenin's was should study this Cold War
lesson closely. Communism was defeated by an alliance spearheaded by 'one
nation under God.'

43. Why would anyone want to be President today? The answer is not one of
glory, or fame; today the burdens of the office outweigh its privileges. Its not
because the Presidency offers a chance to be somebody, but because it offers
a chance to do something.

44. Our peaceful borders and our peaceful history are important symbols, to be
sure. What they symbolize, however, is the spirit of respect and restraint
which allow us to cooperate, despite our differences, in way which help us
both.

45. We must adopt reforms which will expand the range of opportunities for all
Americans. We can fulfill the American dream only when each person has a
fair chance to fulfill his own dreams. This means equal voting rights, equal
employment opportunity and new opportunities for expanded ownership,
because in order to be secure in their human rights, people need access to
property rights.

46. I can see clearly now... that I was wrong in not acting more decisively and
more forthrightly in dealing with Watergate.

47. Yet we can maintain a free society only if we recognize that in a free society
no one can win all the time. No one can have his own way all the time, and
no one is right all the time.

48. It is essential that we take steps to prevent chemical substances from
becoming environmental hazards. Unless we develop better methods to
assure adequate testing of chemicals, we will be inviting the environmental
crisis of the future.

49. While technically I did not commit a crime, an impeachable offense... these
are legalisms, as far as the handling of this matter is concerned; it was so
botched up, I made so many bad judgments. The worst ones, mistakes of the
heart, rather than the head. But let me say, a man in that top job - he's got to
have a heart, but his head must always rule his heart.

50. No words can describe the depths of my regret and pain at the anguish my
mistakes over Watergate have caused the nation and the presidency - a nation
I so deeply love and an institution I so greatly respect.

Gerald R. Ford
George H. W. Bush
George W. Bush

WHAT HAPPENED TO THE OLD G.O.P.?

The Party of Trump (GOP)

Their policies embrace racism, sexism, the NRA, and fake news. Their only interest is to divide the country to maintain control, rig the courts, rig our justice system, and pass laws that favor the rich campaign donors and special interest groups who contribute millions of dollars to their campaigns.

TRUMP WILL DO ANYTHING TO BE REELECTED

Today's Southern Republicans defend the Confederate Flag and Trump considers Confederate Generals heroes and deserving of their statues. However, they all were traitors and deserve no honors in the United States. To the Southern who are still fighting the Civil War, wake up, your side lost, and the Confederate States only were allowed to rejoin the Union until they pledged allegiance to the United States Constitution. (If he was alive today, Lincoln undoubtedly would be a Democrat. Today's Republicans are oft quoted as claiming it was the Republicans who freed the slaves. True of the Republicans in the 1860s, whereas many of the members of the current GOP leadership, especially Trump, are racist. He will do anything to keep in power. Trump will do anything, including plots that are un-constitutional, criminal, hateful, stirring up his base to start a race war, and even a new Civil War. He almost seems to be trying to restart the Wa Between the States, with sides changed, or maybe a race war. He's liable to do anything.

Trump's 2020 Election Campaign Song
SONG LYRICS
"Don't Know Much A..."
Amazon Music Unlimited
(https://lyrics.fandom.com/wiki/Sam_Cooke:Don't_Know_Much_About_History)

Don't know much about history
Don't know much biology
Don't know much about science book
Don't know much about the French I took

But I do know that I love MY supporters
And I know that if they love ME too
What a wonderful world this would be

Don't know much geography
Don't know much trigonometry
Don't know much about algebra
Don't know what a slide rule is for

But I know that one and one is two
And if this one could be with MY supporters
What a wonderful this would be

I don't claim to be an 'A' student
But I'm trying to be
Maybe my being an 'A' student baby
I can win your support for ME

Memo to America: Beware Mr. Trump's playbook. Spread the truth. Stay vigilant. Fight for our democracy. Robert B. Reich, former U.S. Secretary of Labor, is professor of public policy at the University of California at Berkeley and the author of "The System: Who Rigged It, How We Fix It."

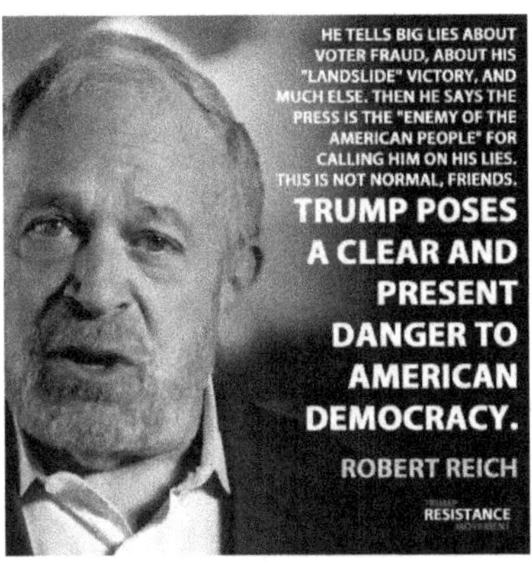

Donald Trump will do anything to be reelected. His opponents are limited because they believe in democracy. Mr. Trump has no limits because he doesn't. Here's Mr. Trump's reelection playbook, in 25 simple steps:

1. Declare yourself above the law. Use racist fearmongering. Demand "law and order" and describe protesters as "thugs," "lowlifes" and "rioters and looters." Describe COVID-19 as "Kung-Flu."

2. Retweet posts from white supremacists.

3. In your campaign ads, use a symbol associated with Nazis.

4. Appoint an attorney general more loyal to you than to America, and politicize the Department of Justice so it's lenient on your loyalists and comes down hard on your enemies. Have it lighten the sentence of a crony convicted of lying under oath. Order investigations of industries you dislike.

5. Fire U.S. attorneys who are investigating you.

6. Fire independent inspectors general who are looking into what you've done. Crush any whistleblowers you find.

7. Demean and ignore the intelligence community. Appoint a director of national intelligence more loyal to you than to America. Demand that the head of the FBI pledge loyalty to you.

8. Pack the federal courts with judges and justices more loyal to you than to the U.S. Constitution.

9. Politicize the Department of Defense so generals will back whatever you order. Refer to them as "my generals." Have them help clear out protesters. Order the military to surveil protesters. Tell governors you'll bring in the military to stop protesters.

10. Purge your party of anyone disloyal to you and turn it into a mindless, brainless, spineless cult.

11. Get rid of accumulated experience and expertise in government. Demean career public servants.

12. Hollow out the State Department, the Department of Justice and the Department of Health and Human Services.

13. Reward donors and cronies with bailouts, tax breaks, subsidies, government contracts, regulatory rollbacks and plum jobs. Put their lobbyists in charge of your agencies. Distribute $500 billion in pandemic assistance to corporations in secret, without any oversight.

14. Coddle dictators. Don't criticize their human rights abuses. Refuse to work with the leaders of other democracies. Withdraw from international treaties.

15. Create scapegoats. Demonize migrants and lock up asylum-seekers at the border even if they're children. Put a white nationalist in charge of immigration policy. Blame Muslims, Mexicans and Chinese.

16. Denigrate and ridicule all critics. Describe opponents as "human scum." Attack the mainstream media as purveyors of "fake news" and "enemies of the people."

17. Conjure up conspiracies against yourself supposedly led by your predecessor and your opponent in the last election. Without any evidence, accuse your predecessor of "treason." Fabricate a "deep state" out to get you.

18. Downplay real threats to the nation, such as a rapidly spreading pandemic. Lie about your utter failure to contain it. Muzzle public health experts. Urge

people to go back to work even as the pandemic worsens in parts of the country.

19. Encourage armed supporters to "liberate" states from elected officials who disagree with you.

20. Bribe other nations to investigate your electoral opponent and flood social media with lies about him.

21. Use right-wing propaganda machines like Fox News and conspiracy-theory-peddling One America News to inundate the country with your lies. Ensure that the morally bankrupt chief executive of Facebook allows you to spread your lies on the biggest media machine in the world.

22. Suppress the votes of people likely to vote against you. Encourage Republican governors to purge voter rolls, demand voter ID and close polling places. Seek to prevent mail-in ballots during the pandemic. Claim they will cause voter fraud, without evidence. Threaten to close the U.S. Postal Service.

23. Get Vladimir Putin to hack into U.S. election machines, as he did in 2016 but can now do with more experience and deftness. Promise him that in return you'll further destabilize America as well as NATO. Allow him to put a bounty on killing U.S. troops in Afghanistan.

24. If it still looks like you'll be voted out, try to postpone the election. If you're voted out of office notwithstanding all this, refuse to leave. Contest the election, claim massive fraud, say it's a conspiracy, get your cult of a political party to support your lies, get your propaganda machine to repeat them, get your Justice Department to back you, get your judges and justices to affirm you, get your generals to suppress any subsequent rebellion.

25. Declare victory.

"Should President Donald Trump lose in the 2020 election, don't expect him to concede defeat — it is simply not in his DNA to do so.

Consider the 2016 race, when then-candidate Trump lost the Iowa caucus to Texas Sen. Ted Cruz. While other losing candidates just moved on, Trump demanded that Cruz's victory be nullified, tweeting the next morning, "Ted Cruz didn't win Iowa, he stole it." And when Colorado gave its convention votes to Cruz after nonbinding caucuses heavily favored the Texas senator, Trump tweeted, "How is it possible that the people of the great State of Colorado never got to vote in the Republican Primary? Great anger — totally unfair!"

For Trump, a personal defeat is always the result of fraud. Why would we expect him to react differently in the event of a Biden victory? He has already telegraphed his intentions, predicting that the 2020 vote will be the most corrupt in our history. In his election script, the only way for our electoral system to demonstrate its trustworthiness would be for him to win; a loss would simply confirm that the election was rigged." (https://www.newsday.com/opinion/commentary/joe-biden-donald-trump-2020-presidential-election-accept-defeat-concede-1.48115520)

I have included the following article in its entirety because if considers a post-election scenario that should frightened all citizens, no matter what party they support.

Will he go? A law professor fears a meltdown this November.
By Sean Illing (@seanillingsean.illing@vox.com Jun 3, 2020, 12:00pm EDT)

"Imagine that it's November 3, 2020, and Joe Biden has just been declared the winner of the presidential election by all the major networks except for Fox News. It was a close, bitter race, but Biden appears to have won with just over 280 electoral votes.

Because Election Day took place in the middle of a second wave of coronavirus infections, turnout was historically low and a huge number of votes were cast via absentee ballot. While Biden is the presumptive winner, the electoral process was bumpy, with thousands of mail-in votes in closely fought states still waiting to be counted. Trump, naturally, refuses to concede and spends election night tweeting about how "fraudulent" the vote was.

We knew this would be coming; he's been previewing this kind of response for a while now.

One day goes by, then a few more, and a month later Trump is still contesting the outcome, calling it "rigged" or a "Deep State plot" or whatever. Republicans, for the most part, are falling in line behind Trump. From that point forward, we're officially in a constitutional crisis.

This is the starting point of a new book by Amherst College law professor Lawrence Douglas called Will He Go? Trump and the Looming Election Meltdown in 2020.

According to Douglas, a scenario like the one above is entirely possible, maybe even probable. And if nothing else, we've learned in the Trump era that we have to take the tail risks seriously. Douglas's book is an attempt to think through how we might deal with the constitutional chaos of an undecided — and perhaps undecidable — presidential election.

I spoke to Douglas by phone about why he thinks our constitutional system isn't prepared for what might happen in November, and why he's not worried about a stolen election so much as an election without an accepted result. "If things go a certain way," he told me, "there's a Chernobyl-like defect built into our system of presidential elections that really could lead to a meltdown."

Sean Illing: What worries you most about the November election?

Lawrence Douglas: To say that we're facing a perfect storm is clichéd, but it does strike me that there are a lot of things coming together that could spell a chaotic election. Foremost among them is the fact that we have a president of the United States who has pretty consistently and aggressively telegraphed his intention not to concede in the face of an electoral defeat, especially if that electoral defeat is of a very narrow margin. And it looks like it probably will be a narrow margin. In all likelihood, the 2020 election is going to turn on the results in probably the three swing states that determined the results in 2016: Michigan, Pennsylvania, and Wisconsin.

The other concern is that if we do fall into an electoral crisis and we start seeing the kinds of challenges to the results that we saw back in year 2000, during Bush v. Gore, then we could really see a meltdown because our contemporary political climate is so polarized. That's what led me to start asking, what types of federal laws do we have in place? What kind of constitutional procedures do we have in place to right the ship? And what I found is that they just don't exist.

Illing:
What does that mean, exactly? Are we racing toward a constitutional crisis?

Douglas: In a word, yes. What makes our situation particularly dangerous is it's not simply the statements that come out of Trump. We're pretty used to Trump making statements that leave us all gobsmacked at this point. What worries me is that if there are going to be any guardrails protecting us from his attacks on the electoral process, it would have to come from the Republican Party. And we've seen that Republican lawmakers simply are not prepared to hold this guy to account.

We saw that in the impeachment proceeding, where it was really astonishing that you have Mitt Romney as the only Republican voting in the Senate to remove the president. And it was only, what, eight years ago that Mitt Romney was the standard-bearer of the party in the national election. It's a pretty disturbing erosion of Democratic norms.

Illing:
If you're right that the Republican Party isn't going to stand up for the rule of law, where does that leave us legally and politically?

Douglas: If you have a president who is really pushing the argument that fraud cost him the election, he really does have the opportunity to push things to Congress. And what I mean by that is that Congress is the body that ultimately tallies Electoral College votes. It's not inconceivable that you have states that submit competing electoral certificates. And I won't go into the nitty-gritty about how that happens, but it can happen. And if that happens and you have a split Congress between the Senate Republicans and the House Democrats, there is basically no way to resolve the dispute.

Illing: Let's say that happens and we enter January 2021 without a political consensus on who won the election. What then?

Douglas: I'm not trying to be an alarmist here, but it's possible to imagine, come January 20, that we don't have a president. By the terms of the 20th Amendment, Trump ceases to be president at noon on January 20 and [Mike] Pence likewise ceases to be vice president.

At this point, by the terms of the Presidential Succession Act of 1947, the speaker of the House, Nancy Pelosi, could become acting president, but only if she resigns her House seat. But what if Trump continues to insist that he has been reelected and is the rightful president? Imagine if, come January 20, Trump stages his own inauguration ceremony with Clarence Thomas issuing the oath of office.

Then we might have Nancy Pelosi and Trump both claiming to be the commander in chief. This is a world of hurt.

Illing: What about the Supreme Court?

Douglas: I think a lot of people assume the Supreme Court would step in and end things before they got too chaotic. This is more or less what happened in 2000.

But it's very misleading to think that it was the Supreme Court that settled the 2000 election. It really wasn't the Supreme Court in the decision Bush v. Gore that ended things — it was Al Gore. Al Gore, for the good of the country, decided to accept the Supreme Court's ruling. I'd say it's impossible to imagine Trump doing anything like that.

Besides, if it did intervene, I'm not sure that Congress would abide by a court ruling. Because so many experts [here and here] say the Court really doesn't have jurisdiction to resolve an electoral dispute once it hits Congress.

Illing: Let's imagine that the election happens and Biden wins convincingly enough that the vast majority of the country, even most Republicans, accept the outcome. In that case, Trump — and a small wing of hardliners — may refuse to concede, but both parties basically accept the results.

What happens then? Would federal marshals have to go in and drag Trump out of the White House?

Douglas: Here's the thing: That's not the scenario I'm worried about. If Trump loses decisively, I think his opportunities for creating mayhem will be dramatically curtailed.

What worries me is that I don't see him losing in that fashion. I could certainly imagine him losing decisively in the popular vote, as he did in 2016, but I can't imagine him losing that decisively in the Electoral College. And everything will turn on what happens in these swing states.

This is going to be an election that is conducted under very unusual circumstances. There are going to be potentially chaotic scenes at polling stations, and god forbid there's a fresh outbreak of Covid-19 in the fall. Then you're also going to have millions of people voting by mail-in.

Illing: Why is that a problem?

Douglas: Well, these mail-in ballots are not going to get counted by November 3. That gives someone like Trump space to create incredible chaos. Imagine a swing state like Michigan. Imagine the November 3 popular vote appears to go to Trump by a small margin. So, he declares that he's won Michigan. And Michigan defines the margin of victory in the Electoral College, so he declares that he's been reelected.

Well, as these write-in ballots and these mail-in ballots are counted in the next days, there's this phenomenon that we've seen in the last several elections called the "blue shift." It tends to be the case that mail-in ballots break Democratic. It's typically the case that mail-in ballots come from urban areas, which are predominantly Democratic in their voting patterns.

And so, in this case, it's entirely possible that Trump is trailing once all the votes are counted. But then he says, "Those votes are bogus. They shouldn't be counted." And if you look at the political profile of Michigan, again, you find this kind of perfect storm brewing, because the Republicans control the statehouse in Lansing. So, let's say they all support Trump, and they all say, "Yeah, we're going to go with the Election Day results. We're going to give our electoral votes all to Trump."

Then we've got total chaos.

Illing: But the governor of Michigan is a Democrat, and my understanding is that it's the governor, along with the secretary of state and the board of electors, who sends the electoral certificate to Congress. Is that right?

Douglas: That's correct. It's the governor who is responsible under federal law to send the electoral certificate of the state to Congress. But that is not to say that the state legislature is barred from sending its own certificate to Congress. You might say, "Well, then, isn't the governor's certificate the proper certificate?" and the answer is that it's up to Congress to make that determination. And if one House accepts the governor's certificate and the other accepts the legislature's certificate, then we're in a stalemate.

"I'm Not Trying To Be An Alarmist Here, But It's Possible To Imagine, Come January 20, That We Don't Have A President"

Illing: So, your main worry is not that the election will be stolen so much as we'll be left without a result?

Douglas: Exactly.

Illing: The situation you're describing is almost unthinkable: We have an election and there's simply no binding result.

Douglas:
Again, I'm not trying to be an alarmist.

Illing: This is pretty damn alarming, Lawrence.

Douglas: Look, one of the main points of my book was to say, "Hello, people. If things go a certain way, there's a Chernobyl-like defect built into our system of presidential elections that really could lead to a meltdown."

Illing Are there any precedents for this?

Douglas: We came very close to having something like this happen back in 1876. There was this Hayes-Tilden election, in which three separate states submitted competing electoral certificates to Congress. Congress was likewise divided between House Democrats and Senate Republicans, and they couldn't figure anything out. It was a total stalemate. They eventually jerry-rigged a solution, but that solution only worked because Samuel Tilden, the Democratic candidate, agreed to concede. Again, I don't see Trump doing that.
(A fairly complete telling of this near constitutional crisis is found in my book: The American Presidents From Polk to Hayes: What They Did, What They Said & What Was Said About Them, by Robert A Nowlan PhD Outskirts Press | Jan 29, 2016)

Illing: This is an astonishing hole in our Constitution. It's another example of our reliance on norms, not laws or institutions, to keep things humming along.

 Douglas: It's such a great point. When I was researching the book, I was asking myself, well, what does the Constitution and the federal law do in order to secure the peaceful transition of power? And one of the things that I realized is they don't secure the peaceful succession of power. They presuppose it. They assume that it's going to happen. So, if it doesn't happen, well, no one knows ...

Illing: Now, on to another worry: Could the election be postponed?

Douglas: No, I don't think so. The president can't do that, because Election Day is set by federal law. You could have Congress change the election, but that would require bicameral support and bipartisan support, and that seems highly unlikely.

Illing: It feels almost pointless to ask this question, but I'll do it anyway: Are you confident that our constitutional system can handle what's potentially coming in November?

Douglas: No. I have incredible respect and admiration for our constitutional system, but I'll go back to one of the points you made, which is that the system really assumes that political actors have absorbed the norms that make the system work. But if you have a president who ignores those norms; if you have a party that ignores those norms, that continues to facilitate the rejection of those norms; and if you have a fractured media universe that rewards the president for rejecting those norms, then we're in a very dangerous situation.

The only real way to avoid this is to make sure we don't enter into this scenario, and the best way to do that is to ensure that he loses decisively in November. That's the best guarantee. That's the best way that we can secure the future of a healthy constitutional democracy.

WHAT ARE 10 PROS OF VOTING?	WHAT 10 CONS OF VOTING?
1. Voter engagement is a critical part of out non-profit work because,it empowers the people and the community we serve.	1. You can't complain about the government if you don't vote.
2. You can ensure the continuation of a stellar goverment.	2. You also, can't complain about the government you choose to support.
3. Exercise your right to hand over your rights to others.	3. Beliefs don't align with Democrats or Republicans.
4. Every single vote counts, even yours.	4. You have to choose between the lesser number of evils.
5. It's a privilege and a duty, to vote.	5. Your supporting a electoral system designed to push out competing parties.
6. You can help someone achieve his/her goal of reelection.	6. You would have to accept some responsibility from the goverment.
7. It creates great jobs for politicians.	7. There would be anarchy, if a dictatorial government wins.
8. There is no right or wrong choice, it's your vote.	

Throughout my voting life, I was pleased that essentially the nation had only two major parties, unlike the cases of some countries in Europe which had numerous political parties. To form a government often requires the creation of an enough strange bedfellows to agree to work together for the time being. In the United States, the third parties developed positions that in many cases were later adopted as part of the platform of one or both of the major parties. Throughout my life, I have voted for a third-party candidate, when the representatives of both major parties were unsupportable.

The system, certainly not perfect, seemed to work with at a certain time, one party was dominant and the other was the loyal opposition. At those times compromise was not only possible, it was essential to accomplishing anything.

Somewhere along the line this arrangement was abandoned, as the two parties adopted ideologies, which they would never compromise on. Then Congress often was in total gridlock, and the party in power became identified as a "do-nothing congress."

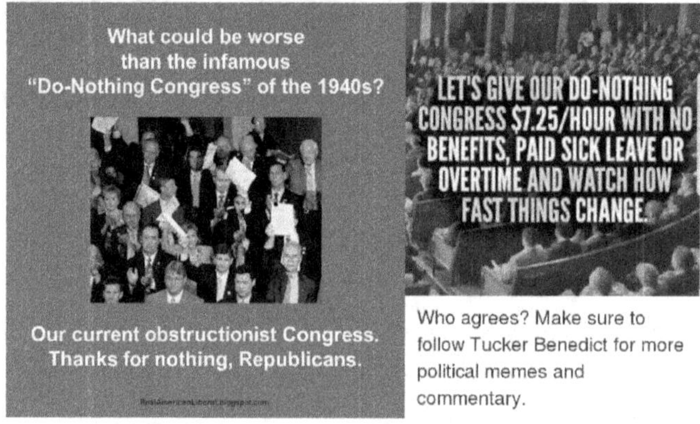

Who agrees? Make sure to follow Tucker Benedict for more political memes and commentary.

And let's not help of the actions of the hard(ly) working (not very)intelligent or qualified doofuses who work at the White House.

SEPARATION OF POWERS AND CHECKS AND BALANCES

Most American citizens are aware of the that the Constitution contains the principles of separation of powers and checks and balances. However, since it becomes more and more apparent that President Trump is trying to erase this sensible division of the government, with help of Republican members of Congress, This another of his attacks on the principles upon which our nation has been based,

"The Constitution nowhere contains an express injunction to preserve the boundaries of the three broad powers it grants, nor does it expressly enjoin maintenance of a system of checks and balances. Yet, it does grant to three separate branches the powers to legislate, to execute, and to adjudicate, and it provides throughout the document the means by which each of the branches could resist the blandishments and incursions of the others. The Framers drew up our basic charter against a background rich in the theorizing of scholars and statesmen regarding the proper ordering in a system of government of conferring sufficient power to govern while withholding the ability to abridge the liberties of the governed.

When the colonies separated from Great Britain following the Revolution, the framers of their constitutions were imbued with the profound tradition of separation of powers, and they freely and expressly embodied the principle in their charters. The theory of checks and balances, however, was not favored, because it was drawn from Great Britain, and, as a consequence, violations of the separation-of-powers doctrine by the legislatures of the states were commonplace prior to the convening of the Convention. Theory as much as experience guided the Framers in the summer of 1787.

The doctrine of separation of powers, as implemented in drafting the Constitution, was based on several generally held principles: the separation of government into three branches, legislative, executive, and judicial; the conception that each branch performs unique and identifiable functions that are appropriate to each; and the limitation of the personnel of each branch to that branch, so that no one person or group should be able to serve in more than one branch simultaneously. To a great extent, the Constitution effectuated these principles, but critics objected to what they regarded as a curious intermixture of functions, in, for example, the veto power of the President over legislation and to the role of the Senate in the appointment of executive officers and judges and in the treaty-making process. It was to these objections that Madison turned in a powerful series of essays.

Madison recurred to "the celebrated" Montesquieu, the "oracle who is always consulted," to disprove the contentions of the critics. "[T]his essential precaution in favor of liberty," that is, the separation of the three great functions of government, had been achieved, but the doctrine did not demand rigid separation. Montesquieu and other theorists "did not mean that these departments ought to have no partial agency in, or control over, the acts of each other," but rather liberty was endangered "where the whole power of one department is exercised by the same hands which possess the whole power of another department." That the doctrine did not demand absolute separation provided the basis for preservation of separation of powers in action.

Institutional devices to achieve these principles pervade the Constitution. Bicameralism reduces legislative predominance, while the presidential veto gives to the President a means of defending his priorities and preventing congressional overreaching. The Senate's role in appointments and treaties checks the President. The courts are assured independence through good-behavior tenure and security of compensation, and the judges through judicial review will check the other two branches. The impeachment power gives to Congress the authority to root out corruption and abuse of power in the other two branches.

Throughout much of our history, the "political branches" have contended between themselves in application of the separation-of-powers doctrine. Many notable political disputes turned on questions involving the doctrine. Because the doctrines of separation of powers and of checks and balances require both separation and intermixture, the role of the Supreme Court in policing the maintenance of the two doctrines is problematic at best. Indeed, it is only in recent decades that cases involving the doctrines have regularly been decided by the Court. Previously, informed understandings of the principles have underlain judicial construction of particular clauses or guided formulation of constitutional common law. That is, the nondelegation doctrine was from the beginning suffused with a separation-of-powers premise, and the effective demise of the doctrine as a judicially enforceable construct reflects the Court's inability to give any meaningful content to it. On the other hand, periodically, the Court has taken a strong separation position on behalf of the President, sometimes unsuccessfully and sometimes successfully.

Following a lengthy period of relative inattention to separation of powers issues, the Court since 1976 has recurred to the doctrine in numerous cases, and the result has been a substantial curtailing of congressional discretion to structure the National Government. Thus, the Court has interposed constitutional barriers to a congressional scheme to provide for a relatively automatic deficit-reduction process because of the critical involvement of an officer with significant legislative ties, to the practice set out in more than 200 congressional enactments establishing a veto of executive actions, and to the vesting of broad judicial powers to handle bankruptcy cases in officers not possessing security of tenure and salary. On the other hand, the highly debated establishment by Congress of a process by which independent special prosecutors could be established to investigate and prosecute cases of alleged corruption in the Executive Branch was sustained by the Court in an opinion that may presage a judicial approach in separation of powers cases more accepting of some blending of functions at the federal level." (https://www.law.cornell.edu/constitution-conan/article-1/section-1/separation-of-powers-and-checks-and-balances)

While there is still the pretense of separation of powers and checks and balances, these elements of the U.S. Constitution has been allowed to erode recently. It has reached a point that there are those of who fear that Trump wishes to become a dictator like his buddies in Russia, North Korea, and Saudi Arabia. There is strong evidence that his plans are to make the legislative and judicial branches of government the puppets of the President. The scariest thing about this is that he seems to be succeeding. Although the judicial still has maintained some authority, the Supreme Court is at the mercy of accepting whomever Trump nominates as an Associate Justice, who must pass his litmus test of suitability (that is, agreeing with Trump.)

In nearly three years in office, President Donald Trump spent federal dollars not authorized by Congress, separated families and incarcerated children at the Texas/Mexico border in defiance of a federal court order, pulled 1,000 American troops out of Syria ignoring a commitment to allies and facilitating war against civilians, and sent 2,000 troops to Saudi Arabia without obtaining a congressional declaration of war.

He has also criminally obstructed a Department of Justice investigation of himself but escaped prosecution because of the intercession of an attorney general more loyal to him than to the U.S. Constitution.

At the outset of his presidency, Mr. Trump took the presidential oath of office promising that he would faithfully execute his obligation to preserve, protect and defend the Constitution. James Madison, the scrivener of the Constitution, insisted that the word "faithfully" be in the presidential oath and that the oath itself be in the Constitution to remind presidents to enforce laws and comply with constitutional provisions, whether or not they agree with them, and to immunize the oath from congressional alteration. (https://www.washingtontimes.com/news/2019/oct/23/how-trump-disparages-the-constitution)

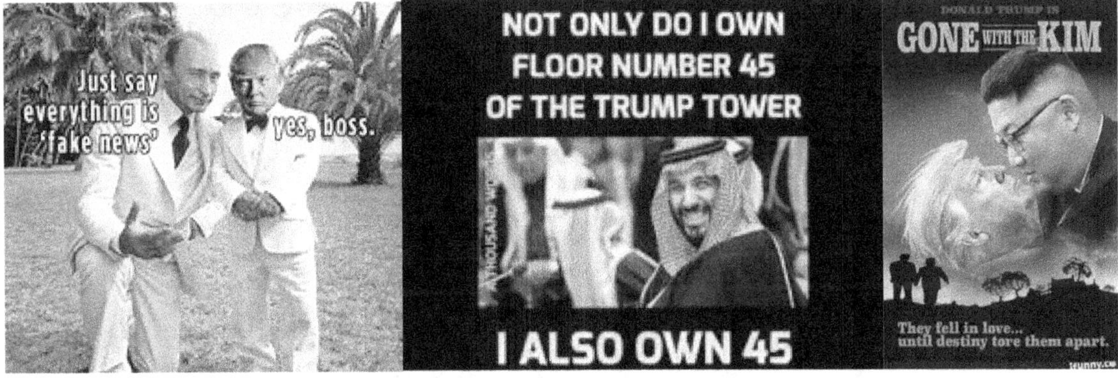

As for the Republican-controlled Senate, the GOP members have no balls to stand up to Trump's most egregious demands, that serves only the very rich and powerful, while destroying the government safety net for ordinary citizens. It is difficult to understand how Republican members of Congress, who we supposed could think for themselves, refuse to do so.

As to Trump supporters who agree with everything he says and advocates, they are not benefitting from his policies, and don't seem to care. The Republican Party has been abducted and infected with a virus far more dangerous that Covid 19. The old Republican Party is dead, It definitely is not the Party of Lincoln, of McKinley, Theodore Roosevelt, Eisenhower, or Reagan. Even Nixon was not as a great a threat to our nation, partially because Republicans stood up and helped force him out of office. As for the Bush's, the less said about them, the better.

Those who hold the values of the traditional Republican Party, must join with the rest of the nation, to see that Trump is defeated on November 3, 2020 so overwhelmingly that even he and his loyal, but stupid followers will accept the verdict of the nation, and block any constitutional crisis that the Trump and his faithful followers who share his values will be forced to accept the results.

TRUMP'S SUPPORTERS

When millions of people voted for Trump in 2016 and claim they will do so again in 2020 stumps a lot of people including myself, asked the question "Why? "I know I could ask the question of Trump loyalists, but I really don't wish to have a debate, perhaps even a heated debate on a subject that we so much disagreed about.

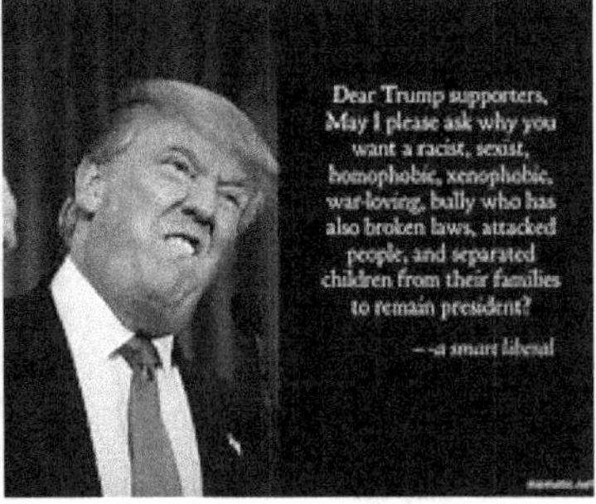

I firmly believe in the sanctity of the ballet and would defend everyone's right to vote for whomever they wish and for whatever reasons. That's one way in which I differ from Trump. He's doing his dirtiest worst to disenfranchise voters. He's doing his rigging with the full support of his base, who sorry, but I have to say it, are so dumb, they are going against their own best interests.

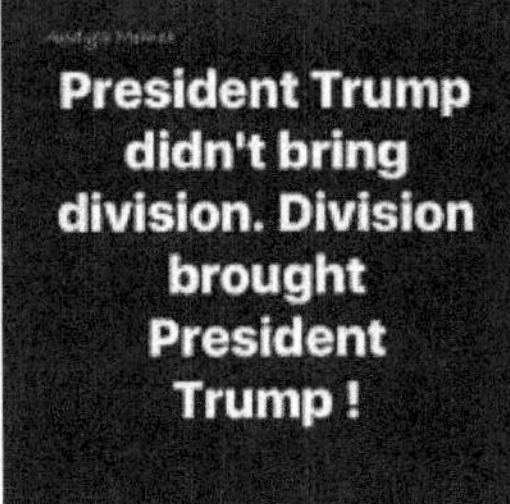

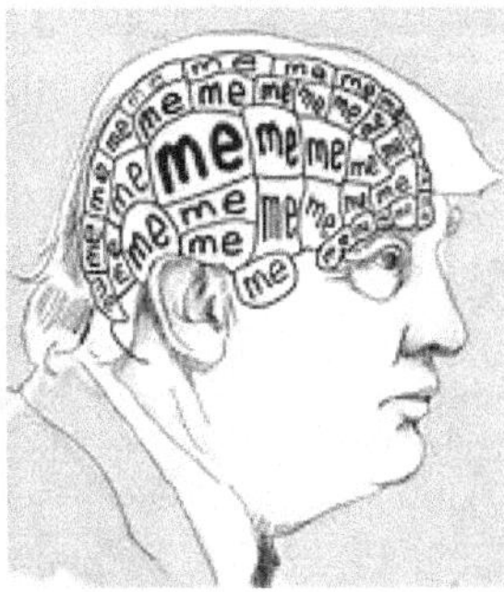

Is it reasonable to believe that Trump supporters favor cutting social security, Medicare and Medicaid, unemployment assistance, at the same time that they are happy is that Trump and his Republican stooges are bailing out the poor billionaires and corporations, even to redo of the White House, and funds to Religious groups that support him, which is a violation of the separation of church and state

IF YOU VOTED FOR
DONALD TRUMP...

"I am tired of trying to see things your way while you sit in your holier-than-thou churches/white power meetups, refusing to see things mine. Did I just lump you in with white supremacists? No, you did that to yourselves. You voted for the same candidate as the KKK. You voted for a candidate endorsed by the KKK. For the rest of your life, you have to know that you voted the same way as the KKK. Does that feel good to you? Here's a hint - it really shouldn't, especially if you call yourself a Christian.

I'm tired of pussyfooting around what offends your morals while couching what offends mine, because racism, misogyny, homophobia, and xenophobia offend mine.

Let me say it right here - if you voted for Trump, I do think you are a racist. I do think you're homophobic. I do think you're a misogynist. Racism, and homophobia, and misogyny are all a spectrum, and you're on it. You might not be a 'cheering while a black man gets lynched' racist, but boy, did you just sell them the rope and look the other way." — Tess Rafferty

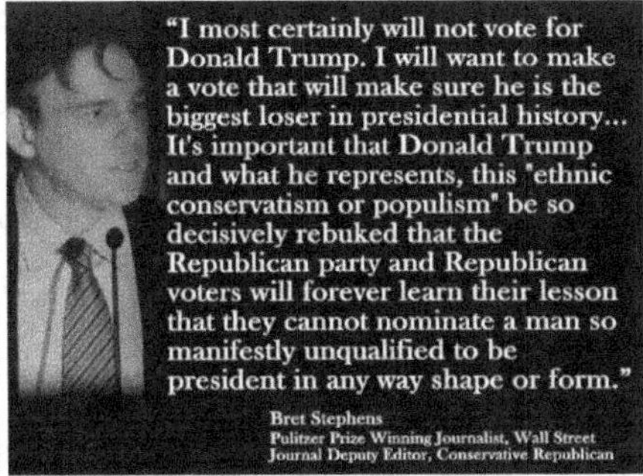

Still, I am curious to know answers to the questions, "why do your support Donald Trump?" "What has he accomplished that you admire and why?" "Does his lies bother you, or do you believe they are not lies, and why?" "Why is he so popular with the religious evangelicals, even though he does behave much like a Christian, or do you believe he does, in what ways?" "What is your opinion of how he has handled the Covid 19 pandemic?" Do you wear masks, practice safe-distancing, wash your hands frequently, and avoid crowds, so not to spread the virus? Please elaborate as much as you can about what you admire about Trump, I really would like to know. One thing that should be certain to all is that his administration certainly has been controversial.

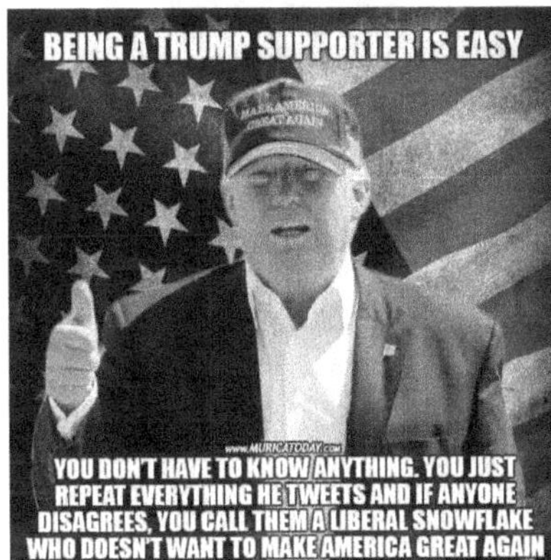

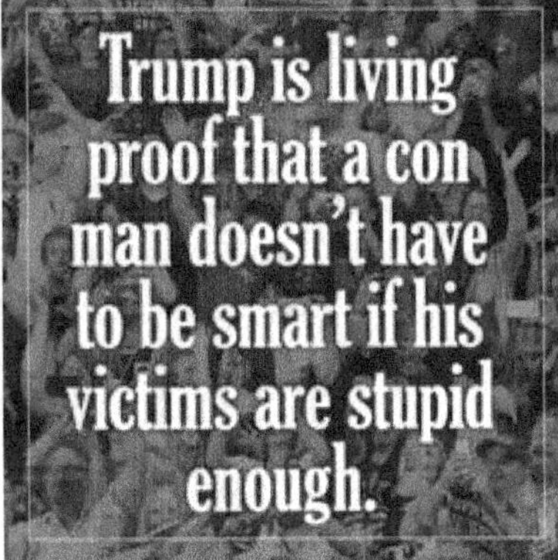

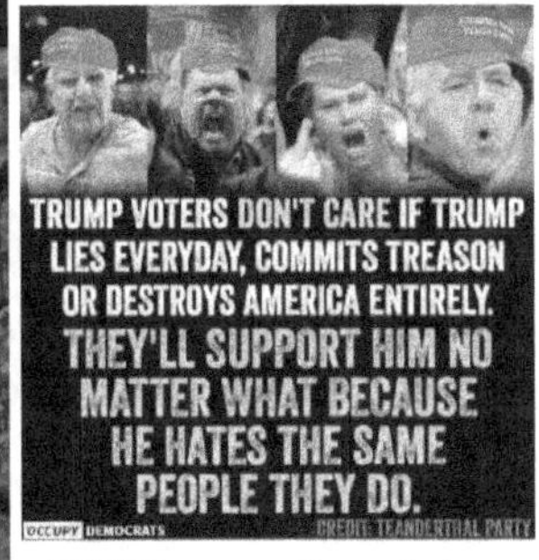

UGH! These people are truly deplorable. Follow Occupy Democrats for more!

"What is your opinion about the tax cuts; do you believe they were fairly divided between the rich and ordinary Americans?" Do you support Trump's efforts to cut health care, social security, and his stands on human rights for all, despite their color, nationality, country of origin, religion, sexual preference, etc.? Do you support his close ties with dictators and his lessening respect for the United States by our longtime friends? Do you think Trump is a racist and his positions seem to have led to greater violence, protests, peaceful, and otherwise? Take on as long as you like, trying to make me understand your position. I don't expect you will convince me, nor I you, but at least we can agree to disagree and continue to value our citizenship.

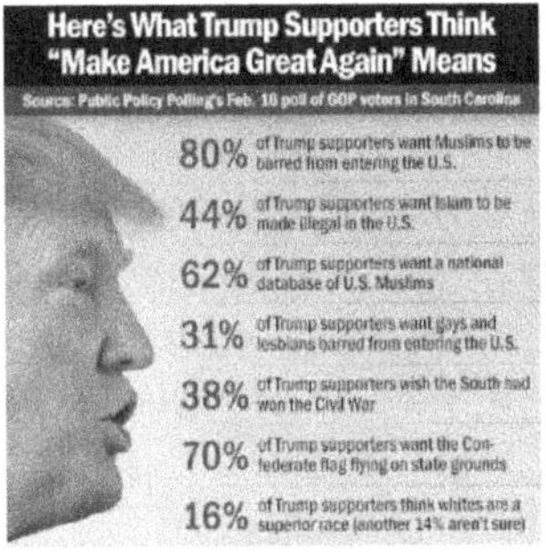

Prior to the Pandemic, before I chose self-imposed quarantine, I did discuss the 2016 election with people who cast their vote for Trump. This was before I concluded that he is a threat to our nation and the Constitution. These were educated, generally well-informed, and neighbors. They didn't adopt the rhetoric of the mobs at Trump's rallies, but always at some point in our discussion, they would bring up the name of Barack Obama. It was no secret that they thought he was a bad president, and could point to some of the failures of his administration. I made sure his accomplishments were considered.

At that point, I still was anxious to raise some of the questions listed above. There was no anger or hatred in our arguments, no shouting, no slogans, jut the words of two people who had different points of view about the 2016 election. Later, it occurred to me these were of the old GOP. Now, I wish I could ask these same individuals if the considered themselves Republicans of the new GOP, Trump's Republicans, and favored all that Trump did and said.

Whereas, I respect everyone's right to vote, I will not be able to resist the temptation to lampoon them a bit. As for Trump, he gets no pass from me. I confess I am biased, and am convinced he is the worst president the United States evrey had, I can't find anything admirable about him. He is a selfish, hateful lout with the brains of an imbecile. He's accomplished nothing positive, however, on the negative side he gets an A+. He lies all the time, brags about himself all the time, and spews hate all the time. He is a racist without any shame.

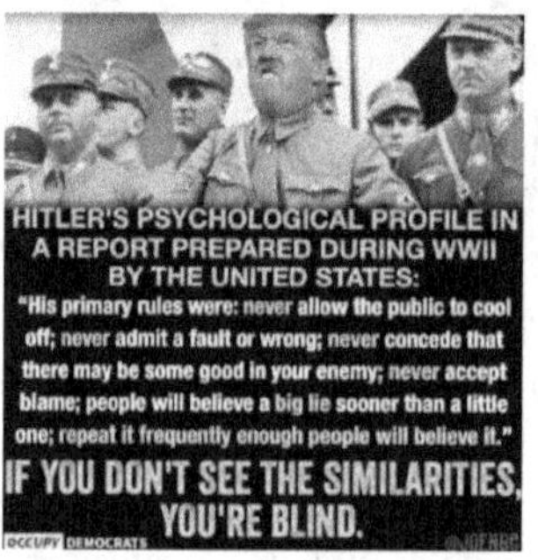

He can't form a coherent simple sentence. He feels he is entitled to receive a Nobel Peace Prize – for what – his only contributions have shown lack of leadership in dealing with any important problem – claiming he takes no responsibility and that things are what they are. He knows nothing of the constitution, except what his buddies in the NRA have told him. He is not familiar with American History, he dismisses science, because he is also ignorant of it as well. Yet he will offer medical advice which is dangerously wrong and is self-serving.

He won't reveal his taxes, because he has sometime to hide, and his fellow citizens wouldn't be so forgiving of his cheating, He has taken nepotism to a level never seen before in a presidency, giving important sounding positions of his children and their spouses for which, they have no credentials, knowledge, or competence. On the other hand, he placed children in cages along the Mexican border. If I didn't consider him such a dangerous threat to our America ideals, I would dismiss him as an ignorant buffoon, who says one irresponsible and untrue thing after another. He appears to be mentally ill, which only makes him more dangerous.

Trump Demeans Women

Trump insults all kinds of people, but he is especially nasty when speaking of women.

"He has a long history of objectifying women with crude jokes, name calling, and worse! Recently a video, taken in 1992, was released of Donald Trump speaking to a 10-year-old little girl. In the video, you can hear Trump asking the little girl, "You going up the elevator?" Immediately after, he turns to someone and says, "I'm going to be dating her in ten years. Can you believe that?" The video was recorded around Christmas time inside Trump Tower." (https://www.youtube.com/watch?v=sircwHwGBWo)

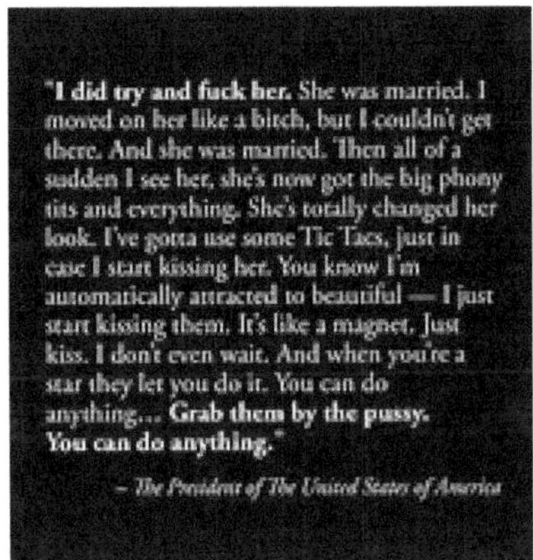

"I did try and fuck her. She was married. I moved on her like a bitch, but I couldn't get there. And she was married. Then all of a sudden I see her, she's now got the big phony tits and everything. She's totally changed her look. I've gotta use some Tic Tacs, just in case I start kissing her. You know I'm automatically attracted to beautiful — I just start kissing them. It's like a magnet. Just kiss. I don't even wait. And when you're a star they let you do it. You can do anything... Grab them by the pussy. You can do anything."

— *The President of The United States of America*

The following are a few of the many times, the President of the United States demeaned women, both before and after his election.

Trump said of Hillary Clinton: "When she walked in front of me, believe me, I wasn't impressed."

Trump said of his former Republican primary competitor, Carly Fiorina: "Look at that face, would anyone vote for that?"

Trump his former White House aide, Omarosa Manigault Newman, "That dog," after she was ousted from the administration.

Trump said of Megyn Kelly: "You could see there was blood coming out of her eyes. Blood coming out of her wherever."

Trump said of supermodel Heidi Klum: "Sadly, she's no longer a 10."

Trump called the 1996 Miss Universe beauty pageant winner Alicia Machado: "Disgusting" and "Miss Piggy."

Trump said of Arianna Huffington: "Extremely unattractive (both inside and out). I fully understand why her former husband left her for a man- he made a good decision."

Trump said of Cher: "Stop with the bad plastic surgery and nasty statements."

Trump said of actress Anne Hathaway after she and her then-boyfriend, Raffaello Follieri, broke up: "So when he had plenty of money, she liked him. But then after that, not as good, right?

Trump called California Rep. Maxine Waters: "An extraordinarily low IQ person."

Trump mocked Christine Blasey Ford, the California professor who accused his then-Supreme Court nominee Brett Kavanaugh of sexual assault. (https://www.businessinsider.com/trumps-worst-insults-toward-women-2018)

***

At least 25 women have accused President Donald Trump of sexual misconduct since the 1970s.

Renewed attention was brought to the allegations amid the #MeToo movement and a national conversation concerning sexual misconduct.

Trump has repeatedly denied the accusations, denouncing his accusers as "liars."

In June 2019, columnist E. Jean Carroll accused President Donald Trump of sexually assaulting her by forcing his penis inside her in a Bergdorf Goodman dressing room in the mid-1990s.

***

At least 25 women have made sexual misconduct allegations against Trump since the 1970s.

A deluge of women made their accusations public following the October 2016 release of the "Access Hollywood" tape, in which Trump was recorded boasting about grabbing women's genitals in 2005. Some others made their stories public months before the tape's release, and still others came forward in the months following.

Trump has broadly dismissed the allegations, which include ogling, harassment, groping, and rape, as "fabricated" and politically motivated accounts pushed by the media and his political opponents. He promised to sue all of his accusers during the 2016 election. In some cases, Trump and his lawyer have suggested that he didn't engage in alleged behavior with certain women because they weren't attractive enough for him to be interested in.

"Every woman lied when they came forward to hurt my campaign," the Republican nominee said during a 2016 rally. "Total fabrication. The events never happened. Never. All of these liars will be sued after the election is over."

The president said these "false allegations" against him were made by "women who got paid a lot of money to make up stories about me." And then alleged that the "mainstream media" refused to report on evidence that the accusations were made up.

Trump has not yet made good on his promise to sue any of the women — although two women have sued him – and the White House says that Trump's election proves the American people don't consider the allegations disqualifying.

"The people of this country, at a decisive election, supported President Trump, and we feel like these allegations have been answered through that process," White House press secretary Sarah Huckabee Sanders told reporters in December 2017, after several of the president's accusers appeared on national television to rehash their allegations.

But despite Trump's denials, 50% of voters — 59% of women and 41% of men — surveyed in a December 2017 Quinnipiac poll released think the president should resign as a result of the sexual misconduct allegations against him. Several Democratic lawmakers have previously called on Trump to resign over the accusations.

***

One accuser, Samantha Holvey, who spoke out in 2016 about her experience with Trump as a Miss USA pageant contestant, said in 2017 that while Trump's election was painful, she and others see the #MeToo movement as an opportunity to "try round two."

"We're private citizens, and for us to put ourselves out there to try and show America who this man is and especially how he views women, and for them to say 'meh, we don't care' — it hurts," Holvey said on NBC News' "Megyn Kelly Today" in December 2017. "And so now it's just like, all right, let's try round two. The environment's different. Let's try again."

***

Here are all of the allegations — in chronological order — made by 25 named women:

***

Jessica Leeds told the New York Times in October 2016 that Trump reached his hand up her skirt and groped her while seated next to her on a flight in the late 1970s.

"He was like an octopus. His hands were everywhere," Leeds said, adding that she fled to the back of the plane.

During an interview on NBC News' "Megyn Kelly Today" in December, Leeds added that she was at a gala in New York three years after the incident on the plane when she ran into Trump, who recognized her and called her a c---.

"He called me the worst name ever," she said. "It was shocking. It was like a bucket of cold water being thrown over me."

Trump denied the allegations and during a rally in October 2016, suggested that Leeds wasn't attractive enough for him to assault.

133

"People that are willing to say, 'Oh, I was with Donald Trump in 1980, I was sitting with him on an airplane, and he went after me,'" Trump said. "Believe me, she would not be my first choice."

***

In a 1990 divorce deposition, Trump's first wife and the mother of his three eldest children Ivana Trump accused her then-husband of raping her in a fit of rage in 1989.

Ivana said Trump attacked her after he underwent a painful "scalp reduction" procedure done by a doctor she had recommended, tearing her clothes and yanking out a chunk of her hair.

"Then he jams his penis inside her for the first time in more than 16 months. Ivana is terrified … It is a violent assault," Harry Hurt III, who obtained a copy of the deposition, wrote in a 1993 book about Trump. "According to versions she repeats to some of her closest confidantes, 'he raped me.'"

Ivana later slightly altered her allegation, saying that while she felt "violated" on that occasion, she hadn't accused Trump of raping her "in a literal or criminal sense."

"[O]n one occasion during 1989, Mr. Trump and I had marital relations in which he behaved very differently toward me than he had during our marriage," Ivana wrote in a 1993 statement. "As a woman, I felt violated, as the love and tenderness, which he normally exhibited towards me, was absent. I referred to this as a 'rape,' but I do not want my words to be interpreted in a literal or criminal sense."

Trump's response:

Trump called Hurt's description of Ivana's allegation "obviously false" in 1993, according to Newsday. Trump's lawyer, Michael Cohen, argued in 2015 that his client could not have raped Ivana because "you cannot rape your spouse."

"There's very clear case law," he said.

Cohen later recanted, saying his comment was "inarticulate."

***

Kristin Anderson, a photographer and former model said Trump reached under her skirt and touched her vagina through her underwear at a New York City nightclub in the early 1990s. Anderson, then in her early 20s, said she wasn't talking with Trump at the time and didn't realize he was sitting next to her when he groped her without her consent.

"So, the person on my right who, unbeknownst to me at that time was Donald Trump, put their hand up my skirt. He did touch my vagina through my underwear, absolutely. And as I pushed the hand away and I got up and I turned around and I see these eyebrows, very distinct eyebrows, of Donald Trump," she told The Washington Post in October 2016.

Anderson said she and her friends, who were talking together around a table at the time of the incident, were "very grossed out and weirded out," but thought "Okay, Donald is gross. We all know he's gross. Let's just move on."

Trump's response:

"Mr. Trump strongly denies this phony allegation by someone looking to get some free publicity," Hope Hicks, the president's then-spokeswoman and current White House communications director, told the Post in October 2016. "It is totally ridiculous."

***

Jill Harth, a businesswoman who worked with Trump in the 1990s, told the Guardian in July 2016 that Trump pushed her against a wall, put his hand up her skirt, and tried to kiss her at a dinner at his Mar-a-Lago resort in the early 1990s.

"He was relentless," she told the New York Times. "I didn't know how to handle it. I would go away from him and say I have to go to the restroom. It was the escape route."

Harth sued Trump in 1997 both for sexual harassment and for failing to uphold his end of a business deal with Harth and her then-partner.

Trump's response:

Hicks responded to the Times' reporting, denying Harth's allegations wholesale.

"Mr. Trump denies each and every statement made by Ms. Harth," she said.

***

Lisa Boyne, a health food business entrepreneur, told HuffPost in October 2016 that she attended a 1996 dinner with Trump and modeling agent John Casablancas during which several other women in attendance were forced to walk across a table in order to leave.

As the women walked on the table, Boyne says that Trump looked up their skirts and commented on their underwear and genitals. Trump allegedly asked Boyne for her opinion on which of the women he should sleep with.

Boyne joined Jessica Leeds, Samantha Holvey, Rachel Crooks — three others who have accused Trump of sexual misconduct — in calling on Congress to investigate Trump in December.

Trump's response:

Hicks denied Boyne's allegations. "Mr. Trump never heard of this woman and would never do that," she told HuffPost.

***

Two Miss Teen USA contestants told BuzzFeed News in October 2016 that Trump walked in on them while they were changing in their dressing rooms.

"I remember putting on my dress really quick because I was like, 'Oh my god, there's a man in here,'" Mariah Billado, who represented Vermont in 1997, told BuzzFeed. Billado added that Trump said something along the lines of, "Don't worry, ladies, I've seen it all before."

135

Victoria Hughes, a former Miss New Mexico, said Trump first introduced himself to the teenage contestants when he unexpectedly walked into their dressing room.

"It was certainly the most inappropriate time to meet us all for the first time," she told BuzzFeed.

Trump's response:

Trump appeared to admit to this behavior when he boasted in an April 2005 interview with radio host Howard Stern that he regularly walked into contestants' dressing rooms on the beauty pageants he owned while women were unclothed.

"I'll go backstage before a show and everyone's getting dressed and ready and everything else. And you know, no men are anywhere. And I'm allowed to go in because I'm the owner of the pageant," he said. "You know they're standing there with no clothes. And you see these incredible-looking women. And so, I sort of get away with things like that."

In October 2016, the Trump campaign called the allegations politically motivated lies.

"These accusations have no merit and have already been disproven by many other individuals who were present," the campaign said in a statement. "When you see questionable attacks like this magically put out there in the final month of a presidential campaign, you have to ask yourself what the political motivations are and why the media is pushing it."

***

Temple Taggart, a former Miss Utah, told the New York Times in May 2016 that Trump "kissed me directly on the lips" when she met him at the Miss USA pageant in 1997. Trump did the same thing when Taggart met with him again at Trump Tower in Manhattan after he offered to aid her modeling career, she said.

In November 2017, Taggart spoke out again, telling the Times that the allegations against Trump were "brushed under the rug."

Trump's response:

Trump "emphatically" denies Taggart's claims.

"I don't even know who she is," Trump told NBC News in October 2016. "She claims this took place in a public area. I never kissed her. I emphatically deny this ridiculous claim."

***

Cathy Heller told the Guardian in October 2016 that she was attending a Mother's Day brunch with her husband, children, and in-laws at Mar-a-Lago in the 1990s when Trump approached her table, introduced himself to her, and forcibly kissed her.

"He took my hand, and grabbed me, and went for the lips," she said, and added that she was "angry and shaken" as a result of the incident.

Trump's response:

A Trump campaign spokesman denied Heller's allegation, arguing that it couldn't have happened in public.

"There is no way that something like this would have happened in a public place on Mother's Day at Mr. Trump's resort," Jason Miller said. "It would have been the talk of Palm Beach for the past two decades."

***

Karena Virginia, a yoga instructor and life coach, told the Washington Post in October 2016 that Trump groped her as she waited for her car outside the US Open in New York in 1998.

Virginia, then 27, said she overheard Trump talking with a group of men about her legs and that Trump then approached her, grabbed her arm, and touched her breast before asking, "Don't you know who I am?"

Trump's response:

"Give me a break," Trump representative Jessica Ditto said in response to Virginia's allegation. "Voters are tired of these circus-like antics and reject these fictional stories and the clear efforts to benefit Hillary Clinton."

***

Two Miss USA contestants said Trump walked into their dressing rooms, where female participants were changing, and ogled them.

Tasha Dixon, a former Miss Arizona who competed in the 2001 Miss USA pageant, told CBS in October 2016 that Trump walked into the contestants' dressing room while they were changing.

"He just came strolling right in," Dixon said. "There was no second to put a robe on or any sort of clothing or anything. Some girls were topless, other girls were naked."

She added, "To have the owner come waltzing in when we're naked or half naked in a very physically vulnerable position, and then to have the pressure of the people that work for him telling us to go fawn all over him, go walk up to him, talk to him."

Dixon said there was "no one to complain to" because Trump owned the pageant and everyone employed there reported to him.

Bridget Sullivan, Miss New Hampshire in 2000, told BuzzFeed News in May 2016 that Trump walked into the contestants' dressing room unannounced and hugged her inappropriately.

"The time that he walked through the dressing rooms was really shocking. We were all naked," Sullivan said, comparing Trump to a "creepy uncle." "He'd hug you just a little low on your back."

Trump's response:

In October 2016, the Trump campaign denied Dixon's allegations, calling them politically motivated fabrications.

"These accusations have no merit and have already been disproven by many other individuals who were present," the campaign said in a statement. "When you see questionable attacks like this magically put out there in the final month of a presidential campaign, you have to ask yourself what the political motivations are and why the media is pushing it."

***

Melinda "Mindy" McGillivray told the Palm Beach Post in October 2016 that Trump grabbed her buttocks while they were backstage during a Ray Charles concert at Mar-a-Lago in 2003.

Ken Davidoff, a photographer present at the concert, said McGillivray, then 23, approached him soon after the incident and said, "Donald just grabbed my a--!"

McGillivray spoke out again on "Megyn Kelly Today" in December, calling for a congressional investigation into the accusations of sexual misconduct against Trump.

"He has to face the music; he can't get away with this," McGillivray said. "I want justice."

Trump's response:

The Post reported that Trump did not respond to requests for comment concerning McGillivray's accusation, but the president has broadly denied all of the sexual misconduct accusations made against him.

"The timing and absurdity of these false claims speaks volumes and the publicity tour that has begun only further confirms the political motives behind them," White House press secretary Sanders said after the TV appearance in December.

***

People magazine reporter Natasha Stoynoff wrote in an October 2016 column that Trump sexually assaulted her in 2005 at Mar-a-Lago. Stoynoff was visiting Trump and his new wife, Melania, at their Florida estate to report on a story about the couple's first year of marriage.

While a pregnant Melania was changing clothes for a photoshoot, Trump offered to show Stoynoff a "tremendous" room at the resort.

"We walked into that room alone, and Trump shut the door behind us. I turned around, and within seconds he was pushing me against the wall and forcing his tongue down my throat," Stoynoff wrote.

She added that Trump told her they would have a sexual affair. "Have you ever been to Peter Luger's for steaks? I'll take you. We're going to have an affair, I'm telling you," he allegedly said.

Trump's response:

Trump denied the allegations, tweeting last year, "Why didn't the writer of the twelve-year-old article in People Magazine mention the 'incident' in her story. Because it did not happen!"

***

Two women have said Trump kissed them without their consent, but that they weren't offended by it at the time.

Juliet Huddy, a former Fox News anchor, said on the "Mornin!!! With Bill Schulz" podcast in December 2017 that Trump kissed her on the lips without her consent after a meeting in Trump Tower in Manhattan in 2005 or 2006.

"He went to say goodbye and he, rather than kiss me on the cheek, he leaned in on the lips," she said. Huddy added that she was surprised by the kiss, but "didn't feel threatened" or "offended" at the time.

"Now that I've matured, I would've said, 'Nope.' At that time, I was making excuses," she said in December.

Jennifer Murphy, a former contestant both in Miss USA and Trump's reality TV show "The Apprentice," told Grazia magazine in December 2016 that Trump kissed her unexpectedly following a job interview in Trump Tower in 2005.

Although Murphy said she was "very taken aback at the time," she later told CNN that she "wasn't offended" by the kiss. She said she voted for him for president, and even created a Katy Perry parody video in which she sang, "I was kissed by Trump and I liked it."

Trump's response:

The White House denied Huddy's account, according to the New York Daily News.

***

Rachel Crooks told the New York Times in October 2016 that Trump kissed her on the mouth without her consent when she introduced herself him in 2005 Trump Tower in Manhattan, where she worked as a receptionist.

She told the Times that she and Trump shook hands and then he kissed her "directly on the mouth."

Crooks told her sister, who confirmed her account to the Times, but said she thought she would lose her job if she told her company anything about the interaction.

"I was shocked, devastated," she said during a December 2017 interview on "Megyn Kelly Today," adding: "I remember hiding in our boss' office because no one else was there, it was early in the morning, and I called my sister ... I felt horrible."

Crooks joined calls for a congressional investigation into Trump's alleged misconduct.

Trump's response:

Trump denied Crooks' account in an interview with the New York Times in October 2016. "None of this ever took place," he said, threatening to sue the Times if it reported on the allegations.

***

THE 22 REPUBLICAN MEN WHO VOTED AGAINST
THE VIOLENCE AGAINST WOMEN ACT

THE VIOLENCE AGAINST WOMEN ACT WAS REAUTHORIZED
IN THE SENATE BY A 78-22 VOTE ON TUESDAY.

THINK PROGRESS

Samantha Holvey, a contestant in the 2006 Miss USA pageant, which Trump owned, told CNN in October 2016 that Trump personally inspected each of the pageant contestants individually.

"He would step in front of each girl and look you over from head to toe like we were just meat, we were just sexual objects, that we were not people," Holvey said, adding that it made her feel "the dirtiest I felt in my entire life."

Then a 20-year-old student at a private Southern Baptist college, Holvey said she "had no desire to win when I understood what it was all about."

Holvey also called for a congressional investigation into Trump's alleged misconduct.

Trump's response:

CNN, who first reported on Holvey's allegations, said Trump did not respond to requests for comment, but the president has broadly denied all of the sexual misconduct accusations made against him.

***

Ninni Laaksonen, a model and former Miss Finland, told Finnish newspaper Ilta-Sanomat in October 2016 that Trump groped her backstage at the "Late Show with David Letterman" in 2006.

"Trump stood right next to me and suddenly he squeezed my butt," Laaksonen said. "He really grabbed my butt. I don't think anybody saw it, but I flinched and thought, 'What is happening?'"

Trump's response:

The newspaper did not include a response from Trump, but the president has broadly denied all of the sexual misconduct accusations made against him.

***

At an October 2016 press conference, adult-film actress Jessica Drake accused Trump of grabbing and kissing her without permission and offering her money to accept a private invitation to his penthouse hotel room in Lake Tahoe in 2006.

"This is not acceptable behavior for anyone, much less a presidential candidate," Drake said. "I understand that I may be called a liar or an opportunist, but I will risk that in order to stand in solidarity with women who share similar accounts that span many, many years."

Trump's response:

Trump called Drake's accusations "total fiction" and implied that Drake was accustomed to being "grabbed" because she is a porn actress.

"One said, 'He grabbed me on the arm.' And she's a porn star. You know, this one that came out recently, 'He grabbed me and he grabbed me on the arm.' Oh, I'm sure she's never been grabbed before," he said on WGIR radio.

***

Summer Zervos, a former contestant on NBC's "The Apprentice," told reporters at an October 2016 press conference that Trump assaulted her during a 2007 meeting at The Beverly Hills Hotel.

"He then grabbed my shoulder and began kissing me again very aggressively and placed his hand on my breast," she said. "I pulled back and walked to another part of the room. He then walked up, grabbed my hand, and pulled me into the bedroom. I walked out." Zervos added that Trump thrust himself on her before she left the room.

Zervos sued Trump for defamation after he accused her of lying about the allegations. Trump's attorneys have moved to dismiss the case, arguing that, as president, he can't be sued in state court and that his remarks about his accusers are political speech. The suit is ongoing.

Trump's response:

"I vaguely remember Ms. Zervos as one of the many contestants on 'The Apprentice' over the years," Trump said in a statement. "To be clear, I never met her at a hotel or greeted her inappropriately a decade ago. That is not who I am as a person, and it is not how I've conducted my life. In fact, Ms. Zervos continued to contact me for help, emailing my office on April 14 of this year asking that I visit her restaurant in California."

***

Cassandra Searles, who represented the state of Washington at the 2013 Miss USA pageant, wrote in a June 2016 Facebook post that Trump treated herself and other female Miss USA contestants "like cattle" and had them "lined up so he could get a closer look at his property."

"He probably doesn't want me telling the story about that time he continually grabbed my ass and invited me to his hotel room," she added.

Trump's response:

Trump has not specifically denied Searles' allegations, but he has broadly denied all of the sexual misconduct accusations made against him.

***

Alva Johnson, a former Trump campaign staffer, said that Trump kissed her without her consent at a Tampa, Florida rally on August 24, 2016.

Johnson, 43, said Trump grabbed her hand and kissed her on the side of her mouth as he exited an RV outside of the rally, according to details in a new federal lawsuit and an interview with the Washington Post.

"Oh, my God, I think he's going to kiss me," Johnson said in a February 2019 interview with the Post. "He's coming straight for my lips. So, I turn my head, and he kisses me right on the corner of my mouth, still holding my hand the entire time. Then he walks on out."

Johnson filed a federal lawsuit against Trump in February.

Trump's response:

White House press secretary Sarah Huckabee Sanders told INSIDER in a statement, "This accusation is absurd on its face. This never happened and is directly contradicted by multiple highly credible eye witness accounts."

***

Former Elle advice columnist E. Jean Carroll accused President Donald Trump of sexually assaulting her by pinning her against the wall and forcing his penis inside of her in a department store dressing room the mid-1990s.

"The moment the dressing-room door is closed, he lunges at me, pushes me against the wall, hitting my head quite badly, and puts his mouth against my lips," Carroll wrote in an excerpt of her 2019 book, "What Do We Need Men For?".

She went on, "The next moment, still wearing correct business attire, shirt, tie, suit jacket, overcoat, he opens the overcoat, unzips his pants, and, forcing his fingers around my private area, thrusts his penis halfway — or completely, I'm not certain — inside me. It turns into a colossal struggle."

Trump's response:

142

The White House denied Carroll's allegations in a statement to New York magazine in June 2019.

"This is a completely false and unrealistic story surfacing 25 years after allegedly taking place and was created simply to make the President look bad," the statement read.

***

President Donald Trump and first lady Melania Trump, with their son Barron, arrive for a New Year's Eve party at his Mar-a-Lago club in Palm Beach, Florida in 2017. Jonathan Ernst/Reuters
Karen Johnson, a regular at Trump's Mar-a-Lago resort in Florida, said Trump pulled her behind a tapestry and kissed and groped her without her consent during a New Year's Eve party there in the early 2000s.

"I'm a tall girl and I had six-inch heels on, and I still remember looking up at him. And he's strong, and he just kissed me," Johnson said. "I was so scared because of who he was ... I don't even know where it came from. I didn't have a say in the matter."

Johnson said Trump forcibly grabbed her genitals.

"When he says that thing, 'Grab them in the pussy,' that hits me hard because when he grabbed me and pulled me into the tapestry, that's where he grabbed me," she said, according to the book excerpt.

Johnson said Trump called her repeatedly after the incident, offering to fly her to New York to visit him. She said she refused his advances and never saw him again or visited Mar-a-Lago, where she'd had her wedding reception years earlier.

Trump's response:

The White House denied the allegation and slammed "All the President's Women."

"That book is trash and those accusations from 20 years ago have been addressed many times," the White House press secretary, Stephanie Grisham, told Insider.
(https://www.businessinsider.com/women-accused-trump-sexual-misconduct-list-2017-12#karena-virginia-9)

Lawyer Elizabeth Beck says that Trump called her 'terrible' and 'disgusting' for attempting to use her breast pump during a break in a meeting. Actor/Comedian, Rosie O'Donnell, has been called "ugly" and other nasty names. Popular TV host, Nancy O'Dell, was hit on by Donald Trump who said, "I moved on her like a b*tch!" (https://fox40.com/news/lawyer-trump-called-me...)

This is a classic example of powerful men consider attractive girls and women fair game for his unwanted sexual advances. It's the kind of behavior of a horny old goat, with no self-control, no respect for woman, no understanding of the word "No', and certainly makes him unfit to be President of the United States. Trump also had plenty to say about his daughter Ivanka that sounded a lot like lustful incestuous fantasies.

Created & posted by Kevin
Karstens... .

In a 2006 appearance on The View, the Trumps were promoting The Celebrity Apprentice when Donald decided to ogle his daughter on national TV. The hosts asked Trump if he'd mind if Ivanka posed for Playboy, and Trump replied:

"I don't think Ivanka would do that inside the magazine although she does have a very nice figure. I've said if Ivanka weren't my daughter perhaps I'd be dating her."

He allegedly once asked a columnist if it was wrong to be more sexually attracted to your daughter than your wife. Ivanka, who was 13 at the time.

In 2013, on her talk show, Wendy Williams asked Donald and Ivanka what favorite activities they had in common. Ivanka said, "Either real estate or golf." Donald grinned and said, "Well, I was going to say sex, but I can't relate that to her," prompting groans from the audience.

In a March 22 CNN interview with Anderson Cooper, former Playboy model Karen McDougal discussed an affair she allegedly had with Trump over a decade ago. McDougal alleged that Trump said McDougal was "beautiful like her," referring to Ivanka.

In a 2004 in-depth interview with New York Magazine, Trump again remarked on Ivanka's appearance — something he almost never fails to mention when he's talking about his family's successes, and an indicator that he links being conventionally attractive with merit.

"Let me tell you one thing: Ivanka is a great, great beauty," Trump told New York in a wide-ranging interview. "Every guy in the country wants to go out with my daughter."

Trump once told Howard Stern it was OK to refer to Ivanka as "a piece of ass."

In another clip discovered by CNN, from 2006, Stern asks Trump, "Did your daughter get breast implants?" Trump says "No, she didn't. I mean, I would know if she did. The answer is no. Why? Did she look a little more stacked?" She looks more voluptuous than ever," Stern replied. No, she didn't get them," Trump said. "She's actually always been very voluptuous ... She's tall, she's almost 6 feet tall and she's been, she's an amazing beauty."

Trump awkwardly touched Ivanka's hips at the Republican National Convention in 2016. This one isn't a quote, per se, but it's very much in line with Trump's brand of creepy. Ivanka introduced her father at the 2016 Republican National Convention (RNC), and when he came on stage, he awkwardly kissed and touched her.

At a rally in North Dakota in September 2017, Trump brought Ivanka on stage and announced that he likes it when his daughter, a senior White House adviser, calls him "daddy." "Come on up, honey," the president said of his 36-year-old daughter before adding that it was her idea to join him at the rally. "She said, 'Dad, can I go with you?'" Trump said. "She actually said, 'Daddy, can I go with you?' I like that. 'Daddy, can I go with you?' I said, 'Yes, you can.'"

Trump made yet another suggestive comment to Rolling Stone reporter Paul Solotaroff in a September 2015 story about Ivanka's beauty. "Yeah, she's really something, and what a beauty, that one. If I weren't happily married and, ya know, her father... ," Trump said. Ya know? I wish Solotaroff said, "No, I don't know. Why don't you elaborate?" (https://www.elitedaily.com/p/9-donald-trump-quotes-about-ivanka-that-are-super-uncomfortable-8646720)

I could go on and on belittled Trump's performance as president, but I am more concerned that he poses a serious threat to the continence of our nation in which the rights and privileges, as well as the responsibilities, of every . , guaranteed by the Constitution. His close friendship with dictators makes one question his patriotism and the sincerity to the oath of office he took at his swearing in ceremony in 2017.

It also concerns me is that he believes he knows better than anyone else about everything, and refuses to listen to those who do know. He is surrounded by inferior people, who also have no regard for the people they are supposed to represent and serve. They, like Trump, seem to be behaving in treasonable ways. It's not enough that Trump lose the election in 2020, and be driven from the White House if that becomes necessary, and have his crimes investigated, charged, convicted and imprisoned.

But, not just him, the list of those who are culpable in enabling him to do his dastardly work, by refusing to stand up to him, and to watch him contributing to tearing the nation apart by refusing to understand what is the purpose of governments; that is providing what all the people require, but aren't able to provide for themselves. Trump likes to throw around the word 'socialism' as a bugaboo to scare his followers. Lile Trump they don't know what Socialism is. In fact, like old '45', they also have little understanding or loyalty to the principle of 'democracy.'

However, like Trump his followers don't know Trump is a reverse Robin Hood; he steals from the poor, and gives to the rich. He rewards the rich and prosperous, who have the resources to help themselves, he siphons revenue which could help people who have lost their jobs, health care, and hope, struggling to make ends meet, to his friends, contributors, corporations, and in violation of the principle of separation of church and state, religious organizations and churches. Trump hides the fact that he and his cronies believe in socialism for the rich and corporations. He has been aided in this horrific effort by Republican politicians who seem to have embrace the new GOP, TRUMPUBLICANs.

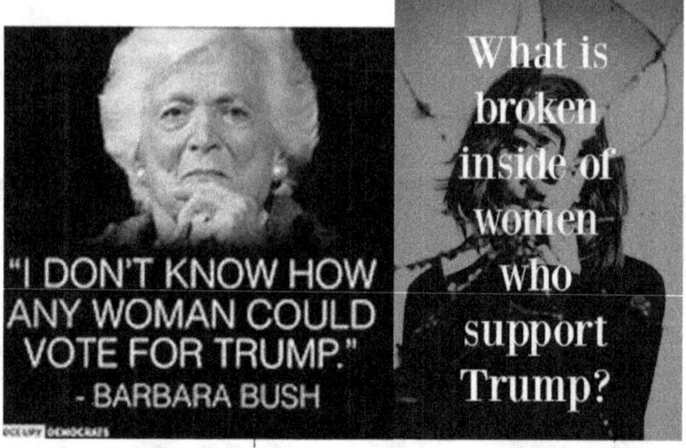

One point I should make clear. I don't believe that all Democrat politicians are good people and all Republicans politicians are bad. I am suspicious of all politicians, no matter what their party. My thoughts on the matter are made clear by the following two cartoons.

The following articles address the question.

"Has the party of Lincoln truly become the party of Trump? Has a former real estate tycoon and reality T.V. star captured the Republican Party and transformed it into the Trumpublican Party? The answer to that question would appear to be "yes," given that some 95% of Republicans claim to support the president, and in a recent survey a majority of Republicans said that Donald Trump is a greater president than Honest Abe. Having worked more than two decades in various capacities for local, state and national Republican elected officials and party leaders, I do not recognize the political organization that today calls itself the Republican Party, and I certainly cannot identify with it. Not only is its titular head a proven liar and poorly informed narcissist, but also under his "leadership," many well-educated, intelligent Republican office holders have begun to act as if they have forgotten their moral and political principles. It is bad enough that a man of Donald Trump's poor character and judgment has become the face of the Republican Party, but it is in some ways even more disturbing that so many other Republicans, including formerly highly respected members of Congress, have seemingly lost all sense of judgment, fairness, decency, and even reality. What has happened to the Grand Old Party? What is driving this madness?" (https://www.dailykos.com/stories/2018/11/28/...)

***

Reflecting on Trump's 2016 victory and on how easily and quickly so many Republican office holders have become Trump apologists and sycophants, I have come to the conclusion that the party that Trump captured in 2016 was not the party of Lincoln — or of Theodore Roosevelt, Eisenhower, or even Ronald Reagan. The party that Trump "captured" was no longer the party controlled by the traditional "old guard" Republicans, but rather a party dominated by evangelicals, tea party activists and nationalists who began making major inroads into the GOP in the late 20th century and had become the party's clear majority by the 2016 election.

Trump did not so much "capture" and reshape the Republican Party as he did recognize the mood, beliefs and frustrations of the party's new majority and become the uncensored, unapologetic voice they sought. I attended the 1988 and 1992 Republican conventions, and looking back, I now recognize that the Party with which I had identified was already disassembling.

In 1988, Rev. Pat Robertson had opposed Vice President George H. W. Bush and Sen. Bob Dole in the primaries and had won four state primaries and a total of 9% of the total vote. In 1992, conservative political commentator Pat Buchanan challenged the Republican incumbent, Bush, and won 23% of the GOP primary vote with a nationalist themed campaign, "Putting and Keeping America First."

By the last two decades of the 20th century, the moderate old guard "country club" wing of the Republican Party was increasingly challenged by highly dedicated and motivated religious and nationalist conservatives, and by 2016, the moderates had lost the battle.

Trump and his advisors recognized that the new Republican majority was not terribly concerned about the old principles, values and issues of the GOP (balanced budgets, strong alliances, free trade, democracy and freedom), but that they cared fervently (in some cases, maniacally) about three issues — abortion, guns, and immigration.

All Trump needed to do to win the nomination was to declare loudly and convincingly that he would "build a great wall," throw abortion doctors in jail, and "protect your Second Amendment rights." It didn't matter to the true believers how crudely Trump said these things or that he had previously been pro-choice and in favor of some gun controls, as long as he could convince the Republican core that he was the most reliable candidate on these three critical issues.

But, how could a brash, womanizing, crude, amoral, untruthful former Democrat convince the new Republican majority of evangelicals and nationalists that he was truly worthy of their support? I think the answer lies at least in part to the fact that Trump and many of today's most rabid Republicans share a deep bond in their common distrust of science, "experts," and 'intellectuals," as well as a desire for simple solutions to complex problems and a propensity to believe myths and conspiracy theories.

It is quite relevant, I believe, that at the time of the 2016 primaries, a Pew research study found that only 40 percent of Republicans accepted as true Darwin's Theory of Evolution, and at the same time — long after President Obama made public his birth certificate — a NBC News/SurveyMonkey poll found that 72 percent of registered Republicans still doubted that Barack Obama was born in the United States.

Given the mindset of the current Republican faithful, is it any wonder that every Republican member of Congress except Mitt Romney chose to reject the strong evidentiary case in favor of impeachment and conviction and chose instead to accept Trump's absurd defense? What happened to the GOP is actually quite clear: Although there are certainly still many highly intelligent, well-educated Republicans who support President Trump for various reasons, including a strong economy, the party's base is now dominated by people with very strongly held beliefs about only a few key issues — abortion, immigration, and gun rights.

Donald Trump did not remake the Republican Party. He simply told the party faithful what they wanted to hear in language that they liked and understood, and he let them know that there was nothing wrong with their values and their skepticism about the mainstream media, scientific theories and opinions of so-called "experts." The president has made it acceptable and comfortable for his followers to reject facts and question inconvenient realities.

Together, Trump and the new Republican majority have created this monster I call the Trumpublican Party. Opinion: Wondering what happened to my old GOP? Feb 07, 2020, By Lee Raudonis. (Lee Raudonis is a former communications director and executive director of the Georgia Republican Party. He also worked for several Republican elected officials in Georgia and the U.S. Congress.) (https://www.ajc.com/news/opinion/opinion-wondering-what-happened-old-gop/qplEObNNjlOeKxUoDQpa4O/)

TRUMP AND THE CHRISTIAN RIGHT

Trump is the darling of the Christian Right, and that's puzzling. Trump has never been affiliated with any religion and hasn't read the bible. He has commit every sin listed in the Ten Commandments and more as well that must have broken off the stone when Moses was carrying in down from the mountain. It is Christian to forgive, and with Trump there is a lot that has to be forgiven. Maybe the rest of us are not so forgiving.

"The pathological hypocrisy of Donald Trump has seeped into the character of the religious right- wing of the party and evangelical Christians. While Democrats quickly turn their backs on colleagues who engage in or are accused of inappropriate sexual or illegal behaviors, Republican right-wingers stay silent or deny undeniable evidence. Hypocrisy and a cult-mentality have replaced the authenticity and decency of millions of so-called Bible-believing Christians.

Trump's sleaze resume is impressive if you're into that sort of thing. He is known to have cheated on all three of his wives. Melania was publicly humiliated by his sexual rendezvous with porn star Stormy Daniels soon after the birth of their son Barron. Playboy Bunny Susan MacDougal has publicly described a 10-month affair with Trump in 2006, which she says was serious and mutual. This affair occurred during his tryst with Daniel's and other women. Adultery is one of the Ten Commandments and is cited pervasively throughout the text as a severe sin. Should we assume Trump's transgressions are now acceptable patterns amongst the evangelical community and Congressional Tea Party Members?

Despite the pervasive nature of the sexual allegations against him, Trump's Christian supporters stand by him, believe his denials and cheer his attacks against his accusers. What if the accused was Obama or any Democratic president? Republicans, especially the religious- right should remember the Bible sees the coveting of sinners as a sin.

Trump also has a pattern of defending men who have been accused of physical abuse against women, involved with prostitution, adultery, and in the case of Roy Moore, pedophilia. When White House Staff Secretary Rob Porter resigned after two ex-wives came forward with claims and evidence of physical violence, Trump only had praise for him, "He is a hard worker, and has a great career ahead of him. He is going through a tough time." No statement was made condemning domestic violence, and no sympathy was shown for his victims. Trump vehemently defends men accused of crimes against women by saying, "He says he's innocent, you have to remember that." That has been his playbook for years.

In addition to the sexual, criminal sleaze surrounding Trump, there exists pervasive political sleaze more accurately referred to as corruption and illegality. He has placed unqualified cronies in positions of power by ignoring, " order of succession regulations," ignores legal subpoenas issued by Congress, and has attempted to suppress the constitutional rights of Americans to full access to vote, to peacefully protest and to express their First Amendment Right to free speech. History will show that Donald J. Trump broke more laws while in office, hired more criminal political figures to protect him, and in doing so, became the worst, most world-wide President in U.S. history. History may also show he became the first U.S. President to be escorted into custody upon leaving the White House."
(https://www.dailykos.com/stories/2020/8/16/1969818/--Donald-Trump-And-The-Religious-Right)

Evangelicals told Trump he was "chosen" by God. Now he says it himself. Religious right leaders say God anointed Trump as a "king." This week he actually declared himself the "chosen one" (salon.com/2019/0...)

The following article offers reasons that the Christian Right have chosen to embrace Donald Trump as a good Christian, doing God's work.

"Jesus Makes America Great" author, Steven Andrew, gives 10 reasons why Christians support President Trump. He says, "The people reaffirming covenant that the USA serves the Lord caused God to raise up and use President Trump."
Donald Trump is a huge improvement over crooked Hillary and Barack Obama. As Christians, we understand God raised up President Trump to undo many of His judgments the nation had for our national sins, explained Andrew.

"Christians support President Trump where he follows Jesus Christ, and thankfully this is many areas," Andrew said. He leads One Million Americans on the Lord's Side, the top Americans saving the USA. Sign Up Here.

To those who doubt Trump, Andrew says, "In God's sovereignty, the Lord knew President Trump would grow closer to Him. No matter what anyone thought about Donald Trump before, we now see President Trump is following God in many ways (John 14:21).

President Trump:

Obeys God that the USA serves God.

"In America we worship God, not government." President Donald Trump
Obeys God by working to destroy the Johnson Amendment
The Johnson Amendment silenced pastors to speak politically, which harmed people's lives and the nation. The Johnson Amendment is illegal, because both God and the First Amendment prohibit Congress from making a law against the free exercise of Christianity. Trump signed an Executive Order opposing the Johnson Amendment. Trump wants Congress to obey God and the Constitution and to remove the Johnson Amendment.

Obeys God that the USA is a Christian nation
"That's just the way it is," said Donald Trump when asked about the USA being a Christian nation. "This is a Christian nation," says the Supreme Court. We know the only way for God to bless the nation is for the USA to serve the LORD. God says, "Blessed is the nation whose God is the LORD" Psalm 33:12. This means the nation would be cursed for not serving the one true God.

Obeys God to end the military's transgender sin

Obeys God by doing all he can to end government funded abortion

Obeys God to say America First

America is dedicated to Jesus Christ. By saying "America First," we are really saying the USA uniquely serves God. No other country has a covenant dedication to God like the USA. "But if any provide not for his own, and especially for those of his own house, he hath denied the faith, and is worse than an infidel." 1 Timothy 5:8

Obeys God to protect the borders

The Bible teaches that dangerous people crossing the borders is God's judgment. God wants us to protect the border. After all, God has the most restrictive border policy. He only allows Christians into Heaven; the Bible says everyone else is cast into hell. Jesus Christ says, "I am the way, the truth, and the life: no man cometh unto the Father, but by me." (John 14:6)

Obeys God to oppose Islamic terrorists.

The Bible teaches God is using President Trump to undo God's judgment of terror. We know terrorism is God's judgment for the nation's sins.

Obeys God to cut taxes.

The Word of God explains high taxes are God's judgment for our national sins, so God is using President Trump to end this judgment. However, by Congress opposing the President, we see that the nation has more repenting to do for God to fully cut taxes.

Obeys God to cut regulations

Regulations and tyranny are also God's judgment for our national sins. So, because of the people reaffirming covenant, God is ending this judgment. Yet, with more people declaring the USA is a Christian nation, people will gain even greater freedom.

The following images and quotes speak for themselves.

EVANGELICALS OVERWHELMINGLY SUPPORT TRUMP DESPITE GLARING MORAL FAILINGS'

NEW MASTER
WHITE EVANGELICALS
TRUMP

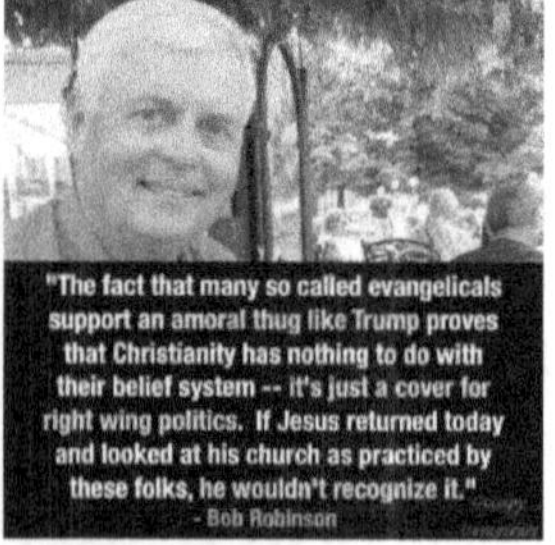
"The fact that many so called evangelicals support an amoral thug like Trump proves that Christianity has nothing to do with their belief system -- it's just a cover for right wing politics. If Jesus returned today and looked at his church as practiced by these folks, he wouldn't recognize it."
- Bob Robinson

Type AMEN
Please
LIKE and SHARE
Thank You,
Lord JESUS,
FOR PRESIDENT
TRUMP

Thank You, Lord, JESUS, PRESIDENT TRUMP

GUN TOTING DEPLORABLE CHRISTIAN WOMEN VOTE TRUMP

US CONSTI TUTION

I'M A BETTER CHRISTIAN THAN ANY TRUMP SUPPORTER AND I'M AN ATHEIST

"I'm sorry I cannot cure any of you."
"You all have pre-existing conditions..."
REPUBLICAN JESUS

TEN COMMANDMENTS TO-DO LIST
Idolatry
Graven Images
False Witness
Adultery
Covet
Covet
WELL... AT LEAST IT SHOWS SOME FAMILIARITY WITH THE CONCEPTS.
EVANGELICALS

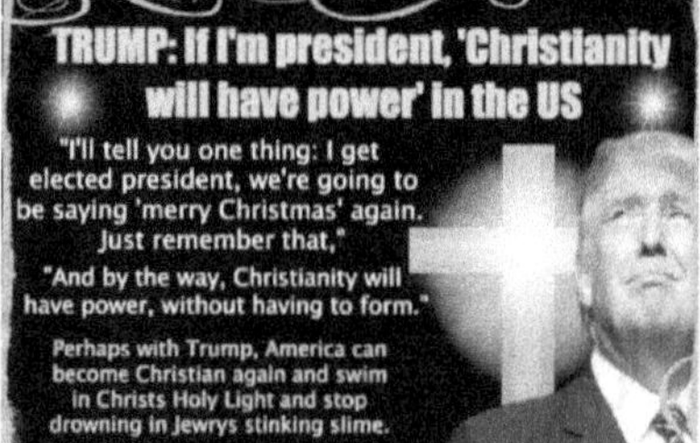
TRUMP: If I'm president, 'Christianity will have power' in the US
"I'll tell you one thing: I get elected president, we're going to be saying 'merry Christmas' again. Just remember that,"
"And by the way, Christianity will have power, without having to form."
Perhaps with Trump, America can become Christian again and swim in Christs Holy Light and stop drowning in Jewrys stinking slime.

DEAR CONSERVATIVES:
THIS IS WHAT JESUS WOULD HAVE DONE.

'So Jesus is in front of thousands of pe right? Huge sold out crowds wherever goes. Bethlehem media doesn't report of it. They're all hungry, again thousan but he feeds them all. Because he's got cash, he doesn't need to borrow.'
AND THEN JESUS SAID "I CAN'T HEAL YOU FOR FREE, THAT'S SOCIALISM"

Evangelicals spent thousands of years warning about the Antichrist. Then, when he shows up, they elect him president.
OCCUPY DEMOCRATS

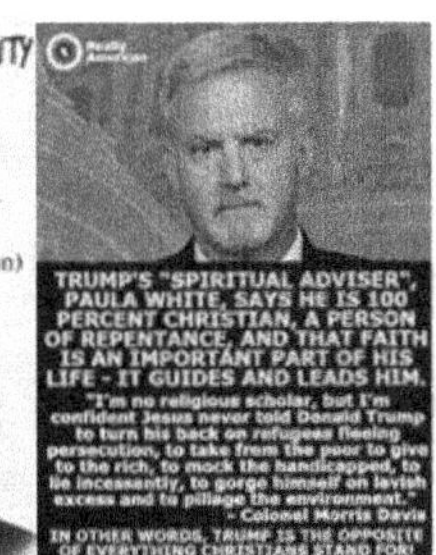

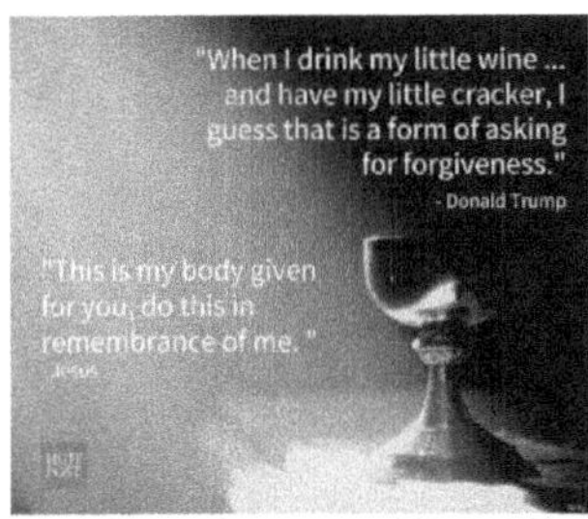

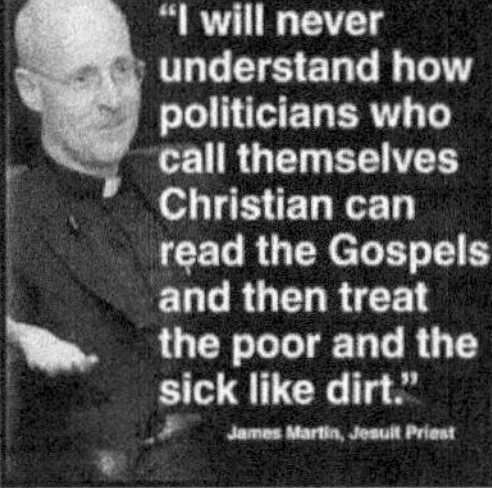

Middle Age Riot
@middleageriot

Evangelicals think God, who didn't protect victims of the Holocaust, two World Wars, the Irish potato famine, Chernobyl, the Bhopal disaster, Hurricane Maria, or the Spanish Flu, will protect them from the coronavirus at church on Easter Sunday because Trump.

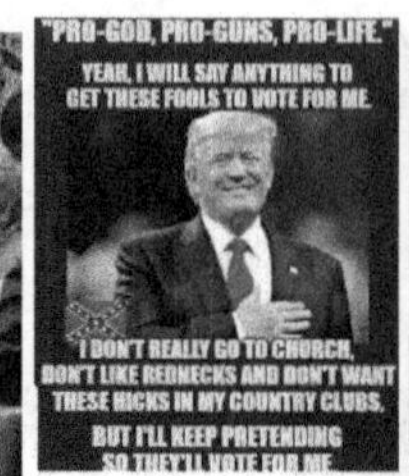

"PRO-GOD, PRO-GUNS, PRO-LIFE."
YEAH, I WILL SAY ANYTHING TO GET THESE FOOLS TO VOTE FOR ME.
I DON'T REALLY GO TO CHURCH, DON'T LIKE REDNECKS AND DON'T WANT THESE HICKS IN MY COUNTRY CLUBS.
BUT I'LL KEEP PRETENDING SO THEY'LL VOTE FOR ME.
as long as he has the R after his name.

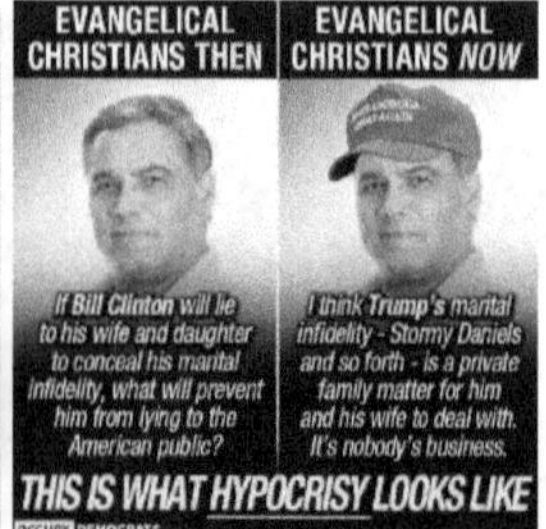

EVANGELICAL CHRISTIANS THEN
EVANGELICAL CHRISTIANS NOW
If Bill Clinton will lie to his wife and daughter to conceal his marital infidelity, what will prevent him from lying to the American public?
I think Trump's marital infidelity - Stormy Daniels and so forth - is a private family matter for him and his wife to deal with. It's nobody's business.
THIS IS WHAT HYPOCRISY LOOKS LIKE
OCCUPY DEMOCRATS

LYING TRUMP

"The Washington Post

Fact Checker: President Trump made 19,127 false or misleading claims in 1,226 days

Glenn Kessler, Salvador Rizzo, Meg Kelly 6/1/2020

The Washington Post logo Fact Checker: President Trump made 19,127 false or misleading claims in 1,226 days

The Toronto Star published a list of trump's lies

It's no longer a question as to whether President Trump will exceed 20,000 false or misleading claims by the time his current term is completed. Instead, we have to ask: Will he top 25,000?

As of May 29, his 1,226th day in office, Trump had made 19,127 false or misleading claims, according to the Fact Checker's database that analyzes, categorizes and tracks every suspect statement he has uttered. That's almost 16 claims a day over the course of his presidency. So far this year, he's averaging just over 22 claims a day, similar to the pace he set in 2019.

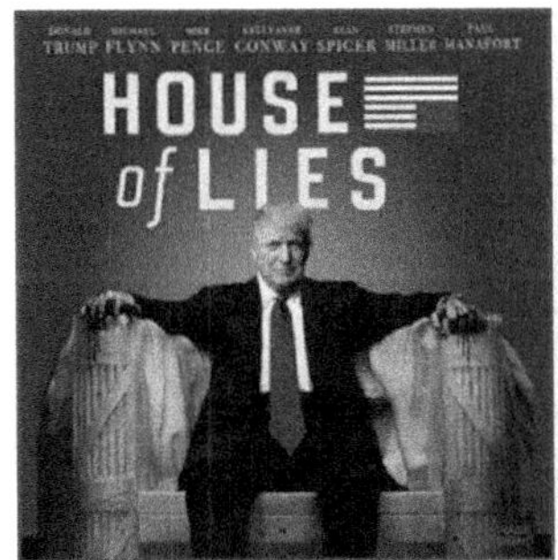

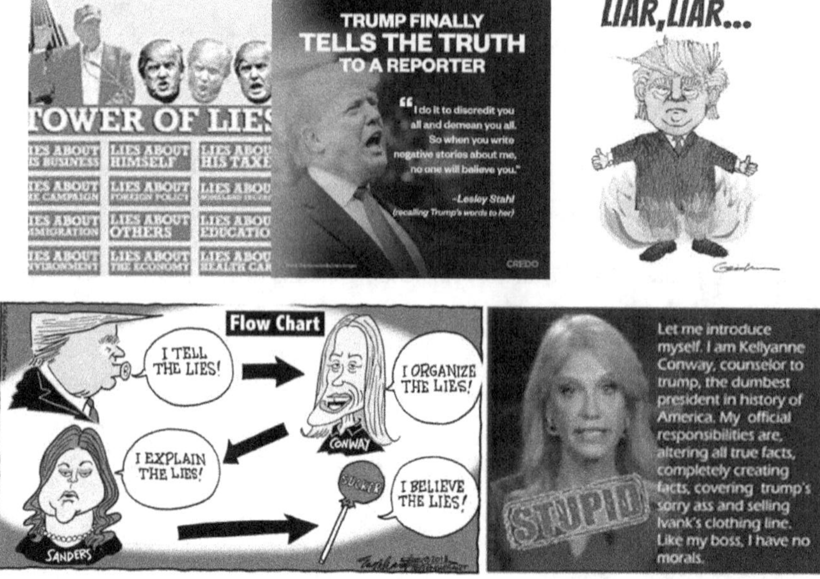

With 235 days to go in his current term, that would leave him just short of 25,000. But we have also found that October is a dangerous month for the truth, especially if an election is nearing. In October 2018, the president tallied 1,205 claims and in October 2019, 1,159 claims. That's a pace of 40 claims a day.

Much depends, of course, on whether the president is able to return to holding campaign rallies for his most loyal supporters. At such rallies, the president runs through a list of exaggerated or false claims that easily tops 60 statements a rally. Since the coronavirus pandemic has more or less shut down the United States, the president has been unable to hold such mass events. He tried substituting a daily news conference at the White House, with the occasional interview with a friendly host, but it's not quite the same thing.

The coronavirus pandemic has spawned a whole new genre of Trump's falsehoods. The category in just a few months has reached 800 claims, with his advocacy for hydroxychloroquine as a possible cure, based on minimal and flimsy evidence, already reaching Bottomless Pinocchio status. It takes at least 20 repeats of a Three- or Four-Pinocchio claim to merit a Bottomless Pinocchio, and there are now 39 entries.

Trump's penchant for repeating false claims is demonstrated by the fact that the Fact Checker database has recorded more than 450 instances in which he has repeated a variation of the same claim at least three times.

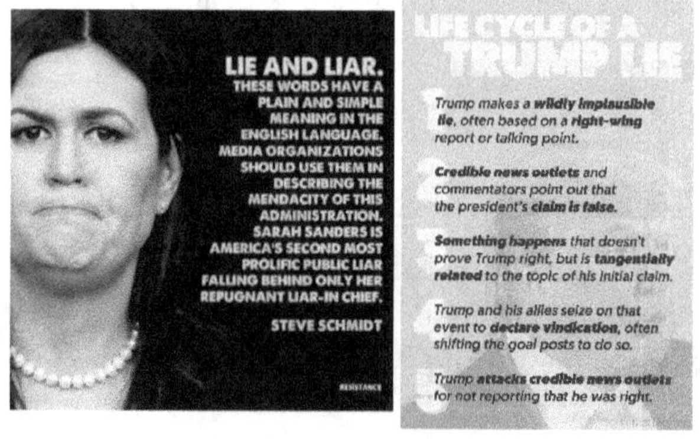

Biggest Liars			Most Honest		
Name	Honesty Index	Percent Lies	Name	Honesty Index	Percent Lies
1. Ben Carson (R)	0.31	82%	1. Dennis Kucinish (D)	0.77	16%
2. Michele Bachmann (R)	0.32	75%	2. Sheldon Whitehouse (D)	0.76	21%
3. Donald Trump (R)	0.35	72%	3. Rob Portman (R)	0.71	20%
4. Herman Cain (R)	0.35	69%	4. Sherrod Brown (D)	0.71	25%
5. Allen West (R)	0.38	73%	5. Bill Nelson (D)	0.70	16%
6. Reince Priebus (R)	0.41	55%	6. Tim Kaine (D)	0.69	22%
7. Ted Cruz (R)	0.44	65%	7. Nathan Deal (R)	0.67	29%
8. Newt Gingrich (R)	0.45	54%	8. Hillary Clinton (D)	0.67	27%
9. Tommy Thompson (R)	0.45	63%	9. Barack Obama (D)	0.66	25%
10. Dan Patrick (R)	0.46	57%	10. Bill Clinton (D)	0.65	26%

Data from PolitiFact.com. Analysis by AmericanNewsX.com.

Trump's most repeated claim — 334 times — is that the U.S. economy today is the best in history. He began making this claim in June 2018, and it quickly became one of his favorites. He's been forced to adapt for the tough economic times, and doing so has made it even more fantastic. Whereas he used to say it was the best economy in U.S. history, he now often recalls he had achieved "the best economy in the history of the world."

Nope. The president once could brag about the state of the economy, but he ran into trouble when he made a play for the history books. By just about any important measure, the pre-coronavirus economy was not doing as well as it did under Presidents Dwight D. Eisenhower, Lyndon B. Johnson or Bill Clinton — or Ulysses S. Grant. Moreover, the economy already was beginning to hit the head winds caused by Trump's trade wars, with the manufacturing sector in an apparent recession.

Trump's second-most repeated claim — 261 times — is that his border wall is being built. Congress balked at funding the concrete barrier he envisioned, so the project evolved into the replacement of smaller, older barriers with steel bollard fencing. (Only three miles of the barrier is on land that previously did not have a barrier.) The Washington Post has reported the bollard fencing is easily breached, with smugglers sawing through it, despite Trump's claims it is impossible to get past. Nevertheless, the project has diverted billions in military and counter narcotics funding to become one of the largest infrastructure projects in U.S. history, seizing private land, cutting off wildlife corridors and disrupting Native American cultural sites.

Trump has falsely said 206 times that he passed the biggest tax cut in history. Even before his tax cut was crafted, he promised it would be the biggest in U.S. history — bigger than President Ronald Reagan's in 1981. Reagan's tax cut amounted to 2.9 percent of the gross domestic product, and none of the proposals under consideration came close to that level. Yet Trump persisted in this fiction even when the tax cut was eventually crafted to be the equivalent of 0.9 percent of gross domestic product, making it the eighth-largest tax cut in 100 years. This continues to be an all-purpose applause line at the president's rallies.

Note: The Fact Checker welcomes academic research of the Trump claims database. Recent examples include work done by Erasmus University of Rotterdam, University College London and the University of California at Santa Barbara. You can request our data files with an explanation of your research plans by contacting us at factchecker@washpost.com.

(The Fact Checker is a verified signatory to the International Fact-Checking Network code of principles."
https://www.msn.com/en-us/news/factcheck/fact-checker-president-trump-made-19127-false-or-misleading-claims-in-1226-days/ar-BB14RCpH)

The Old GOP versus The New GOP
REPUBLICAN PARTY PLATFORM OF 1956
The Republican Party supports an immigration policy which is in keeping with the traditions of America in providing a haven for oppressed peoples
"The Dream Act will be a nightmare for the American people."
Rep. Mike Coffman (Colorado)
The Old GOP versus The New GOP
REPUBLICAN PARTY PLATFORM OF 1956
This Administration has conserved and safeguarded our natural resources for the greatest good of all, now and in the future.
"(T)he idea that carbon dioxide is a carcinogen that is harmful to our environment is almost comical."
Rep. John Boehner (Ohio)

The Modern "New Right" GOP Congressman...
Fox News: unfair and unbalanced
Birther nutters
Tea Party loons
TYPICAL GOP CONGRESSMAN

The Old GOP versus The New GOP
REPUBLICAN PARTY PLATFORM OF 1956
The protection of the right of workers to organize into unions and to bargain collectively is the firm and permanent policy of the Eisenhower Administration.
"We discourage any companies that have unions from wanting to come to South Carolina."
Gov. Nikki Haley

GOODBYE CRUEL WORLD

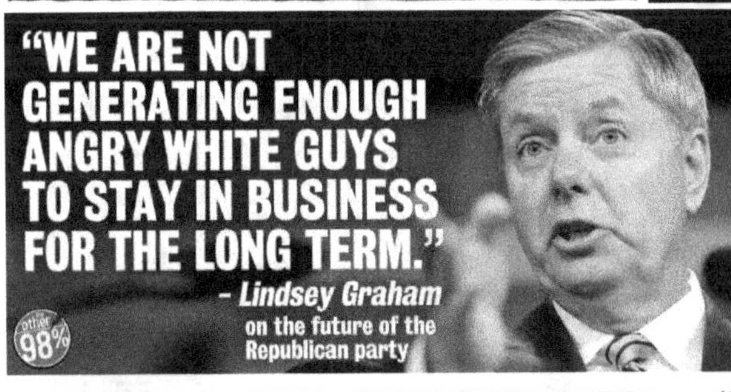

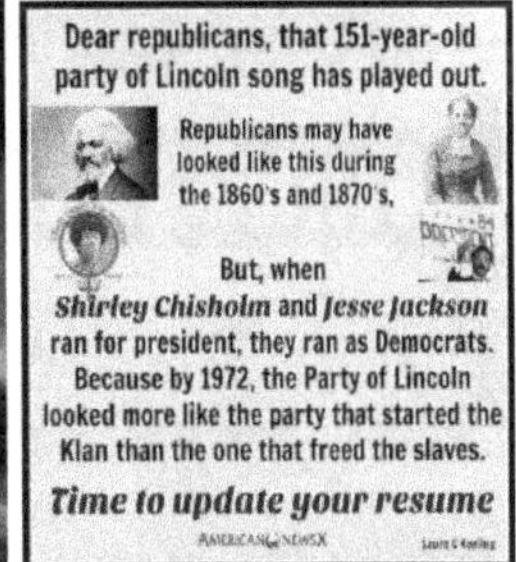
1956 REPUBLICAN PLATFORM
1. Provide federal assistance to low-income communities
2. Protect Social Security
3. Provide asylum for refugees
4. Extend minimum wage
5. Improve unemployment benefit system so it covers more people
6. Strengthen labor laws so workers can easily join a union
7. Assure equal pay for equal work regardless of sex
SHARE IF YOU MISS THE GOOD OLD DAYS!

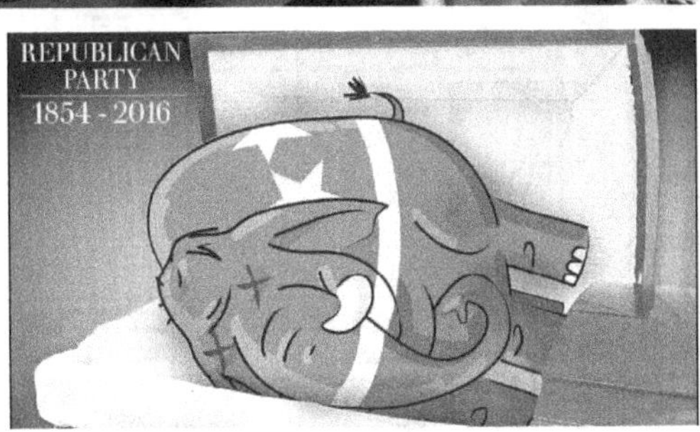
"WE ARE NOT GENERATING ENOUGH ANGRY WHITE GUYS TO STAY IN BUSINESS FOR THE LONG TERM."
- Lindsey Graham
on the future of the Republican party
98%

Dear republicans, that 151-year-old party of Lincoln song has played out.
Republicans may have looked like this during the 1860's and 1870's,
But, when Shirley Chisholm and Jesse Jackson ran for president, they ran as Democrats. Because by 1972, the Party of Lincoln looked more like the party that started the Klan than the one that freed the slaves.
Time to update your resume
AMERICANS NEWSX

REPUBLICAN PARTY 1854 - 2016

WHAT THIS PARTY BADLY NEEDS IS A BIGGER TENT!
GOP
RUSH
HARDLINERS ONLY
MODERATES

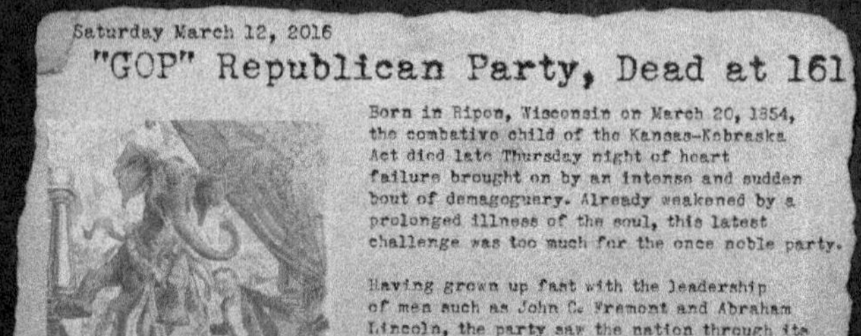

Saturday March 12, 2016

"GOP" Republican Party, Dead at 161

Born in Ripon, Wisconsin on March 20, 1854, the combative child of the Kansas-Nebraska Act died late Thursday night of heart failure brought on by an intense and sudden bout of demagoguery. Already weakened by a prolonged illness of the soul, this latest challenge was too much for the once noble party.

Having grown up fast with the leadership of men such as John C. Fremont and Abraham Lincoln, the party saw the nation through its greatest crisis. Over the years growing wise and strong under Roosevelt and Eisenhower, it eventually began to weaken when infected with a virulent strain of Conservatism under Reagan, the Bushes, and others.

The party is survived by newly disenfranchised fiscal conservatives and a grieving nation that remembers the days of the Grand Old Party. May the Party of Lincoln rest in peace.

The Grand Old Party with Teddy

The Hellfire Federalist

JESUS vs. the GOP

	Jesus	GOP
Favors the poor over the rich	✓	✗
Encourages help for the sick and elderly	✓	✗
Welcomes the outsider/foreigner	✓	✗
Turns the other cheek (non-violence)	✓	✗
Loves money and capitalism	✗	✓

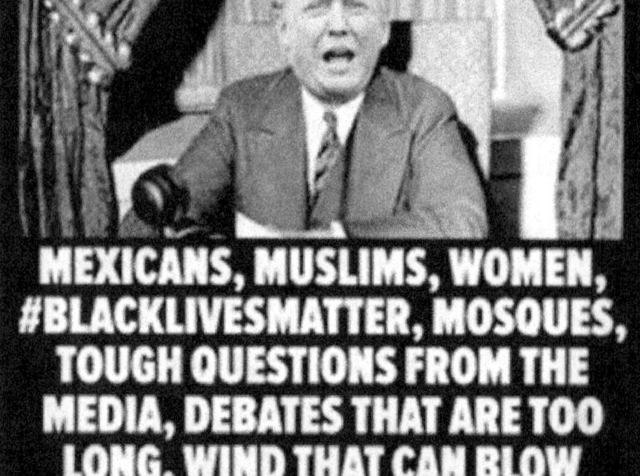

Old GOP vs. New GOP

© 2012 R.S. Janes www.fishink.us

REPUBLICAN PARTY OF 1860	REPUBLICAN PARTY OF TODAY
Abraham Lincoln — First Republican President 1860-1865	**Mitt Romney** — Leading 2012 GOP Presidential Candidate
Dwight D. Eisenhower — President 1952-1960	**Rick Santorum** — 2012 GOP Presidential Candidate
Ronald Reagan — President 1980-1988	**Newt Gingrich** — 2012 GOP Presidential Candidate

OLD GOP
MR. GORBACHEV, TEAR DOWN THIS WALL!
NEW GOP
HEY VLAD! I GOT YOU SOME MORE BRICKS.
M. WERNER

REPUBLICAN PARTY

TRUMP

TRUMP GRABBED THE REPUBLICAN PARTY
BY THE P*$$Y

Its fun seeing all the Republicans back-pedaling on their opinion of Trump. "What? No he is great! I dont remember saying otherwise."

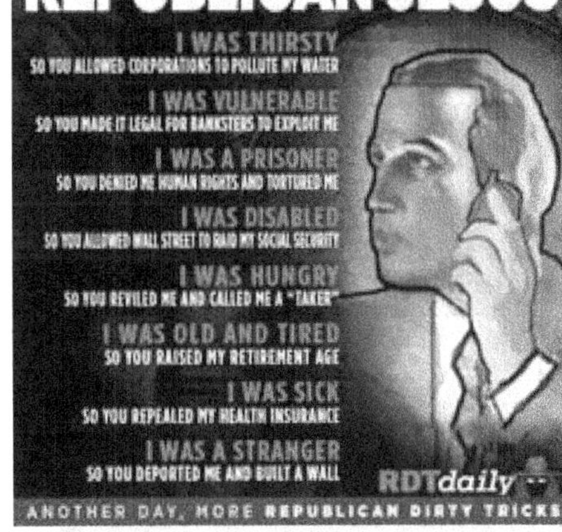

REPUBLICAN JESUS
I WAS THIRSTY
SO YOU ALLOWED CORPORATIONS TO POLLUTE MY WATER
I WAS VULNERABLE
SO YOU MADE IT LEGAL FOR BANKSTERS TO EXPLOIT ME
I WAS A PRISONER
SO YOU DENIED ME HUMAN RIGHTS AND TORTURED ME
I WAS DISABLED
SO YOU ALLOWED WALL STREET TO RAID MY SOCIAL SECURITY
I WAS HUNGRY
SO YOU REVILED ME AND CALLED ME A "TAKER"
I WAS OLD AND TIRED
SO YOU RAISED MY RETIREMENT AGE
I WAS SICK
SO YOU REPEALED MY HEALTH INSURANCE
I WAS A STRANGER
SO YOU DEPORTED ME AND BUILT A WALL
RDTdaily
ANOTHER DAY, MORE REPUBLICAN DIRTY TRICKS

IT HAS NO SPINE
GOP

SHAME ON YOU

NOT A DEMOCRAT

NOT A REPUBLICAN

I'M AN AMERICAN
AND I WANT MY COUNTRY BACK

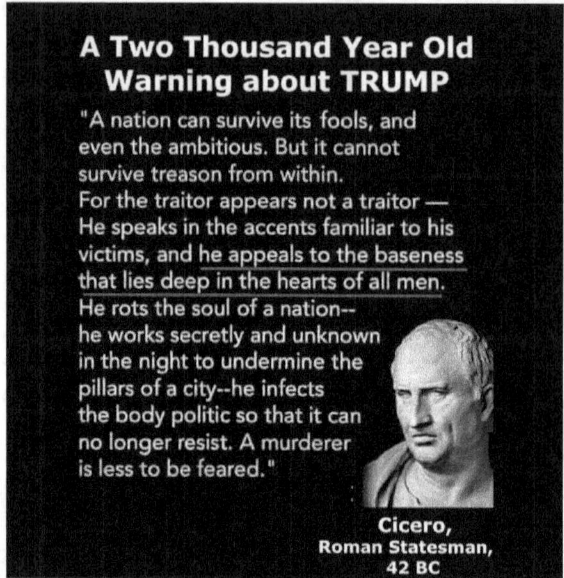

A 2000-year-old warning about Trump

The marriage between Donald Trump and the Republican Establishment was born of convenience not love. The buttoned-up, Burke-quoting worshippers of Mammon (and/or white patriarchal Jesus) who occupy the commanding heights of American conservatism didn't get into bed with a gauche, grimy Clinton donor until they saw no better way to move up in the world.

In January 2016, National Review spoke for most of the GOP's old guard when it declared Trump "a menace to American conservatism." Once the mogul secured the Republican nomination, most of the party's donor class and congressional membership reconciled themselves to his candidacy. But the contingent nature of this partnership revealed itself each time the Trump campaign's fortunes flagged. When America heard Trump's reflections on the joys of sexual assault — and his poll numbers briefly tanked — then–House Speaker Paul Ryan backed out of a campaign appearance with his party's standard-bearer, and refused to affirm his support for the mogul's candidacy. After the American people's amnesia, and James Comey's letter, put the Republican nominee back into contention, Ryan found his way back onto the Trump train.

And from November 8, 2016, to April 2020, the bulk of the respectable right rode that locomotive quite contentedly. Trump remained an irksome vessel for the conservative project, what with the protectionist tantrums, embarrassing tweets, high crimes, and misdemeanors. But in other ways, the reality star was actually a more faithful servant of the movement's cause than an ordinary Republican president would have been.

Trump's dearth of ideological conviction and policy knowledge may have unnerved conservatives at first. But once in office, it enabled the Heritage Foundation and Koch Network to dictate the lion's share of the administration regulatory policies and legislative priorities — without any interference from presidential pollsters who might wish to balance conservatives' ideological objectives against public opinion. Meanwhile, so long as the unemployment rate kept falling, the combination of a strong economy, the biases of the Electoral College, and advantages of incumbency looked sufficient to overwhelm the political detriments of Trump's incompetence and indiscretion — and keep the Executive branch red for another four years.

(Eric Levitz Trump and the GOP Establishment Are Falling Out of Love, AUG. 1, 2020, https://nymag.com/intelligencer/2020/08/trump-republican-party-mcconnell-2020-coronavirus-bill.html)

***

Mark my word, if and when these preachers get control of the [Republican] party, and they're sure trying to do so, it's going to be a terrible damn problem. Frankly, these people frighten me. Politics and governing demand compromise. But these Christians believe they are acting in the name of God, so they can't and won't compromise. I know, I've tried to deal with them.

~ Republican Barry Goldwater

"Donald Trump is not at the fringe of the Republican Party and his poll numbers are not a fluke. He is a product of the modern paranoid conservative media complex and the failure of Republican leaders to condemn the worst of their party's instincts. Trump is what the Republican Party has become."

- Krystall Ball

OCCUPY DEMOCRATS

"Literally every policy position of the Republican party can be explained in this light:

Obstructing or denying equal access to healthcare, public education, equitable taxation, legal protection; obstructing or denying marriage equality, workplace safety, voting rights, a living wage; obstructing or denying a woman's right to choose, and a fair-minded Supreme Court that would value the freedom of the individual over the power of corporations— this is how you create a permanent aristocracy, where only the rich can afford 'equality.'

If you're ok with America being changed like this, then do nothing, let it happen. If you're nauseated by it, vote. It's that simple."

— MICHAEL STIPE & TOM GILROY

REPUBLICAN HISTORIAN MAX BOOTH TELLS THE HARSH TRUTH ABOUT HIS OWN PARTY:

"I'm a lifelong Republican, but the Donald Trump surge proves that every bad thing Democrats have ever said about the Republican Party is basically true."

OCCUPY DEMOCRATS

(Whither Trumpism? With the president's reelection uncertain, Republicans battle over their future. By Janet Hook, staff Writer, Aug. 4, 2020, 5:30 am Updated 7:30 pm)

WASHINGTON — President Trump has transformed the Republican Party over the last four years, but now, with his reelection in doubt, Republicans have begun to sharply divide on whether those changes will — or should — outlast his presidency. Old Guard Republicans acknowledge that there is no going back to the pre-Trump status quo, but see a political opening to steer the party away from Trumpism. At the same time, Trump's allies have started to jockey for primacy in a potential post-Trump party.

Those tensions have already begun to have an impact on legislation, leadership power struggles and campaign strategy in Congress and across the country. In two Senate GOP primaries this week, Trump allies have been facing stiff challenges — from the right in Tennessee and the center in Kansas.

Divisions have surfaced among congressional Republicans over how to handle the next installment of COVID-19 relief funding, with many of the splits directly related to jockeying over the party's future. And after years of nearly unbroken fealty to the president, Republicans have increasingly defied Trump's wishes on issues, including his proposal for a payroll tax cut, funding for a new FBI building — and most resoundingly, his suggestion of a possible delay of election day, which Republican leaders in the House and Senate rebuffed. Trump can't postpone the election, but officials worry he and the GOP could starve it.

July 31, 2020
"This is a party that knows it's going to get beaten and get beaten badly," said Peter Wehner, a Trump critic and former White House advisor to President George W. Bush. "Intra-party turmoil, attacks on each other, the language gets super-heated."

Still, Trump loyalists remain on guard against apostasy. Wyoming Rep. Liz Cheney, a rising GOP star critical of the president on some issues, recently came under fire from a back-bencher who called for her to be booted from the House leadership. Anti-Trump Republicans are fighting back in the 2020 campaign by forming political groups dedicated to keeping Trump from being reelected.

But they face formidable hurdles in rolling back the broader changes Trump has wrought because the voting base of the GOP has been transformed. Country-club Republicanism has been routed, eclipsed by an influx of blue-collar populists who care more about cutting immigration than traditional GOP issues such as deregulation or free trade. At the same time, Trump has alienated many suburban voters who once were mainstays of the party.

That's why many Republicans — both Trump supporters and his opponents — believe his influence will persist even if his presidency does not.

"Donald Trump will have as big an impact on the profile of the Republican Party as Ronald Reagan did," said Kevin Madden, a veteran of several GOP presidential campaigns including Mitt Romney's in 2012, who has since left the party.

"This party and how it wages battles on issues, with the media and with Democrats will be led by him for the foreseeable future." The biggest fight within the party may be over who can claim to be Trump's heir.

Aug. 4, 2020

"Whether he wins or loses in 2020, you're going to see a contest between people trying to carry the mantle of Trumpism," said Andy Surabian, a former Trump aide who now advises the president's son Donald Trump Jr.

"He is going to be the most influential Republican figure, whether he wins or loses," said Surabian. "You're not going to see a pro-amnesty, pro-foreign-intervention, pro-unrestricted trade Republican get the nomination for president in 2024."

The battle over the post-Trump shape of the party will be waged in part on Capitol Hill, where Trump has remade the GOP by sweeping in a new generation of more populist, nationalist Republican legislators, while driving out more traditional Republicans and those who crossed him. One-third of the House's 198 Republican members were elected since 2016, most on Trump's agenda and coattails, and many will stay in Washington long after Trump leaves.
Senate primaries continue to be feuds over which Republican will be the president's most loyal ally, and Trump has often bragged about his ability to carry GOP candidates to primary victories. But the campaigns for this week's primaries in Tennessee and Kansas showed signs of Trump's weakening grip.

In Tennessee, where Republicans on Thursday are choosing a nominee to succeed GOP Sen. Lamar Alexander, who is retiring, the candidate endorsed by Trump is not a shoo-in. Trump's former ambassador to Japan, Bill Hagerty, is meeting a spirited challenge from the right from Manny Sethi, a surgeon who has been endorsed by conservative stalwarts like Sens. Ted Cruz of Texas and Rand Paul of Kentucky and Jim DeMint, a former senator and head of the conservative Heritage Foundation.
In Kansas, longtime Trump ally Kris Kobach — a polarizing conservative who lost his 2018 gubernatorial bid — lost again in Tuesday's GOP primary for the seat now held by retiring GOP Sen. Pat Roberts.

The GOP establishment — including the U.S. Chamber of Commerce and the Senate Leadership Fund, which is allied with Majority Leader Mitch McConnell of Kentucky — backed a rival they believe is less divisive, Rep. Roger Marshall, because they feared Kobach would lose the Senate general election. Trump did not endorse either, despite pressure from GOP leaders for him to back Marshall.

The party's split from its Old Guard past is illustrated in both primaries, as Republicans seized a new weapon for demonizing their rivals: Linking them to Romney, the only Republican senator to vote against Trump in his impeachment trial.

'Trump is a singular danger': The president faces unprecedented opposition — from his own party
July 15, 2020

In Kansas, the Club for Growth, a conservative political group, has aired ads calling Marshall a friend of "never-Trump politicians like Mitt Romney." In Tennessee, Hagerty has had to defend his service as Romney's finance chair in the 2012 campaign.

On Capitol Hill, intraparty warfare broke out recently when Cheney, No. 3 leader of the House GOP, came under attack from members of the conservative House Freedom Caucus for, among other things, her criticism of Trump's foreign policy and his handling of the coronavirus crisis.

Cheney, daughter of former Vice President Dick Cheney, poked Trump for his refusal to wear a mask to prevent the disease's spread by tweeting a photo of her father wearing one, with the hashtag #realmenwearmasks.

Rep. Matt Gaetz of Florida, a Trump ally, tweeted after a closed-door confrontation, "Liz Cheney has worked behind the scenes (and now in public) against @realDonaldTrump and his agenda. House Republicans deserve better as our Conference Chair. Liz Cheney should step down or be removed #MAGA."

Cheney has supported Trump on most issues, and the call to oust her fizzled. Michael Steel, a former aide to House Speaker John Boehner, said Cheney's attackers "kicked off a new front in the fight to define the future of the Republican Party in the post-Trump era, an era they clearly worry will begin quite soon. "

Writing for the Dispatch, a conservative website, Steel called Cheney a "'back to the future' option for the future of the party — advocating a return to fiscal responsibility, an assertive foreign policy, and competence. And there are many who agree with her."

In the Senate, the divisions among Republicans have worsened the stalemate over the next package of economic relief for the damage caused by COVID-19.

One hallmark of Trumpism is the president's lack of concern about the ballooning federal budget deficit. Republicans have mostly gone along, abandoning their past embrace — at least rhetorically — of fiscal conservatism.

Now, in a sign of Trump's weakened position on the Hill, some Republicans with presidential ambitions like Sens. Josh Hawley of Missouri and Cruz have begun complaining about growing costs — despite the risk that a delayed or smaller relief package might pose to Republicans in tough reelection fights this year.

Trump has had little hand in shaping the package so far, leaving negotiations to his top aides. When he has weighed in, he has been slapped down by fellow Republicans, such as when he proposed a payroll tax cut and when his administration pushed unrelated funding for construction of an FBI headquarters in downtown Washington, D.C., across the street from the hotel Trump owns.

If Trump wins in 2020, he will have another four years to cement the changes he has wrought in the GOP. If he loses, Republicans' reaction will hinge largely on how big and decisive his defeat is. Short of a landslide, however, it is unlikely that Trump's influence on the party will vanish, Republicans on both sides say.

Tim Miller, an anti-Trump Republican who worked for Jeb Bush in the 2016 presidential election, said Trump is not likely to follow the lead of President George W. Bush, who retreated to private life and hobbies on his Texas ranch after leaving the White House.

"He's going to be tweeting. He'll have his own network," Miller said. "He is not the type to go to Midland and paint." (www.latimes.com/politics/story/2020-08-04/trump...)

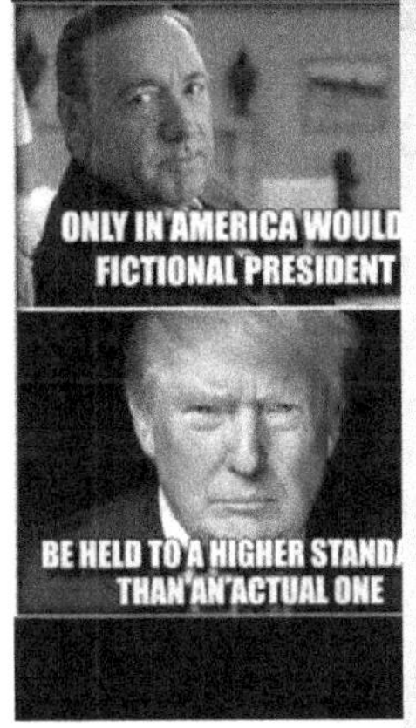

Five things you should know about Gov. Mike Pence

1. He led the push to shut down the government over defunding Planned Parenthood nationwide.
2. He'd totally outlaw abortion.
3. He slashed funding for higher education to pay for corporate tax cuts.
4. He opposes comprehensive immigration reform and birthright citizenship for many children born to immigrant parents.
5. He signed an anti-LGBT law that sparked a national outcry.

LET'S LOOK AT THE RECORD

Alfred Emanuel Smith (December 30, 1873 – October 4, 1944) was an American politician who served four terms as Governor of New York and was the Democratic Party's candidate for president in 1928. He was first Roman Catholic to run for President. His candidacy mobilized Catholic votes, especially from women, who had only recently received federal suffrage. It also brought out the anti-Catholic vote, which was especially strong among white conservative Democrats in the South, although Smith was still successful within the states of the Deep South.

Many Protestants feared his candidacy, including German Lutherans and Southern Baptists, believing that the Pope in Rome would dictate his policies. Incumbent Republican Secretary of Commerce Herbert Hoover was greatly aided by national prosperity and the absence of American involvement in war; Smith lost in a landslide to him, losing six southern states but carrying the Deep South. (Slayton, Robert A. (2001). Empire Statesman: The Rise and Redemption of Al Smith. Free Press; "Deep South". The Free Dictionary. Retrieved January 18, 2007. Neal R. Pierce, The Deep South States of America: People, Politics, and Power in the Seven States of the Deep South (1974), pp 123-61)

To review Trump's disastrous presidency, we follow Al Smith's often repeated quote, "Let's Look at the Record."

A Study in Incompetence, Unconstitutional Behavior, Racism and Lies

Donald J. Trump's ego is so fragile that wants to take credit for everything thing that goes well, and takes no responsibility for anything that goes wrong. Trump is jealous of those who are intelligent and well-liked, such as Barack Obama, and Dr. Fauci. It gnaws at his liver that anyone is admired more than him, failing to understand the reasons for their popularity. He seems unable or unwilling to understand to be admired and respected, you have to accomplish something creditable.

It is seems rather clear that Trump yearns to be a dictator, like his buddies in Russia, North Korea, and Saudi Arabia, where any criticism of the leader almost certainly will get you killed.

Trump knows nothing about science, and doesn't want to. He refuses to listen to experts and doesn't realize that science is a search for truth and not a political tool. He dismisses the threats of Climate Change.

The hardest thing for me to understand is how Trump can find so many people to support him, who like him have no respect for the constitution and cares nothing for citizens, unless they are very wealthy.
In more instances than a politician should not demonstrate is how stupid they are, devoid of any leadership, and are downright nasty.

During the Great Depression, Herbert Hoover was blame for it, which wasn't a title he should share alone. People who saw their wealth and livelihood disappearing swore about Hoover when anything went wrong. I read that when a golfer had a bad shot, they would say, "God damn that Hoover." Americans cannot blame Trump for the Covid 19 pandemic, but he is responsible for mishandling the effort to survive it.

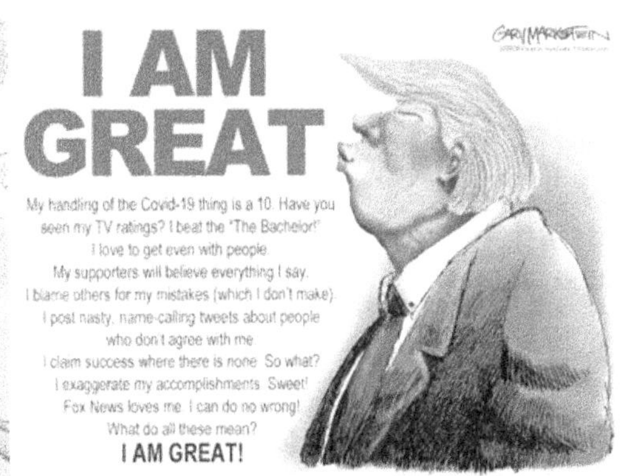

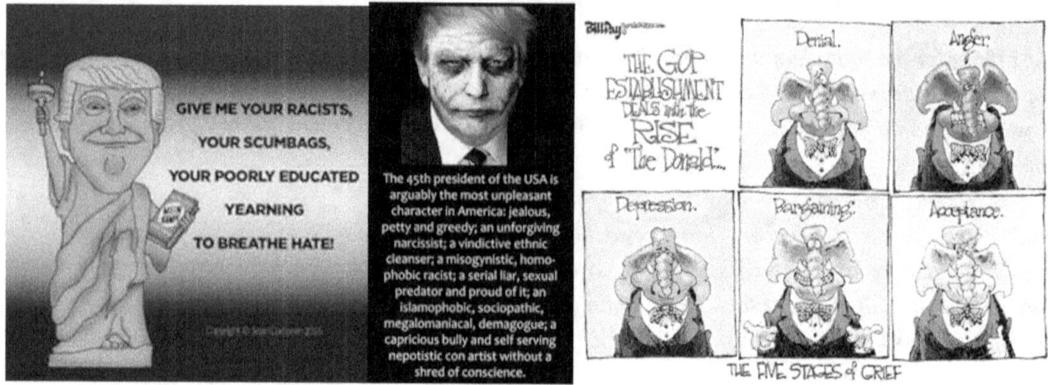

(Source of the following quotations: https://www.brainyquote.com/topics/republican-party-quotes)

There's no doubt that the Christian right has gone to bed with the more conservative elements of the Republican Party. And there's been a melding in their goals when it comes to the separation of church and state. I've always believed in the separation of church and state. Jimmy Carter

Brains, you know, are suspect in the Republican Party. Walter Lippmann

It's time to stop thinking of the Republican Party as an exclusive club where your ideological card is checked at the door, and start thinking about how we can attract more solution-based leaders like Nathan Fletcher and Anthony Adams. Arnold Schwarzenegger

I honestly believe that there's an element in this country, in our politics, that does not want to see a businessman succeed at getting the nomination for the Republican party, and does not want me to succeed at becoming President of the United States of America. Herman Cain

Trump is, in part, a reaction to the intellectual corruption of the Republican Party. That ought to be obvious to his critics, yet somehow it isn't. Tucker Carlson

But in the right-wing media, they do have a right-wing bias. And they also have an agenda. So, their agenda is: we're an adjunct of the Republican Party, and we're going push that agenda every day, and, as you say, brand these stories that help further the right-wing cause. Al Franken

The Republican Party is terrific at determining how a program will impact the federal budget, but we're not nearly as good as the Democrats in explaining to people how our agenda will directly benefit them and their families. J. C. Watts

If the Republican Party does not learn to understand unmarried women as the political force and potent voting bloc that they have become, we risk becoming the minority party. The history of the modern Republican Party is the story of moderates being driven out and conservatives taking over - and then of those conservatives in turn being ousted by those even further to the right. Max Boot

Before Donald Trump, the Republican Party was a majority conservative party with a white nationalist fringe. Now it's a white nationalist party with a conservative fringe. Max Boot

They're anti-government ideologues who dominate the Republican Party. Nancy Pelosi

Even if Donald Trump's successful, it's the beginning of the end if this rhetoric persists in the Republican Party. Gavin Newsom

It has become starkly apparent to me that we lack any sort of strategic foreign policy view, and when I say 'we,' I mean the country in general, but in particular, the Republican Party. Marco Rubio

Economic libertarians and Christian evangelicals, united by their common enemy, are strange bedfellows in today's Republican party, just as the two Georges - the archconservative Wallace and the uberliberal McGovern - found themselves in the same Democratic Party in 1972. Steven Pinker

I just feel abandoned. And I feel, I don't feel represented by the Republican Party. I have always had to defend the social side of the Republican Party by saying that it's not the majority, that it's not their focus, when everything suggests just the opposite. Gary Johnson

If a person wants to be the nominee of the Republican Party, there can be no evasion and no games. They must reject any group or cause that is built on bigotry. This party does not prey on people's prejudices. Paul Ryan

God is not a franchise of the Republican Party. Dick Durbin

We've changed in the sense that we flipped - and this is no longer the Republican party of Lincoln. This is the party of suppression. Andrew Young

So, the Republican party of Teddy Roosevelt and John McCain and Ronald Reagan and George W. Bush is dead. It's over. It doesn't exist anymore. Steve Schmidt

I've spent my life in the Republican party, it gives me no pleasure to say this. This party has demonstrated a complete incapacity to govern. Period. Steve Schmidt

The Republican party has become as hostile towards its own base as the Liberals have always been. Milo Yiannopoulos

The Republican Party is bringing out here onto the floor of Congress an all-out assault on the protection of the rights of people who work in the fields of our country, in the factories of our country, in the offices of our country. Ed Markey

WARNING MEMES

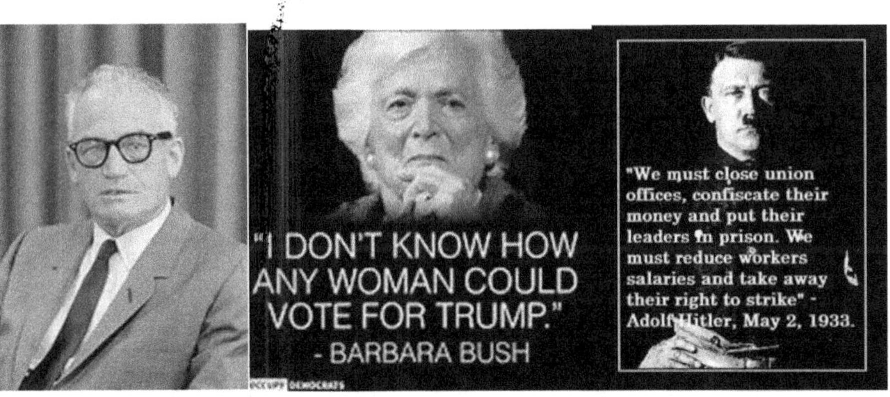

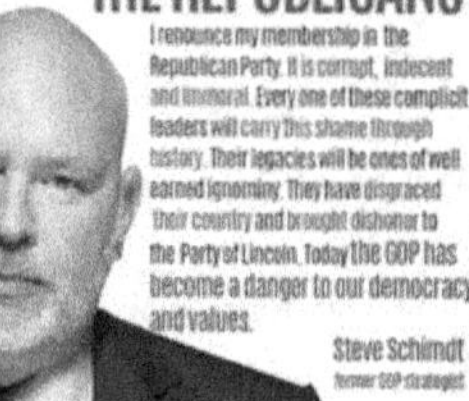

Here's one of the sane, moral ones.

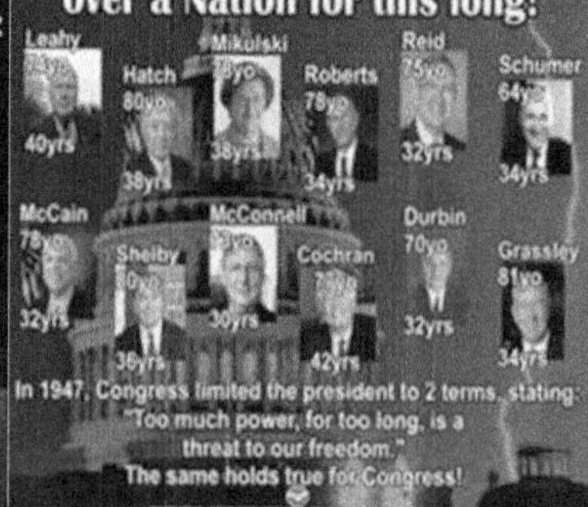

President Trump And The Covid 19 Pandemic

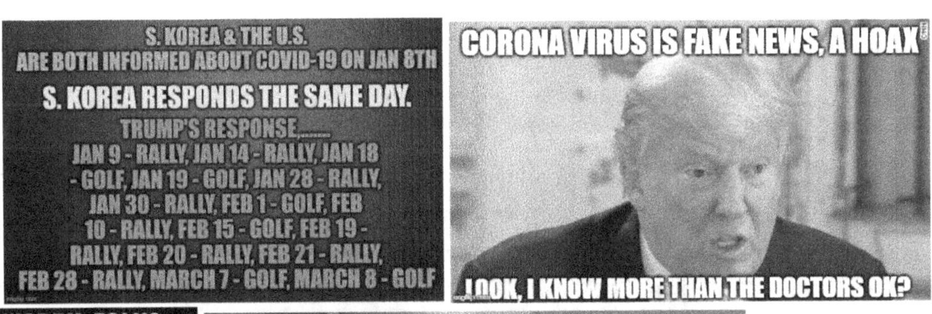

President Trump didn't create the Covid 19 pandemic. He did, however, and still is mishandling the effort to combat it. As a result, the number who contracted the virus and those who died from Covid 19 was far greater than it needed to be, so although he maintains he takes no responsibility, he is responsible for all the extra deaths, if he didn't just treat the pandemic as bad public relations and a threat to his reelection. Trump has refused to follow the advice of scientist, portraying himself as more knowledgeable than they. Secretly, well not so secretly, he is outrage that the public trust the scientists than they do him.

Trump has shown a complete lack of understanding that the pandemic now raging throughout the world, but more so in the United States, is precisely when the President, who represents all the people, must step up and championing a sensible plan by scientists and medical experts that will save the lives of thousands of people. Instead, Trump likes to give medical advice which he has pulled out of his as, which not only won't work, but will only cause more medical problems. Trump likes to find so-called medical experts, who will counter Drs, Fauci and Brix, and swear that only Trump is getting things correct.

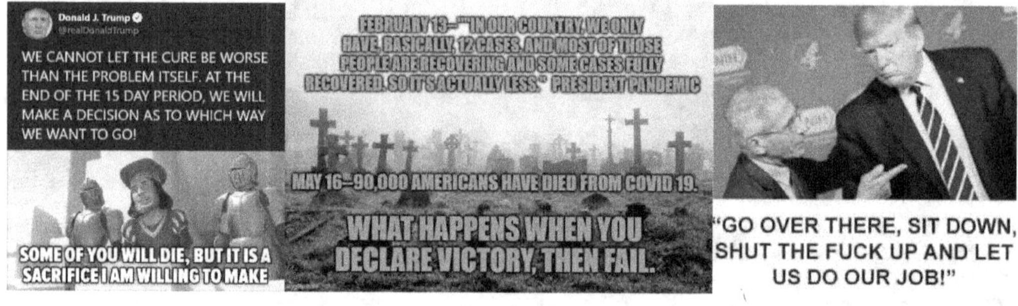

 However, Trump is not concerned about the number of deaths. He is only concerned about being reelected. To do that he is unwilling to take positions that might hurt him with his base, who have decided that being forced to wear masks, avoid crowds, and to anyway be forced to alter their life styles during the crisis. Most other nations have such plans and they seem to be helping reduce the number of new cases of Covid 19.

Covid-19 in the month of July

Place	Population	Cases	Deaths
New Zealand	5 million	32	0
Thailand	70 million	139	0
Vietnam	97 million	191	2
Greece	10 million	1,068	14
South Korea	51 million	1,505	19
Japan	126 million	15,779	34
Netherlands	17 million	4,028	34
Spain	47 million	39,251	90
Australia	25 million	9,069	93
Germany	84 million	14,833	172
Canada	38 million	12,108	253
Italy	60 million	6,938	374
France	67 million	25,118	447
Mississippi	3 million	31,500	590
Alabama	5 million	49,678	630
Louisiana	5 million	58,143	720
Georgia	11 million	105,061	947
South Carolina	5 million	52,617	973
Arizona	7 million	94,759	2,062
Florida	21 million	317,952	3,338
Texas	29 million	275,757	4,197
The USA	331 million	1,976,649	26,442

"We are the envy of the world for how we've handled this" – Donald Trump, July 17th

DR. FAUCI RIPS TRUMP'S FAKE NEWS COVID-19 "VOODOO DOCTORS" VIDEO: "When there's a video out there from a bunch of people spouting something that isn't true, the only recourse you have is to be very, very clear in presenting the scientific data."

SEND THIS ALONG IF YOU STAND WITH DR. FAUCI AND AGAINST TRUMP'S LIES AND PROPAGANDA!

RIDIN' WITH BIDEN

Trump is pushing governors of the various states to declare victory and removing restrictions on their citizens and businesses. When this was tried in several states, the resurgence of the virus was tremendous, and the first stage of the pandemic is not yet open. Trump is also pushing for a vaccine, any vaccine that will protect people, a change from his earlier warnings against vaccines.

Fauci needs to step up to the mic and say "look, I've tried to avoid contradicting this moron but you're going to die if you listen to him. Do not listen to him. He's a fucking moron. I don't care if I get fired, you need to know the truth."

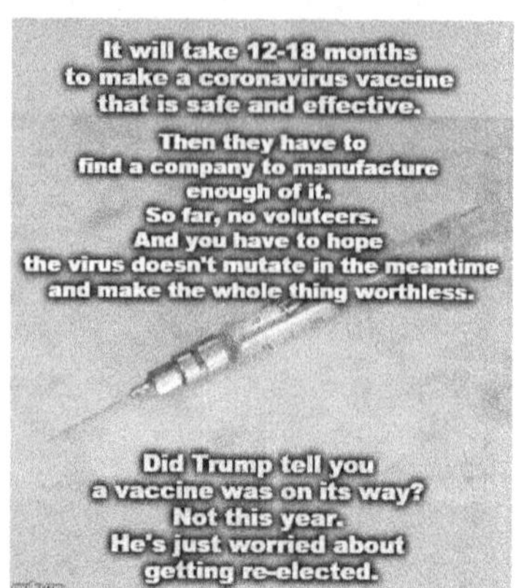

Trump also is pushing hard to have schools reopen, maintaining that youngster are unlikely to contract Covid 19 or spread it at their homes. While, everyone should wish to have children attend schools to get education, how many children and others are they willing to sacrifice if conditions cannot be arranged to have students safe with masks and maintaining safe distancing six or seven hours a day, five days a week. The matter seems to be of no concern to Trump.

Meet Betsy DeVos. Trump's pick for Education Secretary.

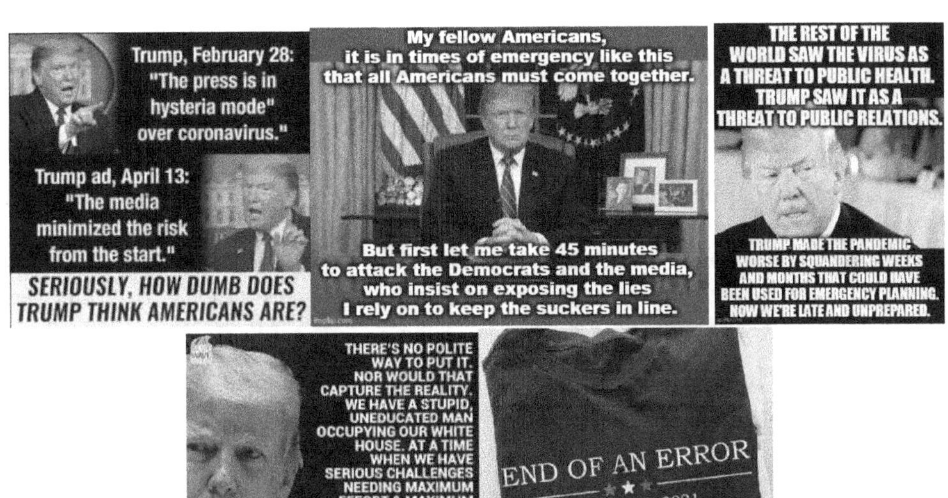

Masks

Aren't you getting very tired of people throwing public fits (see Trump supporters with little education and no sense) whan they are asked to wear masks? They claim being forced to wear masks violates their constitutional rights. You see, that's the problem right now. Requiring people to wear masks during a pandemic is not unconstitutional; it is absolutely necessary and the responsibility of ever US citizen to comply. Like their president, these people probably never read the constitution, knows its history, or understands what it protects.

The outrage of the early colonists against the treatment, and the laws, imposed by the British led to the addition of the Bill of Rights to the Constitution.

The Founding Fathers knew what they wanted in their new nation and what they did not. They only had to look to Europe to recognize the violations of people's natural rights. The villain in these country wasn't the people; it was the rulers and politicians, who operated under the principle that the citzens didn't count for much.

The founders intentionally created a constitution which was it is contract of Negative Rights. The Constitution is nothing more than restrictions upon the government. It is rules that the government cannot break. That is, if the Federal Government is not expressly delegated an authority or 'right' to act, then it cannot act. For instance, the text of the 1st Amendment begins with the statement: Congress shall make no law respecting an establishment of religion, or prohibiting the free exercise thereof; or abridging the freedom of speech, or of the press, or the right of the people peacefully to assemble, and to petition the Government for a redress of grievances.

That's being pretty specific. Why do you suppose the founders emphasized these prohibitions. Simply. because in Europe, the governments did not prohibit them. All of the other amendments put restrictions of what the government could do in dealing with its citizens.

What those who are always screaming about their constitutional rights fail to recognize that the benefits of U.S. citizenship comes with some important responsibilities. Among these are:

The Oath of Allegiance to the United States includes several promises immigrants make when they become U.S. citizens, including promises to: Give up all prior allegiance to any other nation or sovereignty; Swear allegiance to the United States; Support and defend the Constitution and the laws of the United States; and Serve the country when required. All U.S. citizens have many responsibilities other than the ones mentioned in the Oath.

Their rights include: Freedom to express yourself. Freedom to worship as you wish. Right to a prompt, fair trial by jury. Right to vote in elections for public officials. Right to apply for federal employment requiring U.S. citizenship. Right to run for elected office. Freedom to pursue "life, liberty, and the pursuit of happiness."

Their responsibilities include: While voting is a right and privilege of citizenship, it is also a duty or responsibility. U.S. citizens have a responsibility to participate in their government by registering to vote and voting in elections. Support and defend the Constitution. Stay informed of the issues affecting your community. Participate in the democratic process. Respect and obey federal, state, and local laws. Participate in your local community. Pay income and other taxes honestly, and on time, to federal, state, and local authorities. Serve on a jury when called upon. Defend the country if the need should arise.

America is stronger when all of its citizens respect the different opinions, cultures, ethnic groups, and religions found in this country. Tolerance for these differences is also a responsibility of citizenship.

Despite many people causing a fuss about facemasks, the truth is that a face mask requirement does not violate one's constitutional rights. Have you heard and understand the meaning of the phrase: "Your rights end where mine begin?" This statement is very pertinent at this time, when the world is fighting and losing the battle with the coronavirus. It wouldn't seem there are no two sides to the issue of dealing with the pandemic, and it is very dangerous to make it a political football. Are there Americans who still believe the virus is a hoax, or that there is a conspiracy perpetrated by the Democrats to make the president look bad? A lot of these people don't believe in science or facts, or experience or expertise.

Nevertheless, the virus existence and how it spreads is a proven fact and it is not politically motivated or biased. What is known is that If we all wear masks and practice social distancing; the virus can't be passed. If you think your religious faith will protect you, better think again. Now, remember this: you have no rights to spread the disease to others. The masks are not merely protection for you, but also protection for anyone you encounter. Fog God's sake, stop being so selfish.

Back for a moment to the assertion: "Your rights end where mine begin." Maybe, you would prefer other versions of the statement. Victor Hugo put is thusly, "The liberty of one citizen ends where the liberty of another citizen begins." And Abe Lincoln put it rather folksy: "My right to swing my fist ends where your nose begins."

We have laws to ensure that your freedom to live your life as you choose does not impact anyone else's freedom to live their lives as they choose. When these two rights meet, we need laws to decide how to best to handle the situation.

"It is a greater thing to be a good citizen than to be a good Republican or a good Democrat." - Gifford Pinchot

"The whole idea of a public education was to train young people about how our system of government works, so

they could be good citizens and be part of it. We're not doing that today." - Sandra Day O'Connor